Sp[...]ents

spoonfuls

LIQUID

Metric	Imperial	American
5 ml	1 teaspoon	
10 ml	2 teaspoons	
15 ml	1 tablespoon	
30 ml	1 fl oz	1/8 cup
60 ml	2 fl oz	1/4 cup
75 ml	3 fl oz	3/8 cup
125 ml	4 fl oz	1/2 cup
150 ml	5 fl oz	5/8 cup
175 ml	6 fl oz	3/4 cup
200 ml	7 fl oz	7/8 cup
225 ml	8 fl oz	1 cup
300 ml	10 fl oz	1 1/4 cups
350 ml	12 fl oz	1 1/2 cups
375 ml	13 fl oz	1 5/8 cups
400 ml	14 fl oz	1 3/4 cups
500 ml	17 fl oz	2 cups
600 ml	21 fl oz	2 1/2 cups
700 ml	24 fl oz	3 cups
800 ml	28 fl oz	3 1/2 cups
1 l	1 3/4 pints	4 1/4 cups
1.25 l	2 1/4 pints	5 1/4 cups
1.5 l	2 3/4 pints	6 1/2 cups
2 l	3 1/2 pints	8 1/2 cups
2.5 l	4 1/4 pints	11 cups

ABBREVIATIONS

kg	kilogram	C	carbohydrate
g	gram	F	fat
l	litre	P	protein
ml	millilitre	CU	carbohydrate unit
kJ	kilojoule		
kcal	kilocalorie		

	TABLE-SPOON 15 ml	TEA-SPOON 5 ml
Liquid	15 ml	5 ml
Almonds, ground	5 g	1.5 g
Baking powder	13 g	4 g
Black tea	5 g	1.5 g
Breadcrumbs, dried	7 g	2.5 g
Cheese, grated	8 g	3 g
Cinnamon, ground	7 g	2.5 g
Cocoa powder	5 g	1.5 g
Coffee, ground	5 g	1.5 g
Coffee, instant	3 g	1 g
Condensed milk	13 g	4 g
Cooking oil	13 g	4 g
Cornflour (cornstarch)	9 g	3 g
Crème fraîche	14 g	3.5 g
Flour, plain (all purpose)	6 g	2 g
Gelatine, powdered	13 g	4 g
Hazelnuts, ground	5 g	1.5 g
Honey	20 g	7 g
Icing sugar	8 g	3 g
Margarine	13 g	4 g
Mayonnaise	13 g	4 g
Mustard	15 g	5 g
Oat flakes	10 g	3 g
Paprika powder	7 g	2.5 g
Rice	13 g	4 g
Salt	15 g	5 g
Semolina	10 g	3.5 g
Sour cream (10 % fat)	12 g	4 g
Sugar	12 g	4 g
Tomato ketchup	15 g	5 g
Tomato puree	15 g	5 g
Whipping cream (30 % fat)	14 g	5 g

DR. OETKER

GERMAN COOKING TODAY

THE ORIGINAL

DR. OETKER

GERMAN COOKING TODAY

THE ORIGINAL

Dr. Oetker Verlag

You don't fancy the same old scrambled eggs any more, soup-in-a-bag or pot (cup) noodles?
Instead, why not try making ravioli with spinach filling, roast beef rolls
or a saddle of venison: these dishes tastes delicious but they are also
much easier to make than you might think.

German Cooking Today, the standard work on the subject, has been written
for beginners and inexperienced cooks. With this book you will be able to produce
classic dishes such as beef roulade and stuffed bell peppers in no time at all,
and you will also find many new recipes.

Dr. Oetker's Test Kitchen has carefully checked that every dish
is easy to prepare – even for beginners – and that it will taste delicious.
Step-by-step instructions and detailed photographs ensure that the result will be successful.
The new recipes will inspire you to try out and make many of them.

More and more people are discovering the art of cooking, the pleasure of trying out
new recipes and enjoying the result, the careful choosing of ingredients and that
spirit of achievement which will make every day more enjoyable. And the satisfaction
of cutting, chopping, stirring, cooking, frying (sautéing), roasting and braising!

We wish you a lot of pleasure in your culinary experiments and much success.
Now, enjoy yourself!

General advice

To ensure that the food you have prepared tastes as delicious and looks as irresistible as you could possibly wish, here are a few tips for you before you start cooking:

Tip 1 – Preparation
First read the recipe carefully before you start cooking – in fact, read it before you go shopping to buy the ingredients. Often the various cooking processes and the sequence of steps will become clearer as a result. Unless stated otherwise, all the recipe quantities are designed to serve four people. The ingredients are listed in the order in which they are used in preparing the recipe.

Tip 2 – Conversions and equivalents
The conversions and equivalents listed on the inside of the cover of the book are valid for all recipes and will help you to determine accurately the right quantities for the ingredients needed in the recipe.

Tip 3 – Preparation time
The preparation time indicated in the recipes is only given as a guide-line – it is an approximate estimate and will depend on your cooking experience. The preparation time only takes into account the actual time needed to prepare the food. Other waiting times, such as the time needed for cooling, defrosting or marinating are only included if they happen at the same time as other steps in the preparation of the food.

Tip 4 – Cooking temperatures and cooking times
Again, the cooking temperatures and cooking times are only guide-lines which may be increased or de-creased depending on the particular heating output of the oven.

Tip 5 – Information
You will find introductory infor-mation at the beginning of most of the chapters with general explanations, helpful tips and advice regarding the preparation of the food.
In addition, at the end of the book there is also a general glossary of herbs and spices, a description of the various cooking methods and types of cookers as well as useful advice on buying, storing, freezing and defrosting food.
You will also find numerous tips, modifications and recipe variations after the end of each recipe.
Recipe variations are listed in the index.

Tip 6 – Nutritional values
The nutritional values are rough estimates. They apply to one serving of those indicated in the recipes or, in specified cases, the total amounts.

Tip 7 – Serving sizes
Opinions vary about the size of a servings. The indications below are a general guide to the quantities of ingredients needed to make a single serving.

Soup as a starter:
150–250 ml/5–8 fl oz (⅝–1 cup) (finished dish)

Main dishes:
Soup: 375–500 ml/13–17 fl oz (1⅝–2¼ cups, finished dish)
Stews: 500–600 g/18–20 oz (finished dish)
Meat without bones: about 150 g/5 oz (uncooked)
Meat with bones: about 200 g/7 oz (uncooked)
Fish fillet: 150–200 g/5–7 oz (uncooked)
Fish, whole: 200–300 g/7–10 oz (uncooked)
Pasta: 100–125 g/3½–4½ oz (uncooked)

Accompaniments:
Sauce: about 100 ml/3½ fl oz (½ cup) (finished dish)
Vegetables: about 200 g/7 oz (prepared)
Lettuce: 40–50 g/1½–2 oz (prepared)
Potatoes: about 200 g/7 oz (peeled)
Rice, millet, pearl barley etc: 50–75 g/2–3 oz (uncooked)
Pasta: 60–80 g/2–3 oz (uncooked)

Puddings:
Fruit salad: 150–200 g/5–7 oz (finished dish)
Fruit compote: 100–150 g/ 3½–5 oz (finished dish)
Flan: 125–175 g/4½–6 oz (finished dish)

Tip 8 – Kitchen utensils

No kitchen can operate without good cooking utensils and kitchen knives in various shapes and sizes. Kitchen knives are used every day and should therefore be of the highest quality. To ensure that your knives last a long time and remain sharp, the blades must be made of high quality steel. Just as importantly, the knives must sit comfortably in the hand and they must have a good grip so that they do not slip and injure you.

The following kitchen utensils will ensure that your kitchen is perfectly equipped:

1 bread knife
1–2 kitchen knives
1 potato peeler
1 carving knife
1 garlic press
1 pair kitchen shears
1 small and 1 large cooking pot
1 roasting tin
1 saucepan
1 set bowls
1 casserole
1 large and 1 small frying pan
(skillet) with non-stick coating
if preferred
1 timer (preferably digital)
1 large measuring jug
1 small measuring jug
1 electric hand mixer with whisk,
kneading hook and blending
attachments
1–2 chopping boards
1 set of scales
(preferably digital)
1 cake rack

1 potato or spätzle press
1 multi-purpose grater
1 colander
1 tea strainer
1 set of salad servers
1 salad spinner
1 spatula
1 ladle
1 wooden spoon
1 sauce ladle
1 skimming ladle
1 whisk
1 pastry brush
1 can opener
1 bottle opener
1 lemon squeezer
1 pepper mill
1 salt shaker

Tip 9 – Level of difficulty

The level of difficulty is indicated for each recipe, making it easier for you to match the recipe to your resources.

FOR BEGINNERS

FOR EXPERIENCED
COOKS

FOR ADVANCED
COOKS

Soups & stews

Soups are becoming increasingly popular because the word is spreading like wildfire that no dish is so tasty and at the same time so low in calories. In addition it gives you that wonderful feeling that you have actually eaten your fill. Completely safe for your figure! Whether thin or more like its "big brother" the stew or casserole which can form a main meal in itself, soups have become very trendy. They may be clear soups, cream soups, vegetable soups or sweet soups. The basis of a good soup is a good quality stock (bouillon), if possible home-made, such as chicken, vegetable, beef or fish stock. When you make fresh stock, you should make enough for several meals because it can be frozen and will be very useful when you feel like having a little soup again.

This is what you need to make stock (broth):

Regardless of whether you make stock with bones, fish, beef, veal, poultry or venison and vegetables – there is something which you can never do without: the standard **soup vegetables** (photograph 1). These always include 1–2 carrots, a piece of celery and one or two leeks. Depending on the season and region in which you live you can also add a little parsley, parsley root, cauliflower, kohlrabi, bay leaves or thyme and lovage. The broth will be particularly aromatic if you first fry (sauté) these ingredients for a short time over a high heat.

Bouquet garni

A bouquet garni is a bunch of herbs consisting of parsley, thyme and bay leaves that is used to season all kinds of dishes. But you can also add other herbs or make your own selection to make your bouquet garni. By tying the herbs together with cooking string, you can easily remove them from the pan when the stock is ready.

An onion stuck with cloves (photograph 2)

Using a small knife, remove the dry, outer leaves of an onion. Make a slanting incision about 2 cm/¾ in deep and slide 1 bay leaf into the cut. Then push a few cloves into the onion, stalk first.

Starting the stock from cold

When making stock, always put the vegetables in the cold water. The vegetables will yield more flavour and the stock will have a more intense taste.

Exception: In the case of meat stock, if you are using meat you want to use afterwards, for instance as boiled fillet, it is best to wait until the water is boiling before adding the meat.

Degreasing the stock

If you want to use the hot stock immediately, you can remove the fat by skimming it off with a kitchen paper towel (photograph 3). Pull a paper towel over the surface of the stock so that it absorbs the fat. But if you have enough time, it is easier to leave the stock to cool down and refrigerate it. The fat which has risen to the surface will solidify so that it can simply be removed with a spoon (photograph 4).

Freezing the stock

Clear stocks can easily be frozen
after they have cooled. If you freeze
them in small servings, for instance
in an ice-cube tray or in freezer
boxes, they will always be to hand
when needed.

Seasoning with salt

Stock should only be seasoned
with salt towards the end of the
cooking period, and then only a
little because as the liquid reduces
it will soon become too salty. It is
best to adjust the seasoning later
when you use the stock in subse-
quent preparations.

Instant stock

If you not have the time to make
your own stock, you can buy
instant stock which is available in
most shops in the form of granules
or stock cubes. For the amounts,
follow the instructions on the
packet. Another possibility is to
use a jar of ready-made stock.

Concentrated stock

A concentrated stock is a strongly
reduced extract made from crushed
bones, meat cuts, crustaceans, fish,
vegetables, roots vegetables and
herbs. You can make a concentrated
sock by further reducing an already
existing stock. The result will have a
very intense taste, ideal for soups
and for making light sauces and
dark ones.

Easy tips to rescue soup

» Your soup is too thin? Simply stir
in 1–2 tablespoons dried potato
flakes or a little semolina (but not
in the case of clear soups such a
beef broth or chicken soup).
Alternatively thicken the soup with
cornflour (cornstarch); or again,
stir together 20 g/¾ oz (3 tablespoons) plain (all purpose) flour
and 30 g/1 oz (2 tablespoons)
melted butter, then stir this mixture
into the soup and bring it back to
the boil.
» Is your soup too thick? Thin the
soup by adding some stock.

Soup tricks

» Do not cook pasta, rice or
dumplings in clear broth because
they will make it cloudy. These
ingredients are better cooked
separately and then added to the
soup later.
» Serve hot soups really hot and
cold soups really cold. For hot
soups warm the soup plates or
bowls before serving – for
instance in the oven at 50 °C/
120 °F; alternatively you can rinse
the soup plates or bowls in hot
water just before serving.
» You can make delicious cream
soups by thickening them with a
thickening agent such as wheat
flour, cornflour, crème fraîche,
egg yolk or an egg yolk and cream
mixture. If using an egg yolk on
its own or in a mixture to thicken
the soup, make sure that the soup
does not come to the boil or the
egg may curdle.

Chicken broth/ Chicken soup

SOMETHING A LITTLE SPECIAL (ABOUT 6 SERVINGS)

Preparation time:
about 30 minutes
Cooking time: about 1½ hours

2 l/3½ pints (9 cups) water
1 bunch soup vegetables
(celery, carrots, leeks)
1 onion
1 prepared boiling fowl
(1–1.5 kg/2¼–3¼ lb)
salt
200 g/7 oz cooked green and
white asparagus spears
125 g/4½ oz (¾ cup) cooked
long grain rice
2 tablespoons chopped parsley

Per serving (Chicken soup):
P: 32 g, F: 15 g, C: 6 g,
kJ: 1191, kcal: 285, CU: 0.5

1 Bring the water to the boil in a large pan. Meanwhile peel the celery. Top and tail the carrots, then peel them. Wash the celery and carrots, then leave to drain. Prepare the leeks, cut them in half lengthways, wash thoroughly and leave to drain.

2 Coarsely chop the vegetables you have just prepared (photograph 1). Peel the onion. Rinse the boiling fowl inside and out in cold running water and put it in the boiling water. Add 1 teaspoon salt, heat again (but do not bring to the boil), then skim off the foam with a skimming ladle (photograph 2). Add the vegetables and onion to the broth. Cook the chicken over low heat without a lid for about 1½ hours.

3 Pour the broth through a sieve and, if necessary, remove any fat. Season the broth with salt.

4 To make chicken soup, remove the meat from the carcase of the chicken (photograph 3), then remove the skin and cut the meat into small pieces. Add the pieces of meat, the asparagus and the rice to the broth and reheat. Sprinkle parsley on the soup before serving.

TIPS » You can also add a cooked-egg garnish, semolina dumplings, meat dumplings, glass noodles or Oriental mushrooms to the soup.
» If you prepare the chicken soup without adding any ingredients the day before and leave it to cool, you will be able to remove the solidified fat very easily with a spoon the following day.
» Chicken broth without any added ingredients is ideal for freezing.

EXTRA TIP » 150 g/2 oz (¼ cup) uncooked rice makes 125 g/4½ oz (¾ cup) of rice when cooked. Instead of freshly cooked asparagus you can also use canned, bottled or frozen green or white asparagus.

Fish broth

IDEAL FOR PREPARING IN ADVANCE

Preparation time:
about 35 minutes
Cooking time: about 20 minutes

1 bunch soup vegetables
(celery, carrots, leeks)
1 kg/2¼ lb fish pieces and fish
bones, e.g. small pieces of
sole, striped catfish, turbot
1 onion
2 tablespoons cooking oil,
e.g. sunflower or olive oil
2 l/3½ pints (9 cups) water
salt
1 small bay leaf
1 clove
5 peppercorns
freshly ground pepper
1 pinch saffron (optional)

Per serving:
P: 9 g, F: 7 g, C: 4 g,
kJ: 485, kcal: 115, CU: 0.5

1 Peel the celery. Top and tail the carrots, then peel them. Wash the celery and carrots, then leave to drain. Prepare the leeks, cut them in half lengthways, wash thoroughly and leave to drain. Coarsely chop the vegetables you have just prepared.

2 Rinse the fish pieces and fish bones under cold running water until the rinsing water is clear. Peel the onion and cut into quarters.

3 Heat the oil in a large pan. Add the vegetables and sweat while stirring. Add the water, 2 teaspoons salt and the pieces of fish. Now add the quartered onion together with the bay leaf, clove and peppercorns to the broth. Bring to the boil and cook over medium heat without a lid for about 20 minutes.

4 Pour the fish broth through a sieve and season with salt, pepper and, if desired, saffron.

TIPS 》 To make concentrated fish stock, continue boiling the stock until it has reduced by half.
》 You can use the fish broth as a base for fish soups or fish sauces. The fish broth freezes very well.

Recipe variation: To make a more refined fish soup (photograph), take a 150 g/5 oz fennel bulb and cut off the stalk close to the bulb. Cut off the green leaves and put them to one side. Rinse the fennel and pat dry. Top and tail 150 g/5 oz carrots, peel, wash and leave to drain. Prepare 75 g/3 oz leeks, cut in half lengthways, wash thoroughly and leave to drain. Cut the prepared vegetables into thin strips. Peel 1 small onion and 2 cloves of garlic. Dice the onion into small cubes and finely chop the garlic cloves. Rinse 500 g/18 oz fish fillet (such as tilapia or coley) under cold running water, pat dry and if necessary remove any remaining bones; cut the fish into 2.5 cm/1 in cubes. Heat 2 tablespoons cooking oil in a large pan. Add the diced onion, chopped garlic and strips of vegetables and sweat while stirring all the time. Add 1 litre/1¾ pints (4¼ cups) fish stock and bring to the boil. Add the cubed fish fillets and bring back to the boil. Cook the soup over low heat without a lid for about 8 minutes. Rinse 100 g/3½ oz prawns or shrimps under cold running water and pat dry. Season the soup with salt, pepper and cayenne pepper. Add the prawns or shrimps to the soup and cook for a further 2 minutes. Rinse the green fennel leaves, pat dry and sprinkle on the soup at the time of serving.

Beef stock

CLASSIC

Preparation time:
about 30 minutes
Cooking time: 2½–3 hours

750 g/1½ lb beef,
e.g. neck, shin
2 l/3½ pints (9 cups) cold
water
salt
1 bunch soup vegetables
(celery, carrots, leeks)
2 onions
1 bay leaf
3 cloves
5 peppercorns

Per serving:
P: 38 g, F: 7 g, C: 3 g,
kJ: 970, kcal: 230, CU: 0.0

1 Put the beef in a large pan filled with cold water and 2 teaspoons salt. Bring to the boil and cook over medium heat without a lid for 60 minutes, removing the foam regularly with a skimming ladle.

2 Meanwhile peel the celery. Top and tail the carrots, then peel them. Wash the celery and carrots, then leave to drain. Prepare the leeks, cut in half lengthways, wash thoroughly and leave to drain. Coarsely chop the vegetables you have just pre-pared. Peel the onions. Stud 1 onion with a bay leaf and cloves.

3 Add the vegetables, onions and peppercorns to the beef broth and bring back to the boil. Cook over low heat without a lid for 1½–2 hours.

4 Remove the meat and pour the stock through a fine sieve or a sieve lined with a tea towel. Season the broth with salt.

TIPS ›› Beef stock is used as a base in many recipes in which meat stock is used.
›› You can also add meat bones or marrow bones when cooking the stock.
›› You can also serve the beef stock with extra ingredients (photograph) such as asparagus tips, fine noodles and cooked egg garnish as a light soup; sprinkle with parsley before serving. Stock without extra ingredients added can be frozen.

Vegetable stock

GOOD FOR PREPARING IN ADVANCE

Preparation time:
about 30 minutes
Cooking time: about 60 minutes

3 onions
2 cloves garlic
2 bunch soup vegetables
(celery, carrots, leeks)
about 100 g/3½ oz parsley root
200 g/7 oz white cabbage
130 g/1 oz/4½ oz tomatoes
50 ml/1½ fl oz (3 tablespoons)
cooking oil

1 Peel the onions and cloves of garlic, then chop coarsely. Peel the celery. Top and tail the carrots, then peel them. Wash the celery and carrots, then leave to drain. Prepare the leeks, cut them in half lengthways, wash thoroughly and leave to drain. Coarsely chop up the vegetables you have just prepared.

2 Prepare the parsley root, peel and wash; leave to drain, then cut into cubes. Remove the outer yellowish

leaves from the white cabbage, cut into quarters, rinse and leave to drain. Cut out the core and cut the cabbage into strips. Wash the tomatoes, leave to drain, cut in half and cut out the base of the stalk.

3 Heat the oil in a large pan. Add the onions and garlic cloves and sweat while stirring all the time.

4 Add the rest of the vegetables and sweat a little longer. Pour in the

water. Add the salt, bay leaves and peppercorns. Bring to the boil, then cook the vegetables gently over medium heat without a lid for about 60 minutes.

5 Meanwhile rinse the parsley and lovage, then pat dry. Remove the leaves from the stems and chop the leaves.

6 When the stock is cooked, add the herbs and let them steep in the stock for a few minutes over low heat. Season the stock with nutmeg, then pour it through a sieve.

TIP » Vegetable stock can be used as a base for stews, sauces and vegetable recipes.

3 l/5¼ pints (12½ cups) water
1 tablespoon salt
2 bay leaves
1 teaspoon peppercorns
1 bunch parsley
2 sprigs lovage
ground nutmeg

Per serving:
P: 1 g, F: 13 g, C: 1 g,
kJ: 501, kcal: 120, CU: 0.0

Cooked egg garnish

CLASSIC (AT THE FRONT OF THE PHOTOGRAPH)

Preparation time:
about 5 minutes
Cooking time: 25–30 minutes

2 eggs (medium)
125 ml/4 fl oz (½ cup) milk
salt, nutmeg

Per serving: P: 4 g, F: 5 g, C: 2 g,
kJ: 307, kcal: 73, CU: 0.0

1 Whisk together the eggs, milk, salt and nutmeg. Pour the egg and milk mixture into a greased, heat-resistant mould with a lid. Put the lid on the mould and place it in a tall, wide pan, adding enough hot water to reach halfway up the mould.

2 Put the lid on the saucepan and simmer over low heat for 25–30 minutes until the mixture has set. Then loosen the cooked egg garnish from the mould, turn it out and leave to cool a little. Cut the cooked egg garnish into cubes or diamond-shaped pieces.

Semolina dumplings

FOR CHILDREN (AT THE BACK IN THE PHOTOGRAPH)

Preparation time:
about 20 minutes

125 ml/4 fl oz (½ cup) milk
10 g/⅓ oz (2 teaspoons) butter
1 pinch salt
ground nutmeg
50 g/2 oz (⅓ cup) semolina
1 egg (medium)
salted water (1 teaspoon salt
in 1 litre/1¾ pints (4½ cups)
water

Per serving:
P: 4 g, F: 5 g, C: 10 g,
kJ: 428, kcal: 102, CU: 1.0

1 Bring the butter, salt and nutmeg to the boil, then remove the pan from the heat. Stir in the semolina and continue stirring until it forms a smooth ball, then cook for about 1 minute. Put the hot ball of dough in a bowl and stir in the egg.

2 Now bring enough salted water or stock to the boil to enable the dumplings to "swim" in the liquid. Using two teaspoons, previously dipped in hot water, shape the dumplings and put them in the boiling salted water or stock. Simmer very gently without a lid for about 5 minutes (the water should only move very lightly).

Recipe variation 1: To make sweet dumplings, prepare the semolina mixture with a pinch of salt and 1½ teaspoons sugar. Sweet semolina dumplings are delicious served with cold fruit soups or milk soups.

Recipe variation 2: To make meat dumplings, stir 40 g/1½ oz (3 tablespoons) butter or margarine with a wooden spoon until soft. Add 100 g/3½ oz minced (ground) meat (half beef, half pork), 2 egg yolks (from medium eggs) and 40 g/1½ oz (¾ cup) breadcrumbs and mix well. Season with salt and pepper. With moistened hands, shape the meatballs from the meat mixture and cook them for about 5 minutes as described in the recipe.

TIP » Cooked egg garnish and semolina dumplings are ideal for adding to clear broths and soups (for instance chicken soup, p. 10). You can also cook the cooked-egg garnish in the microwave oven. To do this, put the egg and milk mixture in a greased glass or china bowl, cover and cook for about 8 minutes at 450 watts. Add a sophisticated touch by stirring 1–2 tablespoons chopped mixed herbs or 20 g/¾ oz (3 tablespoons) grated cheese into the egg and milk mixture.

Croutons (fried bread cubes)

VERY EASY (ON THE RIGHT IN THE PHOTOGRAPH)

1 Remove the crusts, then cut the bread into cubes. Peel and finely chop the garlic.

2 Heat the butter, margarine or oil in a pan. Add the cubes of bread and fry (sauté) until crispy brown on all sides, stirring them now and again.

3 Stir in the chopped garlic (if used) and fry briefly but do not let it go brown or it will become bitter. Add the croutons to the soup just before serving.

Preparation time: about 10 minutes

3 slices white bread
1 clove garlic (optional)
30 g/1 oz (2 tablespoons) butter or margarine
or 3 tablespoons olive oil

Per serving: P: 1 g, F: 7 g, C: 9 g, kJ: 455, kcal: 109, CU: 1.0

Tomato soup

EASY

Preparation time:
about 30 minutes
Cooking time: about 15 minutes

1.5 kg/3¼ lb beef tomatoes
2 onions
2 cloves garlic
2 tablespoons cooking oil,
e.g. olive oil
500 ml/17 fl oz (2¼ cups)
vegetable or chicken stock
1 pinch sugar
salt, pepper
cayenne pepper
1 bay leaf
dried chopped oregano
a few basil leaves

Per serving:
P: 5 g, F: 6 g, C: 13 g,
kJ: 535, kcal: 126, CU: 0.0

1 Wash the tomatoes, leave to drain, cut into quarters and remove the base of the stalk. Cut the tomatoes into cubes. Peel the onions and garlic and chop finely.

2 Heat the oil in a pan. Add the chopped onions and garlic and sweat lightly until transparent. Now add the cubed tomatoes, stock, sugar, salt, pepper, cayenne pepper, bay leaf and oregano. Bring to the boil, cover and cook over low heat for about 15 minutes.

3 Remove the bay leaf, purée the soup and push it through a sieve. Bring the soup to the boil again and adjust the seasoning with more herbs if necessary. Garnish with basil leaves before serving.

TIP ›› Instead of fresh tomatoes you can also use 1 can of peeled tomatoes (800 g/1¾ lb).

EXTRA TIP ›› Pour a little olive oil into each bowl before serving the soup.

Recipe variation: To make **tomato soup with mozzarella balls** (photograph 1), drain 250 g/9 oz mozzarella cheese, chop finely and purée. Rinse 1 bunch basil, pat dry and remove the leaves from the stalks. Chop the leaves and knead into the puréed mozzarella. Season with salt and pepper. Make 18–24 mozzarella balls, arrange them in the soup bowls and pour the soup on top.

Herb soup

SOPHISTICATED (PHOTOGRAPH 2)

Preparation time:
about 25 minutes
Cooking time: about 15 minutes

4 bunches of various herbs,
e.g. chervil, dill, parsley
100 g/3½ oz leaf spinach or 50 g/
2 oz chopped frozen spinach
1 box garden cress
300 g/10 oz potatoes
1 bunch spring onions (scallions)
1 tablespoon butter, salt, pepper
800 ml/28 fl oz (3½ cups)
vegetable stock
125 g/4½ oz whipping cream or
150 g/5 oz crème fraîche
ground nutmeg

1 Wash the herbs and spinach (if using frozen spinach, defrost it first) and pat dry. Remove the leaves from the stalks and chop up the stalks.

2 Using scissors, cut off the cress but keep a small amount for the garnish. Rinse and pat dry. Peel the potatoes, rinse, drain and cut into small cubes. Prepare the spring onions, wash them, leave to drain and cut into thin slices.

3 Melt the butter in a pan. Add the chopped herb stalks, sliced spring onions and cubed potatoes; leave to sweat and season with salt and pepper. Add the stock and simmer gently over low heat for about 15 minutes.

4 Chop the herb leaves and spinach. Add to the soup. Purée the soup until absolutely smooth. Now add the cream or crème fraîche to the soup and heat briefly but do not allow it to come to the boil.

5 Season the soup with salt, pepper and nutmeg and garnish with the remaining cress.

Per serving: P: 4 g, F: 15 g, C: 16 g, kJ: 931, kcal: 223, CU: 1.0

Pea soup with sausage

FOR CHILDREN

Preparation time:
about 15 minutes
Cooking time: about 25 minutes

250 g/9 oz floury potatoes
2 onions
2–3 tablespoons cooking oil,
e.g. rapeseed (canola) oil
450 g/1 lb frozen peas or
fresh, podded peas
1 litre/1¾ pints (4½ cups)
water
about 2 heaped teaspoons
stock granules
1 teaspoon dried chopped
marjoram
salt
freshly ground pepper
1 tablespoon sugar
4 frankfurters
1–2 tablespoons chopped
peppermint leaves (optional)

Per serving:
P: 17 g, F: 21 g, C: 27 g,
kJ: 1535, kcal: 366, CU: 2.0

1 Peel the potatoes, rinse, leave to drain and chop them coarsely. Peel the onions and chop them coarsely. Heat the oil in a pan, add the chopped onions and potatoes and sweat lightly. Add the peas, then pour in the water and stock granules. Bring to the boil, cover and cook over medium heat for about 25 minutes.

2 Season the soup with more stock granules, marjoram, salt, pepper and sugar.

3 Slice the sausages, add to the soup and leave them to warm up briefly. You can also garnish the soup with peppermint leaves.

TIPS » You can also serve this soup with crème fraîche. If you purée the soup, only add the sausages after.

» Instead of slices of sausage you can add slices of roast lamb fillet and crispy, fried slices of garlic to the soup.

EXTRA TIP » 1 tablespoon chopped herbs (such as parsley, peppermint or chervil) corresponds to about 5 sprigs of the herb in question (rinsed, patted dry and chopped).

Variation: Instead of 1 litre/ 1¾ pints (4¼ cups) of water and stock granules you can use 2 cans – each 400 ml/14 fl oz (1¾ cups) – of unsweetened coconut milk and 200 ml/7 fl oz (⅞ cup) vegetable stock. Replace the slices of sausage with toasted grated coconut and chilli flakes.

Creamed vegetable soup
(Basic recipe)

Preparation time:
about 40 minutes,
including cooking time

650 g–1.1 kg/1½–2½ lb
vegetables
1 onion
25 g/1 oz (2 tablespoons)
butter or 2 tablespoons
cooking oil, e.g. rapeseed
(canola) or olive oil
1 litre/1¾ pints (4½ cups)
vegetable stock
salt, pepper
spices (optional)
soup vegetables (optional)

Per serving (Broccoli variation):
P: 5 g, F: 6 g, C: 4 g,
kJ: 369, kcal: 88, CU: 0.0

1 Prepare the vegetables: top and tail, clean, if necessary peel, rinse and drain them. Chop them up if necessary. Peel and chop the onion. Heat the butter or oil in a pan. Add the chopped onion and sweat until transparent, stirring all the time.

2 Add the vegetables you have just prepared and continue frying (sautéing) gently. Now add the vegetable stock and bring to the boil. Cook until the vegetables are done.

3 Purée the soup, then season with salt, pepper and appropriate herbs. Add the garnish of your choice and serve the soup.

» **Cream of broccoli soup** (on the right in the photograph): Remove the leaves from 700 g/1½ lb broccoli, divide into florets, peel the stalks and cut them into pieces. Wash both florets and stalks, then leave to drain. Add the stalks and florets to the chopped onion in the pan. Pour in the stock, cover and cook over medium heat for about 8 minutes, then purée the soup. Season the soup with freshly grated nutmeg and, optionally, 1–2 teaspoons yoghurt and 1 heaped teaspoon toasted slivered almonds per bowl of soup.

» **Cream of carrot soup** (at the top in the photograph): Clean and prepare 700 g/1½ lb carrots, peel, wash, leave to drain and cut into

slices about 1 cm/⅜ in thick. Add the stock, cover and cook over medium heat for 12–15 minutes, then purée the soup. Add a little sugar to the soup and, optionally, some ground ginger. Garnish with 1–2 teaspoons crème fraîche, 1 teaspoon toasted sesame seeds, or a few strips of smoked salmon if preferred.

» **Cream of squash soup:** Take 1.1 kg/2½ lb squash, cut in half, then remove the seeds and fibres from inside. Peel the squash and cut the flesh into cubes. Add the stock, cover and cook over medium heat for about 15 minutes, then purée. Now season the soup with sugar and curry powder or ground ginger. Garnish each bowl of soup to taste with 1–2 teaspoons crème fraîche, 1–2 teaspoons toasted squash seeds or chopped dill.

» **Cream of pea soup:** Add 650 g/ 1½ lb defrosted frozen peas to the chopped onion. Add the stock, cover and cook for about 8 minutes over medium heat, then purée. Now season the soup with freshly grated nutmeg, sugar and cayenne pepper. Garnish the each bowl of soup with 1–2 teaspoons crème fraîche, 1 teaspoon of roasted almond flakes, a little chopped parsley or chopped chervil or even a few shrimps.

(continued on page 24)

» **Cream of potato soup:** Prepare 1 bunch of soup vegetables. Peel the celery. Top and tail the carrots, then peel them. Wash the celery and carrots, then leave to drain. Prepare the leeks, cut them in half lengthways, wash thoroughly and leave to drain. Peel 400 g/14 oz potatoes, rinse and leave to drain. Chop the vegetables you have just prepared. Add the stock, cover and cook over medium heat for 15–20 minutes, then purée. Season the soup with grated nutmeg. Garnish each bowl of soup to taste with 1–2 teaspoons crème fraîche, a little chopped parsley or chervil or a few croutons.

» **Cream of asparagus soup** (at the front of photograph on p. 23): Wash 500 g/18 oz asparagus and peel thinly from top to bottom. Cut off the ends, removing the woody parts completely. Rinse the asparagus in cold water, leave to drain and cut into pieces about 2 cm/¾ in long. Heat 40 g/1½ oz (3 tablespoons) butter or margarine in a large pan. Add the pieces of asparagus and sweat briefly. Sprinkle 30 g/1 oz (¼ cup) plain (all purpose) flour in the pan with the asparagus. Then stir in 250 ml/8 fl oz (1 cup) chicken stock or white wine and 250 ml/ 8 fl oz (1 cup) milk. Cook the soup

uncovered over medium heat for about 20 minutes, stirring now and again. Purée the soup, stir in 150 g/5 oz crème fraîche, season with salt, pepper, a little sugar and a dash of lemon juice. If liked, garnish with a few leaves of flat parsley, rinsed and patted dry.

Cheese and leek soup

PERFECT TO MAKE AHEAD (6 SERVINGS, PHOTOGRAPH)

Preparation time: about 20 minutes
Cooking time: about 15 minutes

1 kg/2¼ lb leeks
3 tablespoons cooking oil, e.g. sunflower oil
500 g/18 oz minced (ground) meat (half beef, half pork)
salt, pepper
1 litre/1¾ pints (4½ cups) meat stock
1 jar sliced mushrooms (drained weight 315 g/11 oz)
200 g/7 oz cream cheese or soft herb cheese

Per serving:
P: 23 g, F: 29 g, C: 7 g,
kJ: 1589, kcal: 380, CU: 0.5

1 Prepare the leeks, cut in half lengthways, wash thoroughly and leave to drain. Cut them into thin strips.

2 Heat the oil in a large pan. Add the minced (ground) meat and fry (sauté) to seal while stirring, breaking up any lumps which may have formed with a fork or wooden spoon. Season with salt and pepper.

3 Now add the strips of leek and sweat briefly. Pour in the meat stock, bring to the boil, cover and cook over medium heat for about 15 minutes.

4 Drain the mushrooms in a sieve, then add to the pan. Stir in the cheese and let it melt in the hot soup while stirring; do not cook any longer. Season the soup with salt and pepper.

TIP » If you like you can also garnish the soup with a sprig of parsley.

Île flottante (Floating island)

FOR CHILDREN

Preparation time:
about 20 minutes

For the custard:
40 g/1½ oz (5 tablespoons)
custard powder (vanilla
pudding mix)
60 g/2 oz (¼ cup) sugar
1 pinch salt
1 litre/1¾ pints (4½ cups) milk
1 egg yolk (medium)
zest of ½ organic lemon
(untreated, unwaxed)

For the snow balls:
1 egg white (medium)
1 slightly heaped teaspoon
sugar

Per serving:
P: 9 g, F: 9 g, C: 34 g,
kJ: 1174, kcal: 281, CU: 3.0

1 To make the custard, mix the custard powder (vanilla pudding mix) with the sugar and salt. Then add at least 6 tablespoons milk one by one until you obtain a smooth mixture. Stir in the egg yolks. Wash the lemon in hot water and wipe dry. Peel half a lemon, removing only the yellow zest and not the white pith. Add the lemon zest to the milk in a large pan and bring to the boil.

2 Remove the pan from the heat and stir in the custard mixture, using a whisk. Return the pan to the heat and bring to the boil briefly while stirring. Remove the lemon zest from the mixture.

3 To make the egg white balls, beat the egg whites with sugar until stiff. Using 2 teaspoons, make small balls of beaten egg white; place these in the custard mixture, cover and simmer gently for about 5 minutes (the custard must only be moving very slightly).

TIP » Sprinkle the custard with cinnamon-flavoured sugar or add 50 g/2 oz (⅓ cup) raisins while cooking it. You can also garnish the custard with thin slivers of lemon zest and peppermint leaves.

Recipe variation 1: For a **chocolate custard** (photograph 1) make the custard with 1 packet of chocolate flavoured custard powder and 75 g/ 3 oz (⅓ cup) sugar but without lemon zest. You can also add a stick of cinnamon while cooking the custard, but remove it before serving.

Recipe variation 2: To make **semolina soup** (photograph 2), bring 1 litre/1¾ pints (4¼ cups) of milk to the boil with the lemon zest. Mix together 60 g/2 oz (⅜ cup) semolina and 60 g/2 oz (¼ cup) sugar and add to the milk while stirring. Leave to soak for 5 minutes without a lid. Remove the lemon zest if you prefer. Serve hot or cold.

Recipe variation 3: To make this **gruel** (photograph 3), bring 1 litre/ 1¾ pints (4¼ cups) of milk to the boil with the lemon zest. Stir in 40 g/1½ oz (½ cup) oat flakes and 1 pinch of salt. Bring briefly to the boil and simmer very gently over low heat for about 10 minutes without a lid, stirring occasionally. Finally remove the lemon zest and stir in 50 g/2 oz (¼ cup) sugar and 1 packet vanilla sugar. The gruel will have a slightly different consistency depending on the kind of oats used (soft flakes or hard grains).

Pichelsteiner or Three Meat Stew

CLASSIC (PHOTOGRAPH)

Preparation time:
about 20 minutes
Cooking time: about 60 minutes

500 g/18 oz mixed meat
from the shoulder or neck
(lamb, pork, beef)
2 onions
30 g/1 oz (2 tablespoons)
clarified butter or margarine
or 3 tablespoons cooking oil
salt, pepper
chopped marjoram
chopped lovage
500 ml/17 fl oz (2¼ cups)
vegetable stock
250 g/9 oz carrots
375g/13 oz waxy potatoes
350 g/12 oz leeks
300 g/10 oz white cabbage
2 tablespoons chopped parsley

Per serving:
P: 30 g, F: 19 g, C: 19 g,
kJ: 1550, kcal: 370, CU: 1.0

1 Pat the meat dry with a kitchen paper towel and cut into 2 cm/¾ in cubes. Peel the onions, cut them in half and then into slices.

2 Heat the clarified butter, margarine or oil in a pan. Add the cubes of meat and stir to brown them lightly all over. Then add the onion slices and fry (sauté) them briefly with the meat.

3 Season the meat with salt, pepper, marjoram and lovage. Add the vegetable stock, bring to the boil, cover and cook over medium heat for about 40 minutes.

4 Meanwhile top and tail the carrots, peel, wash, then leave to drain. Peel the potatoes, rinse and leave to drain. Cut both vegetables into cubes. Prepare the leeks, cut them in half lengthways, wash thoroughly, leave to drain and cut into slices. Remove any limp, withered outer leaves from the cabbage. Cut the cabbage into quarters, rinse, leave to drain and cut out the core. Cut the cabbage into thin strips.

5 When the meat is cooked, add the vegetables and potatoes you have just prepared and bring to the boil again. Season with salt and pepper, cover and cook for about another 20 minutes.

6 Season the stew again with more herbs and sprinkle with parsley before serving.

Haricot bean stew

EASY (ABOUT 8 SERVINGS)

Preparation time:
about 20 minutes
Cooking time: about 30 minutes

1 can haricot beans
(drained weight 530 g/19 oz)
500 g/18 oz chicken
breast fillet
375 g/13 oz floury potatoes
1 leek (about 200 g/7 oz)
300 g/10 oz carrots
75 g/3 oz celery
2 onions

1 Transfer the haricot beans into a sieve, rinse under cold water and leave to drain. Rinse the chicken breasts under cold running water, pat dry and cut into cubes of about 1 cm/⅜ in.

2 Peel the potatoes, rinse, leave to drain and cut into cubes. Prepare the leeks, cut them in half lengthways, wash thoroughly and leave to drain.

3 Top and tail the carrots, then peel them. Peel the celery. Wash the carrots and celery, then leave to drain. Peel the onions. Cut the vegetables you have just prepared into cubes or slices.

4 Heat the oil in a large pan, add the diced chicken and fry (sauté) to sear.

5 Add the prepared vegetables and potatoes to the pan with the diced chicken and fry (sauté) briefly. Add the drained haricot beans and the stock. Bring the stew to the boil again. Cut the cabanossi (pepperoni) into chunks and add to the stew. Cover and cook over medium heat for about 30 minutes.

6 Season the stew with salt and pepper. Sprinkle with thyme before serving.

TIP » You can prepare the stew in advance and freeze it.

2 tablespoons olive oil
1 litre/1¾ pints (4½ cups) vegetable or chicken stock
200 g/7 oz cabanossi (pepperoni)
salt, pepper
2 tablespoons chopped thyme

Per serving:
P: 24 g, F: 11 g, C: 19 g,
kJ: 1136, kcal: 271, CU: 1.5

Vegetable stew

VEGETARIAN

Preparation time:
about 45 minutes
Cooking time: about 25 minutes

375 g/13 oz carrots
375 g/13 oz floury potatoes
375 g/13 oz green (snap) beans
250 g/9 oz cauliflower
250 g/9 oz tomatoes
2 onions
3 sprigs basil
50 g/2 oz (4 tablespoons)
butter or margarine or
4–5 tablespoons cooking oil
salt, pepper
500 ml/17 fl oz (2¼ cups)
vegetable stock, hot
2 tablespoons chopped parsley

Per serving:
P: 7 g, F: 12 g, C: 22 g,
kJ: 931, kcal: 222, CU: 1.0

1 Top and tail the carrots, peel wash and leave to drain. Then peel the potatoes, rinse and leave to drain. Cut both carrots and potatoes into cubes. Top and tail the green (snap) beans and, if necessary, remove the stringy thread. Wash the beans, leave to drain and cut or break into pieces.

2 Remove the green leaves of the cauliflower and cut out the core. Divide the cauliflower into florets, rinse and leave to dry. Wash the tomatoes, leave to drain, make a cross-shaped incision, plunge briefly in boiling water, then dip into cold water. Peel the tomatoes, cut into quarters and remove the base of the stalk.

3 Peel and chop the onion. Rinse the basil, pat dry and remove the leaves from the stalks. Chop finely and put them to one side for the garnish. Now also finely chop the stalks.

4 Melt the butter, margarine or oil in a pan. Add the chopped onion, cubed potatoes and beans and fry (sauté) together for about 5 minutes, stirring all the time. Season with salt and pepper. Add the chopped basil stalks and vegetable stock, bring to the boil, cover and continue cooking over medium heat for about 5 minutes.

5 Add the chopped carrots and cauliflower florets, cover and cook a further 15 minutes.

6 Add the quartered tomatoes and cook for a further 2 minutes. Season the stew with salt and pepper. Decorate with parsley and basil before serving.

Variation: For a **vegetable stew with meatballs** (photograph 1), squeeze about 300 g/10 oz fresh sausage meat out of the skins, shape into small balls and add to the stew so that they cook in it for the last 5 minutes.

Recipe variation: To make **minestrone** (photograph 2), prepare 200 g/7 oz carrots, 300 g/10 oz waxy boiling potatoes, 150 g/5 oz courgettes (zucchini), 200 g/7 oz leeks, 100 g/3½ oz celery sticks (stalks) and 100 g/3½ oz green (snap) beans. Clean, if necessary peel, rinse and leave to drain. Peel 2 onions and slice. Finely chop 75 g/ 3 oz streaky bacon. Peel 2 beef tomatoes (see step 2 above), cut them in half and remove the seeds. Finely chop the vegetables you have prepared. Heat 2 tablespoons olive oil in a large pan. Add the diced bacon and chopped onion, then fry (sauté) lightly, stirring all the time. Now add the finely chopped carrots, potatoes, celery and beans and continue frying. Add 1 litre/ 1¾ pints (4¼ cups) vegetable stock, bring to the boil, cover and cook for 10–12 minutes. Then add the courgettes (zucchini), leeks, 100 g/ 3½ oz frozen peas and 50 g/2 oz crescent-shaped noodles, bring to the boil again, cover and cook for a further 5–7 minutes. Add the tomatoes with 2 tablespoons chopped parsley and 2 tablespoons chopped basil. Season with salt and pepper as well as sweet paprika powder.

Sprinkle with 70 g/3 oz (½ cup) freshly grated Parmesan before serving.

Savoy cabbage stew (lamb stew)

CLASSIC

Preparation time:
about 30 minutes
Cooking time: about 45 minutes

500 g/18 oz beef or lamb
(shoulder)
2 onions
3 tablespoons cooking oil,
e.g. sunflower or rapeseed
(canola) oil
salt, pepper
ground caraway seeds
750 ml/1¼ pints (3½ cups)
vegetable stock, hot
1 kg/2¼ lb savoy cabbage
375 g/13 oz floury potatoes
2 tablespoons chopped parsley
(optional)

Per serving:
P: 33 g, F: 16 g, C: 17 g,
kJ: 1458, kcal: 349, CU: 1.0

1 Pat the meat dry with a kitchen paper towel and cut into 2 cm/¾ in cubes. Peel the onions, cut in half and slice.

2 Heat the oil in large pan. Add the meat cubes and fry (sauté) lightly to sear, stirring all the time.

3 Now add the sliced onions and fry lightly with the meat.

4 Season the meat with salt, pepper and caraway. Add the vegetable stock, bring to the boil, cover and cook over medium heat for about 30 minutes.

5 Meanwhile remove the outer, yellowish leaves of the savoy cabbage. Cut the cabbage into quarters, rinse, leave to drain, cut out the core and cut the cabbage into strips. Peel the potatoes, rinse and cut into cubes.

6 When the meat is done, add the cabbage and potatoes, bring to the boil, cover and cook for a further 15 minutes.

7 Adjust the seasoning again and, optionally, sprinkle with parsley before serving.

TIP » To obtain about 500 g/18 oz lean and boneless lamb meat, you need a shoulder on the bone weighing about 900 g/2 lb. This stew can be frozen.

Green (snap) bean stew

FOR VISITORS

1 Rinse the beef under running cold water, pat dry and cut into 2 cm/ ¾ in cubes. Peel and chop the onion. Rinse the savory and pat dry.

2 Heat the clarified butter, margarine or oil in a pan. Add the cubes of beef and brown lightly while turning them. Shortly before the meat is fully browned, add the chopped onions and fry (sauté) briefly with the meat.

3 Season the meat with salt and pepper. Add the savory and vegetable stock, bring everything to the boil, cover and cook over medium heat for about 40 minutes.

4 Meanwhile, top and tail the beans, removing the stringy fibres. Wash them, then cut or break them into small pieces. Wash the potatoes, peel, rinse and cut into small cubes.

5 Add the bean pieces and cubed potatoes. Season with salt and pepper, bring to the boil again, cover and cook everything for a further 20 minutes.

6 Remove the savory from the stew. Adjust the seasoning by adding more salt and pepper if necessary and sprinkle with parsley just before serving.

TIP » This stew is also suitable for freezing.

Recipe variation: To make lamb stew with green (snap) beans and tomatoes, use shoulder of lamb instead of beef. Also wash 2 or 3 tomatoes and leave to drain. Make a cross-shaped incision, plunge briefly in boiling water, then dip into cold water. Peel the tomatoes and cut out the base of the stalks. Now cut the peeled tomatoes into cubes and add to the stew shortly before the end of the cooking time. Sprinkle with basil if desired.

Preparation time: about 30 minutes
Cooking time: about 60 minutes

500 g/18 oz beef (shoulder)
1 onion
2–3 sprigs summer savory
30 g/1 oz (2 tablespoons) clarified butter or margarine or 3 tablespoons cooking oil, e.g. sunflower oil
salt
freshly ground pepper
500 ml/17 fl oz (2¼ cups) vegetable stock
1 kg/2¼ lb green (snap) beans
500 g/18 oz waxy potatoes
1–2 tablespoons chopped parsley

Per serving:
P: 34 g, F: 15 g, C: 23 g,
kJ: 1529, kcal: 364, CU: 2.0

Lentil and mettwurst sausage stew

EASY

Preparation time:
about 25 minutes
Cooking time: about 25 minutes

1 bunch soup vegetables
(celery, carrots, leeks)
250 g/9 oz (1½ cups) dried
lentils
375 g/13 oz waxy potatoes
2 onions
2 tablespoons cooking oil,
e.g. sunflower or rapeseed
(canola) oil
1.5 litres/2¾ pints (7 cups)
vegetable stock
4 Mettwurst sausages
(cured and smoked, about
90 g/3 oz each)
white wine vinegar
salt
freshly ground pepper
pinch of sugar
2 tablespoons chopped parsley

Per serving:
P: 34 g, F: 38 g, C: 50 g,
kJ: 2851, kcal: 685, CU: 3.5

1 Peel the celery. Top and tail the carrots, then peel. Wash the celery and carrots, then leave to drain. Prepare the leeks, cut in half lengthways, wash thoroughly, leave to drain. Chop up the soup vegetables.

2 Put the lentils in a sieve and rinse under cold water. Peel the potatoes, rinse, leave to drain and cut into cubes. Peel the onions, cut in half, then slice.

3 Heat the oil in a pan, add the prepared vegetables and potatoes, then fry (sauté) lightly. Add the vegetable stock and lentils, bring to the boil, cover and cook over medium heat for about 15 minutes.

4 Add the sausages and cook for a further 10 minutes.

5 Season the stew with vinegar, salt, pepper and a little sugar. Sprinkle with parsley before serving.

TIP » If you like, add 1 bay leaf and remove just before serving.

Recipe variation 1: To make a quick lentil stew, use tinned lentils. Cook the cubed potatoes in 750 ml/ 1¼ pints (3½ cups) vegetable stock, with the lid on, over medium heat for about 10 minutes. Then add the sausages, cover and cook for a further 5 minutes. Finally add 1 can of lentils with soup vegetables (800 g/1¾ lb), then cook all together for another 5 minutes. Season with salt, pepper, vinegar and sugar.

Recipe variation 2: To make a vegetarian lentil stew (photograph 1), increase the amount of potatoes to 500–600 g/18–20 oz and leave out the sausages. Optionally, sprinkle with grated Parmesan just before serving.

Recipe variation 3: To make a squash and lentil stew (photograph 2), peel 3 onions and 2 cloves of garlic and finely chop both. Remove the seeds from 500 g/18 oz squash, peel and cut the flesh into chunks. Prepare 200 g/7 oz celery sticks (stalks) and remove the outer stringy fibres. Rinse the celery, leave to drain and chop into pieces. Peel 450 g/1 lb potatoes, rinse, leave to drain and cut into cubes. Rinse 100 g/3½ oz lentils in cold water and leave to drain. Heat 2 tablespoons pumpkin seed oil (or if not available, sunflower oil) in a pan. Add the chopped onion and garlic and fry (sauté) lightly. Add the prepared vegetables together with the lentils and 1 litre/1¾ pints (4¼ cups) vegetable stock. Bring to the boil, cover and cook for 20–25 minutes over medium heat. Meanwhile cut 200 g/7 oz frankfurters into thick slices. Rinse 1 bunch of lemon thyme, pat dry and remove the leaves from the stems. Add the sliced sausage and lemon thyme to the hot-pot, cover and cook for a further 10 minutes. Adjust the seasoning with salt and pepper just before serving and, optionally, sprinkle 2 tablespoons pumpkin seed oil on top.

Meat

Since taste and flavour are so important, always buy first-class quality meat. You can assess the quality of meat by checking its colour, smell, taste and texture. Quality also depends on the age, weight and breed of the animal from which it came. But meat does more than contribute to the pleasure of your palate; it also contains important proteins and is rich in amino acids. Meat protein is biologically more efficient than plant protein. This means that meat protein is more easily converted into the kind of protein naturally produced in the body, and protein is the basic component of all the cells in the body. Meat is also rich in vitamins, minerals (for instance zinc and iron) and trace elements. The nutritional value of meat depends on the type and cut of the meat and how it was produced.

Texture of the meat
The meat of well-fed animals contains variable amounts of fat, depending on the piece. Even relatively lean meat benefits from the presence of fat because fat enhances the succulence and flavour of the meat. Meat which is streaked with thin veins of fat is described as marbled; this marbling is particularly distinguishable in rump steak and bee sirloin. When the fat is located between the muscle tissue of meat, such as in pork spare rib chops, the meat is said to be marbled (photograph 1).

Veal –
A particularly delicate flavour
Veal comes from calves which are not older than three months. Compared to beef, veal is a more tender meat and has a more delicate flavour.

Lamb –
A slightly different taste
Lamb has a strongly aromatic flavour which adds a special touch to dishes. Fresh lamb, normally relatively local in origin, is widely available in supermarkets and from the butcher. Frozen lamb, on the other hand, usually comes from New Zealand.

Important: Only the meat from animals less than 12 months old can be called lamb. Suckling or milk-fed lamb comes from lambs no older than 3–6 months (or very often younger) which have never grazed.

Pork –
Versatile and tasty
Pork comes mainly from pigs which are 7–8 months old and are not yet sexually mature. After 2 days the meat will have already matured sufficiently and developed its distinctive taste.

Beef –
Dark and hearty
Usually only meat from young beef cattle is available in the shops. After hanging for a certain time in a refrigerated warehouse, it develops its characteristic aroma and becomes tender and mellow.

Mince –
Popular and versatile
Minced (ground) meat (photograph 2) can be made from all kinds of meat but the only kinds normally available in the shops are beef, pork, lamb and poultry.
» Ground beef (a) is used to make "steak hâché" or "steak tartare";

it is made from lean and boneless muscular meat from beef cattle and at 6% it has the lowest fat content.

» Minced beef (b) consists of meat with the sinews coarsely removed and must not contain more than 20% fat.

» Pork mince (c) is made from meat from which the fat has been roughly removed and then minced; it has a maximum fat content of 35%.

» Ground pork (d) is minced pork which has already been seasoned with spices – for instance Thüringian mince.

» Mixed mince (e) is made from half beef and half pork and has a fat content of 30%.

» "Kalbsbrät" is sausage meat made from lean veal, with the sinews roughly removed.

To make minced meat dishes even more attractive, you can add either 1 roll, previously soaked and squeezed to remove as much liquid as possible, or 1 large, mashed, boiled potato, or 1–2 tablespoons cooked rice, or 1–2 slices of toasted bread previously soaked and squeezed to remove as much liquid as possible, or a few tablespoons of quark (curd cheese) or 2 table-

Because minced (ground) meat goes bad very quickly there are strict rules for dealing with it. When buying mince always check the date on which it was prepared. Whether you buy mince ready-made or mince it yourself in a mincing machine, you should always either process it immediately or within one day. It must be kept in the refrigerator until you use it.

spoons soaked and drained cereals (for instance, oats).

To make a meat loaf, meatballs or rissoles from minced meat, first moisten your hands with a little water to stop the meat from sticking to your hands, then shape the minced meat into the shape desired. The result will be even more success-ful if you add 1 egg white or 1 whole egg to the minced meat – egg white will make the mince more compact and help it to stick together while a whole egg will make the mince lighter.

Storing meat properly

If you will not be using the meat immediately, you can wrap it up and freeze it. Then, before you want to use it later, leave it covered in the refrigerator to defrost. When it has done so, pour the defrosting liquid away immediately since it might contain bacteria which could be dangerous to you health. Once the meat has been defrosted it must on no account be frozen again because bacteria will have multiplied during the defrosting process which would not be killed when frozen again. When buying shrink-wrapped meat, check the "use-by" date and the recommended storage temperature.

Preparing the meat properly
Meat should always be as fresh as possible when you buy it because it goes bad very quickly as a result of its protein and water content. Do not wash the meat before preparing it; just pat it dry. Then prepare the meat as described in the recipe. If you are not using the meat at once, cover it and store in the refrigerator.

Before cutting the meat into pieces to be served, carefully remove any traces of skin and sinews. Add cooking oil, butter or margarine, depending on the recipe, then heat the pan or skillet until it is very hot and add the meat. When one side has browned, turn the meat over to cook the other side – it is best to do this with tongs (photograph 1) or a spatula, not a fork. In this way you will avoid pricking the meat so the juices will remain inside; it will remain tender and moist as a result.

Cooking the meat properly
» **Pan-frying (sautéing):** For pan-frying it is best to use tender meat from young animals. Usually the meat is cut into individual servings because flat surfaces are better for frying. For a tasty crust, it is recommended that the meat should be seasoned before frying.
Important: seasoning with salt should only be done immediately before frying because salt will draw moisture out of the meat which then becomes dried out. Red meat such as beef is fried "au naturel" and may be cooked so as to be more or less done. White meat such as veal or pork can be coated in breadcrumbs or flour and then

fried. This makes a beautiful, tasty crust while also preventing the meat from drying out.

» **Roasting:** When meat is cooked in the oven, it is usually cooked in a roasting tin and, depending on the recipe, with or without a lid. This makes it possible to brown the meat beautifully with or without adding extra fat. Roasting is particularly suitable for large pieces of meat or poultry. It is important to preheat the oven to the temperature indicated in the recipe. Meanwhile fry (sauté) the meat in hot fat in the roasting tin on the stove until brown all over. When the oven is hot enough, put the meat in it on the shelf recommended in the recipe. If the liquid in roasting tin should evaporate, add more. Also baste the meat regularly with the meat juices in the roasting tin to make it even more flavourful.

» **Braising:** In braising, the meat is cooked on the stove in a pan with the lid on over low heat. First add a little fat to the pan and heat it up. Season the chunks or pieces of

meat, put the meat in the hot fat in the pan and brown on all sides. The meat can be cooked with a selection of onions, garlic, carrots, celery, leeks (photograph 2) and tomatoes, depending on the recipe. Add a little water, wine or stock and scrape the cooking residues from the bottom of the pan; then add more liquid until the meat is one-third covered by the liquid. Bring to the boil, then turn the heat down. Season with herbs and spices. Cover the pan and continue cooking over low heat on the stove or in the oven. Turn or stir the meat occasionally during the cooking and, if necessary, add more water, stock or wine, depending on the recipe. The meat is cooked when it feels almost completely soft when you press it. Braising is especially recommended to beginners because precise cooking times are not vital with this method of cooking – half-an-hour too long will do no harm to the meat.

» **Testing when it is "done":** The juices exuded by the meat when it is cut will give you an idea of whether it is cooked enough or not. When a

Meat will be particularly tender and moist if it is cooked according to the "slow-cooking" method. First you must seal the meat by browning it vigorously on all sides in a pan on the stove. Now put the pan with the meat into the preheated oven (top and bottom heat: 80–95 °C/180–200 °F for poultry and large roasts) and cook following the instructions in the recipe. With this cooking method it is important that the low cooking temperature should be carefully maintained; therefore it is advisable to use an oven thermometer to check the temperature during the cooking. When cooked the internal temperature of the meat must be at least 60 °C/140 °F in the case of beef and lamb, while in the case of poultry, venison and pork, the internal temperature of the meat must be at least 70 °C/160 °F. It is best to check the internal temperature of the meat with a digital probe thermometer.

piece of meat cooked, the meat juices should run clear, not pink or red. You can also check whether the meat is adequately cooked by pressing it with a spoon. If the meat gives a lot and feels soft, then that piece of meat is still red inside. If the meat is springy, it is pink inside. When the meat does not give at all when pressed with a spoon, it means that the meat is cooked through.

» **Carving meat:** Large roasted pieces of meat in particular but steaks as well should be allowed to stand for at least 10 minutes, covered with a sufficiently large plate or foil to keep it hot. This will let the meat juices settle evenly so that the meat is juicy and tender. Always carve meat across the grain. Reserve the meat juices which run from the meat while carving it and use them in the sauce.

» **A delicious sauce:** The sauce is often the perfect finishing touch when serving a roast or fried (sautéed) meat. It usually prepared using the cooking residues on the bottom the pan after the meat has finished cooking. The flavour of the cooking residues is enhanced by the addition of vegetables such as onions, garlic, carrots, celery and leeks, cut very small. You can also add tomatoes and tomato purée. To make a perfect sauce, remove the meat from the roasting tin and put it in a warm place; then carefully remove the fat from the cooking juices. Now loosen the cooking residue in the pan with wine, water or stock. This will give you the basis for a delicious sauce to accompany the meat.

Meatballs

EASY (AT THE BACK OF THE PHOTOGRAPH)

Preparation time:
about 35 minutes,
excluding cooling time

1 day-old bread roll
2 onions
1–2 tablespoons cooking oil,
e.g. sunflower oil
600 g/1¼ lb minced (ground)
meat (half beef, half pork)
1 egg (medium)
salt
freshly ground pepper
sweet paprika
40 g/1½ oz (3 tablespoons)
margarine or 5 tablespoons
cooking oil, e.g. sunflower
or rapeseed (canola) oil

Per serving:
P: 32 g, F: 33 g, C: 10 g,
kJ: 1921, kcal: 459, CU: 0.5

1 Soak the bread roll in cold water. Peel and finely chop the onions. Heat the oil in a pan. Add the chopped onions and sweat for 2–3 minutes until transparent, stirring all the time. Remove the fried onions from the pan and leave to drain on a kitchen paper towel as well as to cool a little.

2 Squeeze as much liquid as possible from the bread roll (photograph 1) and mix with the minced (ground) meat, chopped onion and egg (photograph 2). Season the meat mixture with salt, pepper and ground paprika. Moisten your hands and make 8 meatballs (photograph 3).

3 Heat the oil in the pan. Add the meatballs and fry (sauté) over medium heat for about 10 minutes, turning them over occasionally until both sides are brown and the meatballs are cooked.

TIP » Serve in the traditional way with mashed potatoes (p. 166), peas (p. 119) and carrots (p. 118).

Recipe variation 1: To make meatballs with sheep's cheese filling (bottom of photograph), add a teaspoon of dried thyme leaves to the meat mixture and divide into 8 servings. Cut 200 g/7 oz sheep's cheese in to 8 equal-sized cubes. Make 8 flat shapes from the meat mixture, put 1 cube of cheese on each and wrap the meat mixture round it. Fry as described in the recipe.

Recipe variation 2: To make Königsberger Klopse (meatballs with capers and anchovies), soak 1 day-old bread roll in cold water for about 10 minutes. Peel and finely chop 1 onion. Mix 500 g/18 oz minced meat (half beef, half pork) with the well-squeezed bread roll, chopped onion, 1 large egg or 1 egg white and 2 level teaspoons mustard. Season with salt and pepper. Meanwhile bring to the boil 750 ml/ 1¼ pints (3½ cups) vegetable stock. Make 8–10 meatballs from the meat mixture, then drop them into the vegetable stock. Bring back to the boil and simmer the meatballs over low heat for about 15 minutes. Pour the meatballs into a sieve, collect the stock and reserve about 500 ml/ 17 fl oz (2¼ cups). For the sauce, melt 30 g/1 oz (2 tablespoons) butter or margarine in a pan. Stir in 30 g/ 1 oz (¼ cup) plain (all purpose) flour and continue stirring until the mixture has become smooth and light yellow. Pour the 500 ml/17 fl oz (2¼ cups) stock you have put aside into the mixture and stir well with a whisk, making sure there are no lumps. Bring the sauce to the boil and simmer over low heat without a lid for about 5 minutes. Stir together 1 egg yolk (from a small egg) and 2 tablespoons milk, then stir slowly into the sauce. Do not let the sauce boil again. Add a small jar of capers, including the liquid (drained weight 20 g/¾ oz). Season with salt, pepper, sugar and lemon juice. Add the meatballs to the sauce and simmer for about 5 minutes over low heat. Sprinkle a little dill on top.

Sausages

FOR CHILDREN

1 Pat the sausages dry with a kitchen paper towel. Then prick them several times all over with a fork.

2 Heat the oil or margarine in a pan. Add the sausages and fry (sauté) them without a lid over medium heat for about 10 minutes, turning them occasionally, until beautifully brown all over.

Serve with: mashed potatoes (p. 166) and red cabbage (p. 120) or sauerkraut (p. 128).

TIP » You can also make meatballs with the sausage meat. Just squeeze the sausage meat out of its skin and shape into small balls. Fry for about 10 minutes until nice and brown.

Preparation time: about 15 minutes

4 boiled or fresh bratwurst
30 g/1 oz margarine
or 3 tablespoons cooking oil

Per serving:
P: 15 g, F: 26 g, C: 0 g,
kJ: 1227, kcal: 293, CU: 0.0

Pork escalopes in mushroom sauce

CLASSIC

Preparation time:
about 35 minutes

1 onion
250 g/9 oz mushrooms
4 pork escalopes (about
200 g/7 oz each)
salt
freshly ground pepper
sweet paprika
40 g/1½ oz (⅜ cup) plain
(all purpose) flour
50 g/2 oz (4 tablespoons)
margarine or 5 tablespoons
cooking oil, e.g. sunflower oil
1 carton (150 g/5 oz)
crème fraîche
1 tablespoon chopped parsley

Per serving:
P: 49 g, F: 26 g, C: 6 g,
kJ: 1905, kcal: 457, CU: 0.5

1 Peel and chop 1 onion. Prepare the mushrooms, rub clean with a kitchen paper towel and cut them into slices.

2 Pat the escalopes dry with a kitchen paper towel, then season with salt, pepper and ground paprika. Turn the cutlets over in the flour. Gently shake off the loose flour.

3 Heat the oil or margarine in a pan. Add the escalopes and fry (sauté) on both sides over medium heat for 10–12 minutes (depending on the thickness), turning them from time to time. Then remove the escalopes from the pan and keep in a warm place.

4 Now add the chopped onion to the remaining fat in the pan and fry while stirring. Add the sliced mushrooms and fry with the onions. Stir in the crème fraîche. Season the sauce with salt and pepper and simmer without a lid over low heat for 2–3 minutes. Stir in the parsley. Serve the sauce with the escalopes.

Serve with: fried potatoes (p. 168) and leaf salad.

Recipe variation 1: To make Gypsy Schnitzel, prepare the escalopes as described in steps 2 and 3. Then add 1 jar (500 g/18 oz) of gypsy sauce (Zigeuner sauce) to the cooking residues in the pan, heat up and serve with the cutlets.

Recipe variation 2: To make veal escalopes cordon bleu, ask the butcher to cut a pouch in 4 veal escalopes (about 200 g/7 oz each). Dry the escalopes with a kitchen paper towel, season with salt and pepper and stuff each one with 1 slice each of cheese and ham. Turn the veal escalopes first in about 40 g/1½ oz (⅜ cup) plain (all purpose) flour (photograph 1), then in 2 beaten eggs (photograph 2) and finally in about 60 g/2 oz (¾ cup) dried breadcrumbs (photograph 3); gently shake off the loose breadcrumbs. Fry the escalopes for about 10 minutes, turning them over very gently from time to time. Instead of using veal escalopes you can use pork or turkey escalopes.

Recipe variation 3: For pork chops coated in breadcrumbs, pat dry 4 pork chops (about 200 g/7 oz each) with a kitchen paper towel. Season on both sides with salt, pepper and sweet paprika. Then turn over the chops first in 20 g/¾ oz (3 tablespoons) plain (all purpose) flour, then in beaten egg and finally in 40 g/1½ oz dried breadcrumbs. Press hard into the breadcrumbs and gently shake off the loose breadcrumbs. Heat 5 tablespoons cooking oil in a pan. Add the chops and fry on both sides for about 8 minutes over medium heat, then place on a previously warmed dish. Serve the chops with parsley potatoes (p. 158), a mushroom sauce or mixed vegetables (p. 118).

German pot roast

WITH WINE

Preparation time:
about 45 minutes,
excluding marinating time
Braising time: 1½–2 hours

750 g/1½ lb beef topside
(round)

For the marinade:
2 onions
1 bunch soup vegetables
(celery, carrots, leeks)
5 juniper berries
15 peppercorns
5 allspice corns
2 cloves
1 bay leaf
250 ml/8 fl oz (1 cup) white
wine vinegar
375 ml/13 fl oz (1⅝ cups)
water or red wine
3 tablespoons cooking oil,
e.g. sunflower or rape seed
(canola) oil
salt, pepper
375 ml/13 fl oz (1⅝ cups)
reserved marinade liquid
50 g/2 oz pumpernickel or
gingerbread
a little sugar

Per serving:
P: 43 g, F: 13 g, C: 14 g,
kJ: 1538, kcal: 368, CU: 1.0

1 Pat the meat dry with a kitchen paper towel.

2 For the marinade, peel the onion and cut into slices. Prepare the celery and carrots, peel and wash; then leave to drain. Prepare the leeks, cut in half lengthways, wash thoroughly and leave them to drain. Cut up the vegetables you have just prepared into small pieces.

3 Stir the onions and soup vegetables together with the juniper berries, peppercorns, allspice corns, cloves, bay leaf, vinegar and water or red wine. Put the meat in a bowl and pour in the marinade (photograph 1). Cover the bowl with a lid or clingfilm (plastic wrap) and leave to marinade in the refrigerator for about 2 days, stirring occasionally.

4 Then remove the marinated meat from the marinade and pat dry. Pour the marinade through a sieve and reserve 375 ml/13 fl oz (1⅝ cups). Put the marinade and the vegetables to one side.

5 Heat the oil in a heavy-based saucepan. Add the meat and brown briskly on all sides, then season with salt and pepper. Add the drained vegetables and continue frying (sautéing) briefly. Add a little of the reserved marinade to the meat and vegetables. Cover and braise over medium heat for about 30 minutes, stirring occasionally. As the liquid in the pan evaporates, gradually replace with more marinade.

6 Crumble the pumpernickel or gingerbread finely, add to the pan and continue cooking for about another 1½ hours.

7 When cooked, remove from the heat and leave to rest for about 10 minutes so that the meat juices have time to settle.

8 Rub the cooking juices together with the vegetables through a sieve and heat up the liquid again. Season this sauce with salt, pepper and sugar. Slice the meat and arrange on a preheated dish. Serve the sauce with the meat.

Serve with: macaroni or boiled potato dumplings (p. 170), red cabbage (p. 120).

Recipe variation 1: For a sweet pot roast (photograph 2), add to the sauce 50 g/2 oz (⅓ cup) raisins or 100 g/3½ oz halved grapes with the seeds removed. Instead of gingerbread, use 20 g/¾ oz (¼ cup) grated plain (unsweetened) chocolate.

Recipe variation 2: For a beef stew in the Sauerland style (photograph 3): Pat the meat dry with a kitchen paper towel, cut up into largish chunks and put in a shallow bowl. Prepare the marinade as described above but add only 200 ml/7 fl oz (⅞ cup) red wine, water and 5 tablespoons white wine vinegar. Coarsely chop 250 g/9 oz (1⅔ cups) mixed dried fruit (for instance, plums, apples, apricots, raisins) and soak in 500 ml/17 fl oz (2¼ cups) lukewarm water. Leave the meat to drain in a sieve and

reserve the marinade. Now fry the meat and vegetables as described in the recipe and season. Add the dried fruit together with the

soaking and marinade liquids and braise for about 40 minutes, stirring occasionally. Finally season with salt and pepper.

1

2

3

Cured pork loin
EASY (ABOUT 6 SERVINGS)

Preparation time:
about 20 minutes
Roasting time: about 50 minutes

1.5 kg/3¼ lb cured pork loin
(boned by the butcher and
supplied with the bones
chopped into pieces)
1 onion
1 tomato
1 bunch soup vegetables
(celery, carrots, leeks)
1 small bay leaf
400 ml/14 fl oz (1¾ cups) hot
water
dark gravy thickener
(optional)
salt
freshly ground pepper

Per serving:
P: 36 g, F: 17 g, C: 5 g,
kJ: 1317, kcal: 314, CU: 0.0

1 Pat the meat dry with a kitchen paper towel and make incisions on the top to form a trellis shape. Preheat the oven:
Top and bottom heat:
about 200 °C/400 °F (Gas mark 6)
Fan oven:
about 180 °C/350 °F (Gas mark 4)

2 Peel the onions. Wash the tomatoes, leave to drain, cut into quarters and remove the base of the stalk. Prepare the celery and carrots, peel, wash, then leave to drain. Prepare the leeks, cut them in half lengthways, wash thoroughly and leave to drain. Finely chop up all the soup vegetables.

3 Rinse a roasting tin with water. Place the meat in it with the incised top facing upwards. Add the vegetables, bay leaf and bones. Put the roasting tin without a lid on a shelf in the bottom third of the preheated oven. Cook the meat for about 50 minutes.

4 If the cooking juices begin to burn, add a little more hot water. As the liquid evaporates gradually replace it with hot water. Baste the meat regularly with the cooking juices.

5 When the meat is cooked, remove from the roasting tin together with the bones. Cover the meat and leave to rest so that the meat juices settle.

6 For the sauce, loosen the cooking residues on the bottom of the roasting tin with a little water. Rub the cooking residues and vegetables through a sieve. Put back on the stove and bring to the boil again. If you like you can thicken the sauce with gravy thickener and reduce it a little. Slice the meat and arrange on a preheated dish. Adjust the seasoning of the sauce with salt and pepper and serve with the meat.

Serve with: boiled potatoes or mashed potatoes (p. 166) and sauerkraut (p. 128).

Recipe variation: For cured smoked pork loin with herb pesto, take 750 g/ 1½ lb pork loin and pat dry with a kitchen paper towel. Cut off any fat. Place the meat in an oven roasting bag, seal following the instructions on the packet and place on a baking sheet. Slide the baking sheet into the preheated oven and cook for about 45 minutes at the temperature indicated in the recipe. To make the pesto, fry (sauté) 30 g/1 oz (¼ cup) pine nuts in a pan without fat, then leave to cool. Drain 30 g/1 oz dried tomatoes preserved in oil and chop coarsely. Prepare the mixed herbs: for instance, 1 bunch basil, 1 bunch parsley and 1 box mustard cress. Peel 1 clove garlic. Purée all the ingredients with 150 ml/5 fl oz (⅝ cup) olive oil. Take 30g/1 oz (¼ cup) grated Parmesan and stir into the mixture. Finally season the pesto with salt, pepper and sweet paprika. Leave the meat to rest in the oven roasting bag for about 10 minutes and serve with the pesto.

Crispy pork roast with crackling

POPULAR (ABOUT 6 SERVINGS)

Preparation time:
about 35 minutes
Braising time: about 1½ hours

1.25 kg/5½ lb pork loin with
crackling
salt
3 onions
1 bunch soup vegetables
(carrots, celery, leeks)
20 g/¾ oz (1½ tablespoons)
clarified butter or margarine
500 ml/17 fl oz (2¼ cups) beer
freshly ground pepper
1 teaspoon ground caraway
seeds
6 cloves
a little meat stock or water
(if needed)
1 tablespoon cornflour
(cornstarch)

Per serving:
P: 47 g, F: 17 g, C: 9 g,
kJ: 1682, kcal: 402, CU: 0.5

1 Bring plenty of water to the boil in a large pan. Add salt at the rate of 3 teaspoons salt per 3 litres/5¼ pints (12 cups) water, then add the meat. Cook the joint of pork, letting it simmer gently over low heat for about 45 minutes. Then preheat the oven: top and bottom heat: about 200 °C/400 °F (Gas mark 6), fan oven: about 180 °C/350 °F (Gas mark 4).

2 Meanwhile peel the onion and cut into quarters. Prepare and wash the soup vegetables, leave to drain and cut into pieces. Heat the clarified butter or margarine in a roasting tin, add the vegetables and fry (sauté) briskly. Then add half the beer.

3 Remove the meat from the water, leave to drain and cut the skin about 1 cm/⅜ in deep with a utility knife so as to make a diamond-shaped pattern. Season the meat with salt, pepper and caraway. Insert the cloves at the points where the incisions cross.

4 Place the joint on the vegetables in the roasting tin. Put the roasting tin without a lid on a shelf in the bottom third of the preheated oven. Cook the joint for about 45 minutes.

5 Pour a little beer over the joint now and again. About 10 minutes before the end of the cooking time, pour the rest of the beer over the meat and continue cooking until done. If there is not enough liquid, add a little stock or water.

6 Take the meat out of the roasting tin and leave to rest for a while. Pour the cooking juices through a sieve and bring to the boil. Mix together the cornflour (cornstarch) and a little water until the mixture is smooth, then stir it into the liquid. Cook the sauce for about 5 minutes, stirring occasionally. Season with salt and pepper.

Serve with: Savoy cabbage (p. 132) or thick slices of coarse rye bread.

TIP » While it is easier to cut the thick skin with a utility knife, a very sharp carving knife can also be used.

Cabbage roulade

SUITABLE FOR FREEZING

Preparation time:
about 30 minutes
Braising time: about 45 minutes

water
salt
1 head Savoy cabbage or white
cabbage (about 1.5 kg/3¼ lb)

For the filling:
1 day-old bread roll
1 onion
1 egg (medium)
about 1 teaspoon medium
strong mustard
375g/13 oz minced (ground)
beef
salt
freshly ground pepper
4 tablespoons cooking oil,
e.g. rapeseed (canola) oil
500 ml/17 fl oz (2¼ cups)
vegetable stock
1–2 teaspoons cornflour
(cornstarch)
2 tablespoons cold water

Also:
cooking string or
roulade needles

Per serving:
P: 23 g, F: 25 g, C: 12 g,
kJ: 1517, kcal: 362, CU: 1.0

1 Bring plenty of water to the boil in a large pan. Add salt at the rate of 1 teaspoon salt per 1 litre/1¾ pints (4¼ cups) water. Meanwhile remove any yellowish outer leaves from the Savoy or white cabbage. Rinse the cabbage, leave to drain and cut out the base of the stalk by removing a cone-shaped piece (photograph 1). Place the cabbage in the boiling water until the outer leaves become detached. Repeat this process until you have removed 12 large leaves which are sufficiently soft. Pat the leaves dry and shave off the thick leaf vein in the middle to make it flat.

2 To make the stuffing, soak the roll in cold water. Peel and chop the onion. Squeeze the roll to remove as much water as possible, then mix together with the chopped onion, egg, mustard and minced (ground) meat. Season with salt and pepper.

3 For each serving, place 2–3 large leaves on top of each other and put a quarter of the stuffing on top; then roll them up (photograph 2). Secure the roulades by tying cooking string round each one or secure with roulade needles (photograph 3).

4 Heat the oil in a pan. Add the roulades and brown on all sides. Add the vegetable stock. Cover and cook the roulades over low heat for about 45 minutes, stirring occasionally.

5 Take the cooked roulades out of the pan, remove the cooking string or roulade needles. Arrange the roulades on a previously warmed dish and keep in warm place.

6 Stir together the cornflour (cornstarch) and water. Bring the cooking liquid to the boil and stir in the mixture just prepared with a whisk. Bring the sauce to the boil again and simmer gently for about 5 minutes. Season the sauce with salt and pepper and serve with the roulade.

Serve with: boiled potatoes (p. 158), mashed potatoes (p. 166), bread dumplings (p. 172) or potato dumplings (p. 170).

TIP » Use the rest of the cabbage to make a vegetable accompaniment for another dish (Savoy cabbage, p. 132), for soup or in a stew.

Variation: Instead of the soaked roll, use 50 g/2 oz cooked rice to add to the minced (ground) meat.

Recipe variation: For vegetarian roulades, prepare the cabbage as described in the recipe and detach 12 leaves from it. Cut the rest of the cabbage into strips. Prepare 300 g/ 10 oz carrots, peel, wash, leave to drain and chop. Peel and chop 1 onion. Melt 30 g/1 oz (2 table-spoons) butter or margarine in a pan, stir in the strips of cabbage, chopped carrots and onions, then fry (sauté) while continuing to stir. Add about 125 ml/4 fl oz (½ cup) vegetable stock, bring to the boil and cook for about 5 minutes. Season with salt, pepper and caraway. Then continue as described from step 3 onwards.

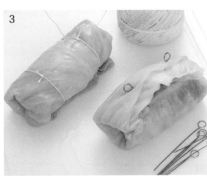

Beef roulade

CLASSIC

Preparation time:
about 20 minutes
Braising time: about 1½ hours

4 slices beef topside (round),
180–200 g/6–7 oz each
salt
freshly ground pepper
medium strong mustard
60 g/2 oz streaky bacon
4 onions
2 medium gherkins
1 bunch soup vegetables
(celery, carrots, leeks)
3 tablespoons cooking oil,
e.g. sunflower oil
about 250 ml/8 fl oz (1 cup)
hot water or vegetable stock
about 1 heaped teaspoon
cornflour (cornstarch)
3 tablespoons water

Also:
roulade needles or cooking
string

Per serving:
P: 44 g, F: 21 g, C: 8 g,
kJ: 1654, kcal: 395, CU: 0.0

1 Pat the slices of beef dry with a kitchen paper towel, then season with salt and pepper. Spread 2–3 teaspoons mustard on the slices of meat. Slice the bacon. Peel 2 onions and cut in half. Now cut the onion halves and gherkins into slices.

2 Arrange the prepared ingredients on the slices of beef. Roll up them up, starting from the short side (photograph 1) and secure with roulade needles or cooking string.

3 Peel the other 2 onions and cut into quarters. Prepare the celery and carrots, peel, wash and leave to drain. Prepare the leeks, cut them in half lengthways, wash thoroughly and leave to drain. Finely chop all the prepared vegetables.

4 Put the oil in a saucepan or roasting tin. Add the roulades and brown briskly on all sides. Add the onions and soup vegetables, then fry (sauté) briefly (photograph 2). Then add half the hot water or stock. Cover and cook the roulades over medium heat for about 1½ hours.

5 Turn the roulades over now and again. Gradually replace the evaporated liquid with more hot water or stock. Take the cooked roulades out of the pan, remove the cooking string or roulade needles, arrange them on a previously warmed dish and keep in a warm place.

6 Rub the cooking juices through a sieve (photograph 3). Add more water or stock to make 375 ml/ 13 fl oz (1⅝ cups) and bring to the boil. Stir some water into the cornflour (cornstarch) until you obtain a smooth paste. Bring the sauce to the boil, stir in the mixture just prepared and simmer without a lid over low heat for about 5 minutes, stirring constantly. Season the sauce with salt, pepper and mustard.

Serve with: cauliflower (p. 118), red cabbage (p. 120) or peas (p. 119) and carrots (p. 118) and boiled potatoes (p. 158).

TIP » If you prefer you can replace 100 ml/3½ fl oz (½ cup) water or vegetable stock with red wine and instead of onions you can use 1 bunch of spring onions.

EXTRA TIP » You can also add 1–2 carrots, cut into strips and braised, to the roulade stuffing. Serve with sugar peas and potatoes.

Goulash

CLASSIC

Preparation time:
about 15 minutes
Braising time: 1¼–1½ hours

500 g/18 oz onions
500 g/18 oz lean beef,
e.g. topside (round)
30 g/1 oz (2 tablespoons)
margarine or 3 tablespoons
cooking oil, e.g. sunflower oil
salt
freshly ground pepper
sweet paprika
2 slightly heaped tablespoons
tomato purée
about 250 ml/8 fl oz (1 cup)
hot water
1–2 drops Tabasco sauce

Per serving:
P: 27 g, F: 14 g, C: 7 g,
kJ: 1101, kcal: 264, CU: 0.0

1 Peel the onions and cut in half. Now cut the onion halves into slices. Pat the meat dry with a kitchen paper towel and cut into cubes of 3 cm/1¼ in.

2 Heat margarine or oil in a pan. Add the meat cubes in two instalments and brown briskly on all sides. Add the rest of the margarine or oil and the sliced onions and fry (sauté) together.

3 Season with salt, pepper and ground paprika, then stir in the tomato purée. Add 250 ml/8 fl oz (1 cup) hot water. Cover and cook for 1¼ to 1½ hours over medium heat. If there appears to be too little liquid at any time, add a little water.

4 Season the goulash with salt, pepper, ground paprika and Tabasco sauce.

TIPS » Use lean pork instead of beef (braise for about 45 minutes). Add a sophisticated touch to the goulash by replacing half the water with red wine.
» Goulash is suitable for freezing.

Serve with: noodles or rice and cucumber salad.

Variation 1: For goulash with mushrooms (photograph 1), prepare 200 g/7 oz mushrooms, rub them clean with a kitchen paper towel, cut into slices and add to the goulash about 10 minutes before the end of the cooking time.

Alternatively, drain 1 jar sliced mushrooms (drained weight 210 g/7½ oz) with a sieve and add just before the goulash is done.

Variation 2: For goulash soup (photograph 2), reduce the amount of onions and beef to 250 g/9 oz each. Add 1 red and 1 yellow bell pepper, coarsely chopped, and increase the amount of water to 1 litre/1¾ pints (4¼ cups).

Recipe variation: For beef stroganoff, pat dry 600 g/1¼ lb fillet of beef and cut into strips. Peel 150 g/5 oz onions. Take 150 g/5 oz mushrooms and rub clean with a kitchen paper towel. Cut 100 g/3½ oz gherkins, the onions and the mushrooms into slices. Brown the meat in 3 tablespoons cooking oil in two servings as described in the recipe, then remove from the pan and put to one side. Add the sliced gherkins, onions and mushrooms to the cooking juices in the pan and fry (sauté) them; then take them out and put with the meat. Pour 200 ml/7 fl oz (⅞ cup) beef stock (bouillon) (p. 104) into the pan with the cooking residues and slightly reduce over high heat without a lid. Stir 1 teaspoon mustard and 2 tablespoons crème fraîche or sour cream into the sauce. Stir the meat and vegetables into the sauce and heat again without allowing it to boil. Season the beef stroganoff with salt and pepper.

Stuffed beef roulade

TAKES A LITTLE WHILE (PHOTOGRAPHS OPPOSITE)

Preparation time:
about 20 minutes
Roasting time: about 6 hours

1 butterflied piece beef
(about 25 x 30 cm/8 x 12 in)
prepared by the butcher
from topside (round)
1 onion
200 g/7 oz minced
(ground) beef
1 egg (medium)
2 tablespoons breadcrumbs
salt, freshly ground pepper
1 level teaspoon ground
sweet paprika
¼ level teaspoon chilli powder
1 red bell pepper
(about 200 g/7 oz)
4 tablespoons cooking oil,
e.g. rapeseed (canola) oil
400 ml/14 fl oz (1¾ cups)
meat stock
1 can (400 g/14 oz)
drained tomatoes

Also:
cooking string or roulade
needles

Per serving:
P: 35 g, F: 23 g, C: 12 g,
kJ: 1667, kcal: 398, CU: 0.5

1 Preheat the oven top and bottom to 80 °C/180 F. Pat the meat dry with a kitchen paper towel and cut off any fat and sinews if necessary.

2 Peel and finely chop the onion. Mix together the minced beef, onion, egg and breadcrumbs. Season with salt, pepper, paprika and chilli powder.

3 Cut the peppes in half, then remove the stalk and the white membranes. Wash, leave to drain and cut each half pepper into four.

4 Sprinkle salt and pepper on the meat. Spread the minced beef on top and arrange the strips of pepper on it (photograph 1). Roll the meat tightly, starting with the small side (photograph 2) and secure with cooking string (photograph 3) or roulade needles.

5 Heat the oil in a large, shallow pan. Add the meat and fry (sauté) briskly on all sides for about 10 minutes. Stir in the stock and drained tomatoes, bring briefly to the boil. Place the pan on a shelf in the bottom third of the preheated oven and cook for about 6 hours, turning the roulade over 2 or 3 times.

6 Remove the cooking string or roulade needles from the roulade. Cut the roulade into slices and serve with the sauce.

Serve with: parsley potatoes (p. 158), kohlrabi (p. 118).

Recipe variation: To make stuffed herb fillet, pat 2 pork fillets (400 g/ 14 oz each) dry with a kitchen paper towel. Preheat the oven: top and bottom heat: about 200 °C/400 °F (Gas mark 6), fan oven: about 180 °C/ 350 °F (Gas mark 4). Make a large incision in each fillet so that they can be pressed open. Season them with salt and pepper. For the stuffing, mix together 4 peeled, finely chopped shallots and 2 teaspoons chopped herbs with 150 g/5 oz herb-flavoured cream cheese and 2 tablespoons herb mustard. Season the stuffing with salt and pepper. Stuff the fillets with the cream cheese mixture and secure with wooden skewers. Heat 3 tablespoons olive oil in a pan. Add the pork fillets and fry (sauté) on all sides, then take out and place in a greased casserole dish. Place the casserole on a shelf in the bottom third of the preheated oven. Cook the fillets for 20–25 minutes.

Knuckle of pork with sauerkraut

CLASSIC

1 Rinse the knuckle of pork under running cold water. Put in a pan with water, bring to the boil, cover and cook over low to medium heat for about 1½ hours.

2 Meanwhile pull the sauerkraut slightly apart to make it looser. Peel the onion. When the meat is cooked, remove it from the pan. Pour the cooking liquid through a sieve and put to one side. Measure about 500 ml/17 fl oz (2¼ cups) of this stock (the amount of liquid depends on the texture of the sauerkraut) and return to the pan.

3 Add the sauerkraut, onion, cloves, bay leaf and juniper berries to the cooking liquid. Now add the knuckle of pork. Bring everything to the boil, cover and cook over medium heat for a further 30 minutes. If necessary, add a little more stock or cooking liquid.

4 Meanwhile wash the potato, peel and rinse it, then leave to drain. When the potato is cooked, grate it and add to the sauerkraut. Bring to the boil again briefly until the mixture becomes creamy. Season the sauerkraut with salt, pepper and sugar. Serve the knuckle with the sauerkraut.

TIP » You can also replace 125 ml/ 4 fl oz (½ cup) of the cooking liquid used to cook the sauerkraut with dry white wine.

Serve with: mashed potatoes (p. 166) or boiled potatoes (p. 158).

Preparation time: about 30 minutes
Cooking time: about 1¾ hours

1.5 kg/3¼ lb cured knuckle of pork (2–3 pieces, ordered from the butcher in advance if necessary)
about 1.25 litres/2¼ pints (5½ cups) water
750 g/1½ lb sauerkraut (fresh or canned)
1 onion
1 bay leaf
3 cloves
5 juniper berries
1 medium floury potato
salt, freshly ground pepper
some sugar

Per serving:
P: 58 g, F: 29 g, C: 7 g,
kJ: 2226, kcal: 532, CU: 0.5

Pot roast

TAKES LONGER

Preparation time:
about 20 minutes
Braising time: about 1½ hours

750 g/1½ lb beef topside
(round)
salt
freshly ground pepper
2 onions
100 g/3½ oz tomatoes
1 bunch soup vegetables
(celery, carrots, leeks)
3 tablespoons cooking oil,
e.g. sunflower or rapeseed
(canola) oil
1 teaspoon dried chopped
thyme
250 ml/8 fl oz (1 cup)
vegetable stock
tomato purée
a little sugar

Per serving:
P: 41 g, F: 16 g, C: 7 g,
kJ: 1413, kcal: 337, CU: 0.0

1 Pat the meat dry with a kitchen paper towel and rub in salt and pepper. Peel and chop the onions. Wash the tomatoes, leave to drain, cut into quarters and remove the base of the stalk. Cut the tomatoes into chunks.

2 Prepare the celery and carrots, peel, wash and leave to drain. Prepare the leeks, cut them in half lengthways, wash thoroughly and leave to drain. Then cut up all the vegetables into very small pieces.

3 Heat the oil in a saucepan with a solid base. Add the meat and briskly brown on all sides. Add the vegetables and fry (sauté) briefly with the meat. Sprinkle thyme on the meat. Pour in a little of the vegetable stock, bring to the boil, cover and cook for about 1½ hours over low to medium heat.

4 Turn the meat over occasionally while cooking. Gradually replace the evaporated liquid by adding vegetable stock whenever necessary.

5 When the meat has cooked, leave to rest for about 10 minutes with the lid on to let the meat juices settle evenly. Cut the meat into slices and arrange on a preheated dish.

6 Purée the cooking residues on the bottom of the pan together with the vegetables or rub through a sieve; if necessary, add a little more vegetables stock. Heat the sauce again, season with salt and pepper, then stir in tomato purée and a little sugar.

TIP » Instead of vegetable stock you can also use half vegetable stock and half red wine. If there is any meat left over, it can be frozen together with the sauce.

Serve with: potato dumplings (p. 170) or boiled potatoes (p. 158) and green (snap) beans (p. 119) or peas (p. 119) and carrots (p. 118).

Recipe variation: For pot roast with marinade, make a marinade with 100 g/3½ oz onions, 50 g/2 oz carrots, 2 cloves garlic (all chopped), 250 ml/8 fl oz (1 cup) red wine, 50 ml/1½ fl oz (3 tablespoons) Cognac, 2 bay leaves and ½ teaspoon thyme. Add the meat and leave to marinade overnight. Then remove the meat, pat the meat dry with a kitchen paper towel, season with salt and pepper, then fry (sauté) in 3 tablespoons cooking oil. Prepare 100 g/3½ oz tomatoes as described in the recipe and add to the meat together with the marinade and vegetables. Cover and cook over medium heat for 1½ to 2 hours. Take the meat out of the pan and keep in a warm place. Rub the sauce with the vegetables through a sieve and add a little water if necessary. Heat the sauce again and season with salt and pepper, tomato purée and sugar; you can also thicken the sauce with 1 teaspoon cornflour (cornstarch).

Boiled beef with horseradish sauce

TAKES A LITTLE WHILE

Preparation time:
about 20 minutes
Cooking time:
about 2 hours 20 minutes

1–1.5 litres/1¾–2¾ pints
(4½–7 cups) water
1 kg/2¼ lb beef topside
(round)
1–1½ teaspoons salt
1 bay leaf
1 tablespoon peppercorns
2 large onions
150 g/5 oz carrots
150 g/5 oz celery sticks
(stalks)
200 g/7 oz leeks

For the horseradish sauce:
30 g/1 oz (2 tablespoons)
butter or margarine
25 g/1 oz (4 tablespoons) plain
(all purpose) flour
375 ml/13 fl oz (1⅝ cups)
beef stock
125 g/4½ oz whipping cream
20 g/¾ oz freshly ground
horseradish
salt
some sugar
about 1 teaspoon lemon juice
1 tablespoon chopped parsley

Per serving:
P: 55 g, F: 21 g, C: 11 g,
kJ: 1982, kcal: 474, CU: 0.5

1 Bring water to the boil in a large pan. Pat the meat dry with a kitchen paper towel and add to the boiling water together with the salt, bay leaf and peppercorns. Cover and simmer the meat for about 2 hours over low to medium heat.

2 Meanwhile peel and chop the onions. Prepare the carrots and celery, peel, wash, leave to drain and cut into slices. Prepare the leeks, cut them in half lengthways, wash thoroughly and leave to drain; cut into pieces about 2 cm/¾ in long.

3 When the meat has cooked, add the vegetables you have just prepared, cover and cook for a further 20 minutes.

4 Cover and leave the meat to rest for about 10 minutes before slicing to let the meat juices settle. Strain the stock with the vegetables through a sieve, reserve the stock and keep 375 ml/13 fl oz (1⅝ cups) for the sauce. Cover the vegetables and keep in a warm place.

5 While the meat is resting, melt the butter or margarine for the horseradish sauce in a small pan. Add the flour and stir until the mixture has become pale yellow. Add the 375 ml/13 fl oz (1⅝ cups) boiled beef stock you have reserved and the cream. Whisk the sauce briskly with a whisk, making sure that there are no lumps. Bring the sauce to the boil while stirring all

the time, then simmer for about 5 minutes without a lid over low heat, stirring occasionally.

6 Stir in the horseradish. Season the sauce with salt, sugar and lemon juice. Cut the meat into slices and arrange them on a previously warmed dish; then pour some hot stock over the meat. Serve the boiled beef with the vegetables and the sauce and sprinkle with parsley if desired.

Serve with: roast potatoes, green salad or carrots (p. 118).

TIPS ›› You can also make the sauce with horseradish from a jar instead of fresh horseradish.
›› Boiled beef can also be frozen in its broth.

Recipe variation 1: To make herb sauce (top left in the photograph), mix together 3 tablespoons mayonnaise, 150 g/5 oz crème fraîche, 150 g/5 oz yoghurt, 100 g/3½ oz whipping cream and ½ teaspoon medium sharp mustard. Stir 3 tablespoons chopped mixed herbs into the sauce. Season with salt and pepper.

Recipe variation 2: To make cold horseradish sauce (top centre in the photograph), mix together 150 g/5 oz crème fraîche with 2 tablespoons horseradish from a jar and season with a little lemon juice, salt, pepper and sugar.

Recipe variation 3: To make a chives sauce (top right in the photograph), finely dice 1 peeled shallot and 1 prepared carrot (about 100 g/3½ oz). Blanch the carrots for about 1 minute in boiling water, then plunge in ice-cold water. Mix together 150 g/5 oz crème fraîche with 4 tablespoons olive oil and 1 tablespoon white wine vinegar. Rinse 1 bunch of chives, pat dry and chop into rings. Stir the vegetables and chives into the sauce. Season with salt and pepper and serve with the boiled beef.

Leg of lamb

FOR GUESTS (4–6 SERVINGS)

Preparation time:
about 25 minutes
Roasting time: about 60 minutes

1 leg of lamb on the bone
(about 1.5 kg/3¼ lb)
salt
freshly ground pepper
1–2 cloves garlic
6 tablespoons cooking oil,
e.g. olive oil
1–2 teaspoons chopped herbs
of Provence
about 375 ml/13 fl oz (1⅝ cups)
vegetable stock (or half red
wine, half vegetable stock)
150 g/5 oz cherry tomatoes
2 yellow bell peppers
1 medium courgette
(zucchini)
4 sprigs thyme
1 teaspoon sugar
2 tablespoons white balsamic
vinegar

Per serving:
P: 53 g, F: 20 g, C: 2 g,
kJ: 1657, kcal: 395, CU: 0.0

1 Preheat the oven:
Top and bottom heat:
about 180 °C/350 °F (Gas mark 4)
Fan oven:
about 160 °C/325 °F (Gas mark 3)

2 Pat the meat dry with a kitchen
paper towel and rub it with salt and
pepper. Peel the cloves of garlic and
push through a garlic press.

3 Heat 4 tablespoons of the oil in a
roasting tin. Add the meat and
brown briskly on all sides. Rub the
pressed cloves of garlic all over the
meat and sprinkle with herbs.

4 Add one third of the vegetable stock
or red wine-vegetable stock mixture.
Put the roasting tin with the meat
without a lid on a shelf in the lower
third of the preheated oven and
cook for about 60 minutes.

5 Gradually replace the liquid that
has evaporated with the remaining
vegetable stock or red wine and
vegetable stock mixture.

6 Meanwhile wash the cocktail
tomatoes, wipe dry and cut in half.
Cut the peppers in half, then remove
the stalks, seeds and white membranes. Wash and leave to drain.
Wash the courgette (zucchini),
pat dry and cut off the ends. Cut
the peppers and courgette into
1–2 cm/⅜–¾ in cubes. Rinse the
thyme and pat dry. Remove the
leaves from the stalks and chop
them up.

7 When the meat has cooked, remove
from the oven and take out of the
roasting tin. Cover and leave to rest
for about 10 minutes to let the meat
juices settle.

8 Heat 2 tablespoons oil in a pan, add
the prepared vegetables and fry
(sauté). Season with sugar, salt and
pepper, then stir in the thyme. Stir in
the balsamic vinegar.

9 Cut the meat into slices and
arrange on a pre-warmed dish.

10 Rub the cooking residues and
juices together with the vegetables
through a sieve. Add more wine or
stock if necessary. Adjust the
seasoning with salt and pepper
and serve with the vegetables and
the meat.

Serve with: baguette.

Recipe variation 1: To make mint
sauce, remove the leaves of 1 bunch
of mint, rinse and pat dry. Then
purée the leaves with a little salt,
pepper, 1 teaspoon icing (confectioner's) sugar, 2 tablespoons white
wine vinegar and 6 tablespoons
olive oil. Season the sauce with salt
and pepper.

Recipe variation 2: To make grilled
(broiled) lamb cutlets, pat dry and
either cut off the fatty edges or
make several incisions in them.
Peel 2 small cloves of garlic, press
through a garlic press, add a little

pepper and stir in 3 tablespoons cooking oil. Coat the cutlets with this oil mixture, place on a dish, cover with clingfilm (plastic wrap) and put in the refrigerator for about 60 minutes. Shortly before the end of the marinading time, preheat the oven grill to about 240 °C/450 °F. Put the cutlets on a grid lined with foil. Put under the preheated grill and grill (broil) the chops for 3 minutes on each side.

Liver with onions

CLASSIC

Preparation time:
about 30 minutes

5 onions
4 slices liver,
about 0. 5 cm/³⁄₁₆ in thick
(100–120 g/3½–4 oz each)
20 g/¾ oz (3 tablespoons) plain
(all purpose) flour
about 50 g/2 oz margarine or
3 tablespoons cooking oil,
e.g. sunflower or rapeseed
(canola) oil
salt
freshly ground pepper
dried chopped marjoram

Per serving:
P: 23 g, F: 13 g, C: 9 g,
kJ: 1027, kcal: 246, CU: 0.5

1 Peel the onions, cut into thin slices and separate into rings. Pat the liver dry with a kitchen paper towel and coat in flour. Gently shake off any excess flour.

2 Heat half the margarine or oil in a pan. Add the slices of liver and brown on each side for 2–3 minutes. Afterwards season the liver with salt, pepper and marjoram and arrange on a previously warmed dish, then keep in a warm place.

3 Add the rest of the margarine or oil to the residue in the pan. Add the onion rings and brown over medium heat for about 2 minutes, stirring all the time. Season the onion rings with salt and pepper and serve with the liver.

TIPS » This dish can be prepared with pork liver, beef liver or calf's liver. The various kinds differ in both taste and texture. Calf's liver is more tender in texture and has a sweeter taste than pork liver; it needs less cooking than the other kinds of liver. Beef liver has a strong flavour and a firmer texture. Cooking time also depends on the thickness of the slices. But liver should never be fried over excessively high heat because the meat will quickly become tough and dry.
» If desired you can also garnish the liver with sprigs of chervil.

Serve with: mashed potatoes (p. 166) and apple sauce (p. 210).

Recipe variation: For Berlin Style liver, fry (sauté) apple rings or segments from 2 medium-sized apples together with the onions.

Poultry

Poultry is popular and is also delicious. The meat is tender and white, its flavour – depending on the preparation – subtle and delicate. Poultry is much more than just roast chicken. Poultry includes the following domestic fowl:

» **Chicken** is available either fresh or frozen: chickens 5–7 weeks old weighing 800 g–1.2 kg/1¾-2½ lb. Chicken fed on special food such as corn, for instance, is particularly tasty. **Boiling fowls** are laying hens which are slaughtered after 12–15 months. They are bred for the purpose of laying eggs and not fattened, reaching a weight of 1.1–2 kg/2½ lb–4½ lb when finally slaughtered. Boiling fowls are used to make chicken stock and ragouts.

» **Ducks** are usually slaughtered after reaching sexual maturity when they are over 1 year old. They usually weigh between 1.8 and 2.5 kg/ 4 and 5½ lb.

Barbary ducks are very popular because of their leanness and the large proportion of breast meat.

» **Geese** are usually about 9 months old. By then they are already very large, weighing between 4 and 6 kg/9 and 13 lb.

» **Turkeys** are the heavyweights of the poultry world: mature female turkeys can weigh up to 12 kg/26 lb and males up to 20 kg/44 lb! In shops turkeys are usually available already cut up (breast, leg). Young turkeys slaughtered when about 8 weeks old weigh between 3 and 4 kg/6½ and 9 lb and are available either whole or already cut up.

Baby turkeys also called poults, weigh only 2–3 kg/4 1/2–6½ lb.

Ready jointed poultry

All types of poultry are available fresh or frozen, either whole or as pieces. They are available as half-fowls, breasts, breast fillets, escalopes (only in the case of chicken and turkey), legs (thighs and lower legs) and wings. The rather dry chicken and turkey breast meat is particularly delicious in dishes where it is served cut up into strips or as a basic ingredient in eastern cuisine.

Correct preparation and cooking

Fresh poultry must be stored in the refrigerator as soon as possible after being purchased. If you buy frozen poultry for storing in the freezer, make sure that it does not defrost between leaving the shop and reaching your house. Use a freezer bag with a thermal lining. Poultry can be infected with bacteria, such as salmonella, which can be dangerous to health. It is therefore important to follow a few safety rules when preparing and cooking poultry:

» Always make sure that the fowl is well refrigerated or sufficiently deep-frozen.

» Always wash your hands and thoroughly clean all equipment which has come into contact with the poultry during its preparation (such as the knife and chopping board) immediately afterwards, using water and washing-up liquid.

» Always leave the frozen poultry to defrost overnight in the refrigerator. In addition, make sure that the poultry or thawing water does not come into contact with other food

Turkey

Goose

Boiling fowl

Duck

Roasting chicken

in the fridge; throw away the thawing water immediately.

» Poultry can only be eaten if it is thoroughly cooked through. It is considered "cooked" when the juices exuded by the chicken are as clear as water or when the legs pull away easily from the body. If you use a digital probe food thermometer to measure the temperature inside poultry (which should reach a minimum of 70 °C/160 °F), make sure that the probe is not too close to a bone or the reading will be distorted.

The right way to defrost

Poultry should defrost as slowly as possible, preferably in the refrigerator to preserve the cell structure and to ensure that the meat remains beautifully tender.

» Remove all the packaging and throw it away.

» Then put the poultry in a colander or large metal strainer over a large bowl, so that the defrosting liquid can drain away. The poultry must not lie in the defrosting liquid!

» Now cover the bowl.

» Throw away the defrosting liquid immediately. It is important that the defrosting liquid should not come into contact with other food because of the danger of salmonella.

» Finally clean all work surfaces and equipment thoroughly with water and washing-up liquid and wash your hands with soap.

Trussing poultry (photograph 2)

When a bird is trussed, it is arranged in such a way that it dries out less when cooking and therefore also tastes better – but it also looks more delicious. If you cook the bird whole, secure all projecting parts, such as wings and legs, with cooking string and tie them as close as possible to the body. To do this,

place the prepared bird on its back, bend the ends of the wings backwards and slide the wings under the body. Now cut the ends of the wings and tie the wings together under the body with cooking string. Tie the legs together with cooking string.

Stuffing

Large birds in particular, such as geese and turkeys, are ideally suited for stuffing. Prepared according to the recipe, stuffing can be served with the bird as an accompaniment. To stuff the prepared bird, put it on its back and put the stuffing inside the bird's abdomen. Then close the opening by sewing it with cooking string or secure it with wooden skewers. Finally, truss the stuffed bird with cooking string.

Carving

Carving is the process of cutting the cooked bird into individual servings. Before you start, prepare a platter on which the servings will be arranged. First separate the legs with a sharp knife, for instance a carving knife. To do this, first cut the legs as far as the joint, then slightly twist the joint and cut through the tendons. Then cut the wings off at the joints. Now slice off the breast meat on each side of the bone and present it as individual servings. Finally arrange the meat on a pre-warmed dish. Poultry shears can also be helpful in carving the bird.

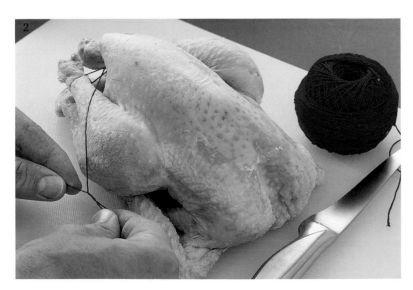

Chicken legs
POPULAR

Preparation time:
about 10 minutes
Roasting time: about 45 minutes

**4 chicken legs (about
250 g/9 oz each)
½ teaspoon salt
1 pinch freshly ground pepper
1 teaspoon sweet paprika
2–3 tablespoons cooking oil,
e.g. sunflower oil**

Per serving:
P: 34 g, F: 24 g, C: 0 g,
kJ: 1458, kcal: 349, CU: 0.0

1 Preheat the oven:
Top and bottom heat:
about 200 °C/400 °F (Gas mark 6)
Fan oven:
about 180 °C/350 °F (Gas mark 4)

2 Rinse the chicken legs under cold
running water, then pat dry.

3 Stir together the salt, pepper and
paprika powder with the oil. Rub
the oil mixture all over the chicken
legs and put in a roasting tin. Put
the roasting tin on the middle shelf
in the preheated oven and cook the
chicken legs for about 45 minutes.

Serve with: potato salad (p. 152)
or fried potatoes (p. 168) and peas
(p. 119) or carrots (p. 118).

Recipe variation 1: For **chicken
legs coated with herb-flavoured
breadcrumbs**, prepare the chicken
as described in step 1. Rub the
chicken legs with salt, pepper and
sweet paprika powder. Mix together 4–5 tablespoons mixed chopped herbs (fresh or deep-frozen,
for instance parsley, tarragon and
chives) and 6 tablespoons breadcrumbs. Then coat the chicken legs
first in plain (all purpose) flour,
then in 1 beaten egg and finally in
the breadcrumbs and herb mixture.
Press this breadcrumb coating onto
the chicken legs to make it stick;
gently shake off any excess coating.
Put the chicken legs in a roasting
tin, sprinkle 3-4 tablespoons cooking oil over them and cook as described in the recipe.

Recipe variation 2: To make roast
chicken, preheat the oven: top and
bottom heat: about 200 °C/400 °F
(Gas mark 6), fan oven: about 180 °C/
350 °F (Gas mark 4). Rinse a chicken
(about 1.3 kg/2¾ lb) inside and
outside under cold running water
and pat dry. Rub the chicken all
over with salt, pepper and sweet
paprika. Now coat the chicken with
20 g/¾ oz (1½ tablespoons) melted
butter or 2 tablespoons cooking oil.
Peel and chop 1 onion. Prepare 200 g/
7 oz carrots, peel, rinse, leave to
drain and cut into slices. Peel
130 g/4½ oz tomatoes (see p. 114,
step 1), cut into quarters and cut
out the stalk and its base. Mix together 1–2 teaspoons finely chopped
rosemary, 1 bay leaf broken into
pieces, the prepared vegetables
and 125 ml/4 fl oz (½ cup) chicken
stock. Pour into the roasting tin
and add the chicken. Put the roasting tin without a lid on the middle
shelf of the preheated oven. Cook
the chicken for about 60 minutes.
Then remove the chicken from the
roasting tin. Cover and leave to rest
for 5–10 minutes so that the meat
juices can settle. If necessary add
a little more water to the cooking
residues and rub the vegetables
through a sieve. Season the sauce
with salt, pepper and paprika
powder. Cut the chicken into pieces
with chicken shears, arrange on a
serving dish and serve with the
sauce.

Chicken fricassee
WITH ALCOHOL

Preparation time:
about 30 minutes,
excluding cooling time
Cooking time: about 60 minutes

1.5 litres/2¾ pints (7 cups)
water
1 bunch soup vegetables
(celery, carrots, leeks)
1 onion
1 bay leaf
1 clove
1 prepared boiling fowl
(1–1.2 kg/2¼–2½ lb)
1½ teaspoons salt

For the sauce:
25 g/1 oz (2 tablespoons)
butter
30 g/1 oz (5 tablespoons) plain
(all purpose) flour
500 ml/17 fl oz (2¼ cups)
chicken stock
1 jar asparagus spears
(drained weight 175 g/3 oz)
1 jar mushrooms (drained
weight 150 g/5 oz)
4 tablespoons white wine
about 1 tablespoon
lemon juice
1 teaspoon sugar
2 egg yolks (medium)
4 tablespoons whipping cream
salt
freshly ground pepper
Worcestershire sauce

Per serving:
P: 49 g, F: 22 g, C: 8 g,
kJ: 1835, kcal: 439, CU: 0.5

1 Bring the water to the boil in large pan. Peel the celery. Prepare and peel the carrots. Rinse the celery and carrots and leave to drain. Prepare the leeks, cut in half lengthways, wash them thoroughly and leave to drain. Cut the soup vegetables into large chunks. Peel the onion and stud with a bay leaf and cloves (photograph 1).

2 Rinse the boiling fowl inside and out under cold running water. Put the chicken together with a little salt in the boiling water, bring to the boil again and skim off the foam that forms.

3 Put the soup vegetables in the pan with the chicken, cover and cook over low heat for about 60 minutes.

4 Take the chicken out of the cooking liquid and leave to cool a little. Pour the liquid through a sieve, remove excess fat and put 500 ml/17 fl oz (2¼ cups) to one side for the sauce. Remove the meat from the bones (photograph 2), remove the skin (photograph 3) and cut up the meat into bite-size pieces.

5 To make the sauce, melt the butter in a pan. Add the flour and stir until you obtain a smooth pale yellow mixture. Now add the liquid you put to one side and stir briskly with a whisk, making sure that there are no lumps. Bring the sauce to the boil and simmer gently for 5 minutes, stirring occasionally.

6 Leave the asparagus pieces and mushrooms to drain in a sieve and, if necessary, cut the larger mushrooms into quarters. Add the pieces of asparagus and mushrooms to the chicken pieces and bring briefly to the boil. Add the white wine, lemon juice and sugar.

7 Whisk together the egg yolk and cream and stir slowly into the fricassee until it thickens, being careful not let the fricassee boil again. Season with salt, pepper, Worcestershire sauce and lemon juice.

Serve with: rice and salad.

TIPS » Use fresh mushrooms, prepared and cleaned, cut into slices and fried in 1 tablespoon butter instead of mushrooms from a jar.
» If you are in a rush you can use 600 g/1¼ lb chicken breast fillets instead of a whole chicken. Cook the chicken fillets with the vegetables in salted water for about 2 minutes. Put about 500 ml/17 fl oz (2¼ cups) of the cooking liquid to one side for the sauce. Cut the meat into large chunks, then continue to follow the instructions in the recipe.

EXTRA TIP » **Thickening.** To thicken liquids such as milk, sauces, meat stock or spicy soups, stir in a mixture of cream and egg yolk. But do not let it come to the boil again.

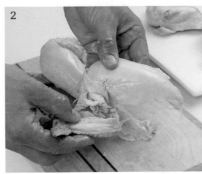

Chicken breasts with mozzarella

QUICK

Preparation time:
about 30 minutes

4 chicken breast fillets
excluding skin (about
150 g/5 oz each)
salt
freshly ground pepper
2 large tomatoes
125 g/4½ oz mozzarella
3 tablespoons cooking oil,
e.g. sunflower oil
a few basil leaves

Per serving:
P: 42 g, F: 9 g, C: 1 g,
kJ: 1076, kcal: 257, CU: 0.0

1 Preheat the oven grill to about 240 °C/465 °F. Rinse the chicken fillets under cold running water and pat the meat dry with a kitchen paper towel. Season the fillets with salt and pepper.

2 Wash the tomatoes, pat dry and cut out the stalks including the base. Then cut each tomato into 4 slices. Leave the mozzarella to drain and cut into 8 slices.

3 Heat the oil in an ovenproof pan. Add the fillets and fry (sauté) for about 10 minutes on each side.

4 Put 2 tomato slices on each fillet and sprinkle with pepper. Then put 2 slices of mozzarella on top and sprinkle again with pepper.

5 Put the pan with the chicken fillets on the shelf under the preheated grill and grill (broil) them for 5–10 minutes until the cheese begins to melt. (If you do no have an ovenproof dish, transfer the chicken fillets into a casserole after frying them.)

6 Finally garnish the chicken fillets with a few basil leaves.

Serve with: rice (p. 182) or garlic bread.

TIP » If you do not have an oven grill, put the pan or casserole on a shelf in the oven, preheated top and bottom to about 220 °C/425 °F (Gas mark 7) or fan oven 200 °C/ 400 °F (Gas mark 6). Bake until the cheese melts.

EXTRA TIP » Chicken is also very delicious with fresh goat's cheese or gorgonzola, melted under the grill.

Roast duck

CLASSIC

Preparation time:
about 30 minutes
Roasting time: 2¼–2½ hours

1 oven-ready duck
(2 –2.5 kg/4½–5½ lb)
salt
freshly ground pepper
about 850 ml/1½ pints
(3½ cups) water

For the sauce:
1 heaped tablespoon cornflour
(cornstarch)
50 ml/1½ fl oz (3 tablespoons)
cold water

Also:
cooking string

Per serving:
P: 71 g, F: 33 g, C: 3 g,
kJ: 2479, kcal: 593, CU: 0.5

1 Preheat the oven.
Top and bottom heat:
about 180 °C/350 °F (Gas mark 4)
Fan oven:
about 160 °C/325 °F (Gas mark 3)

2 Rinse the duck inside and out under cold running water, pat dry and, if necessary, remove the fat inside the body cavity (photograph 1). Rub the duck all over with salt and pepper inside and out.

3 Tie the legs and wings together (photograph 2). Put 50 ml/1½ fl oz (3 tablespoons) of water in a roasting tin. Place the duck breast down in the roasting tin and put it uncovered in the preheated oven on a shelf in the bottom third of the oven. Cook the duck for 2¼ to 2½ hours.

4 Meanwhile rinse the giblets under cold running water and put in a pan with 750 ml/1¼ pints (3½ cups) water. Add 1 teaspoon salt, cover, bring to the boil and simmer over low heat for about 30 minutes. Then pour through a sieve and reserve the broth.

5 Prick the duck several times under the wings and legs while roasting the oven to allow the fat escape as it melts. After about 30 minutes remove the fat which has melted from the duck; repeat the process several times. As soon as the cooking residues begin to brown, add a little stock. Meanwhile replace the evaporated liquid throughout the cooking process. After about 60 minutes, turn the duck over.

6 Stir together 100 ml/3½ fl oz (½ cup) water and ½ teaspoon salt. Brush this over the duck about 10 minutes before the end of the cooking time and increase the oven temperature by about 20° C/35 °F so that the skin becomes nice and crispy.

7 Remove the duck from the roasting tin, cover and leave to rest for 5–10 minutes.

8 Scrape the cooking residues off the bottom while adding a little water, pour through a sieve, remove the fat (photograph 3), top up with water to make 375 ml/13 fl oz (1⅝ cups) of liquid and bring to the boil on the cooker. Mix the cornflour (cornstarch) and water together until smooth and stir into the boiling liquid using a whisk, making sure that there are no lumps. Simmer the sauce gently without a lid over low heat for about 5 minutes, stirring from time to time. Season the sauce with salt and pepper.

9 Carve the duck into individual servings, arrange on a pre-warmed platter and serve with the sauce.

Serve with: bread dumplings (p. 172), potato dumplings (p. 170) and Savoy cabbage (p. 132).

TIP » The sauce will taste even better if you degrease the resulting stock (bouillon) and further reduce it in a pan to only half the quantity.

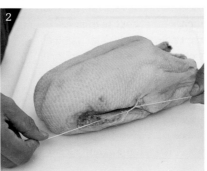

Turkey thigh with vegetables

FOR GUESTS

Preparation time:
about 25 minutes
Roasting time: about 90 minutes

4 tablespoons cooking oil,
e.g. sunflower oil
1 turkey thigh (with bone,
about 1 kg/2¼ lb)
salt
freshly ground pepper
1 litre/1¾ pints (4½ cups) hot
water or vegetable stock
500 g/18 oz onions
200 g/7 oz carrots
200 g/7 oz celery
1 small parsley root
200 g/7 oz leeks
250 g/9 oz tomatoes
1–2 sprigs rosemary or thyme
150 g/5 oz sour cream
1 tablespoon cornflour
(cornstarch)
1 tablespoon thyme leaves
(optional)

Per serving:
P: 50 g, F: 42 g, C: 17 g,
kJ: 2723, kcal: 652, CU: 0.5

1 Put the oil in a roasting tin, put in the oven on the middle shelf and preheat the oven:
Top and bottom heat:
about 200 °C/400 °F (Gas mark 6)
Fan oven:
about 180 °C/350 °F (Gas mark 4)

2 Rinse the turkey thigh under cold running water and pat dry. Rub with salt and pepper, put into the hot roasting tin and roast for about 70 minutes.

3 As soon as the cooking residues begin to brown add a little hot water or vegetable stock. Regularly baste the turkey thigh with the cooking juices. Gradually replace the evaporated liquid with water or stock.

4 Meanwhile peel and chop the onions. Prepare and peel the carrots, the celery and the parsley root. Rinse the vegetables and leave to drain. Cut the carrots into slices 1.5 cm/½ in thick. Coarsely chop the celery and parsley.

5 Prepare the leeks, cut in half lengthways, wash them thoroughly and leave to drain. Cut into pieces about 3 cm/1¼ in length. Wash the tomatoes, wipe dry, cut in half and cut out the stalks together with the base. Chop up the tomatoes.

6 Rinse the sprigs of rosemary and thyme; pat dry, remove the leaves from the stems and coarsely chop. When the turkey thigh has been in the oven for about 50 minutes, add the onions and the vegetables you have just prepared and, if necessary, add a little more water or stock. Season the turkey with salt, pepper, rosemary or thyme. Roast the vegetables for about 20 minutes at the temperature indicated.

7 Arrange the turkey thigh with the vegetables on a pre-warmed serving dish and keep in a warm place.

8 Loosen the cooking residues from the bottom of the pan with a little water and pour through a sieve. Add more water to make the quantity up to 400 ml/14 fl oz (1¾ cups) and bring to the boil again.

9 Stir the cornflour (cornstarch) into the sour cream, then whisk this mixture into the boiling liquid using a whisk, making sure that there are no lumps. Bring the sauce to the boil again and simmer gently without a lid over low heat for about 5 minutes, stirring occasionally. Season the sauce with salt and pepper. Serve the turkey leg with the vegetables and sauce. Garnish with a little thyme if desired.

Serve with: boiled potatoes (p. 158), noodles or rice (p. 182).

Variation: Slow cooking of the turkey thigh at 95 °C/200 °F. Preheat the oven to 95 °C/200 °F (top and bottom heat). Rinse the turkey thigh under cold running water, pat dry, remove the bone and tie the meat together with cooking string. Season with salt and pepper. Heat 2 tablespoons olive oil in a large shallow pan or roasting tin, add the turkey thigh and fry (sauté) briskly on all sides. Put the pan in the oven in the bottom third of the oven and cook for about 5 hours. The vegetables should be prepared as described in the recipe and added with the herbs to the turkey in the pan about 1½ hours before the end of the cooking time. Then take the turkey out of the oven, remove the cooking string, carve and serve with the vegetables.

Stuffed goose

FOR GUESTS (ABOUT 8 PORTIONS)

Preparation time:
about 45 minutes
Roasting time: about 4½ hours

1 oven-ready goose
(4–4.5 kg/9–10 lb)
salt, pepper
dried chopped marjoram

For the stuffing:
50 g/2 oz streaky bacon
2 onions
20 g/¾ oz (½ tablespoon)
butter or margarine
about 8 day-old bread rolls
(300 g/10 oz)
300 ml/10 fl oz (1¼ cups) milk
4 eggs (medium)
2 tablespoons chopped parsley
salt
2 apples

about 500 ml/17 fl oz
(2¼ cups) hot water
1 bunch soup vegetables
(celery, carrots, leeks)
about 100 ml/3½ fl oz (½ cup)
cold water
10 g/⅓ oz (1½ tablespoons)
plain (all purpose) flour

Also:
cooking string or wooden
skewers

Per serving:
P: 77 g, F: 75 g, C: 27 g,
kJ: 4552, kcal: 1087, CU: 2.0

1 Rinse the goose under running cold water and pat dry. Rub the goose inside and out with salt, pepper and marjoram.

2 To make the stuffing, cut the bacon into cubes, peel and finely chop the onion. Melt the butter or margarine in a pan. Add the diced bacon and fry (sauté) until crisp. Then add the chopped onions, sweat until transparent and put to one side.

3 Preheat the oven:
Top and bottom heat:
about 200 °C/400 °F (Gas mark 6)
Fan oven:
about 180 °C/350 °F (Gas mark 4)

4 Cut the rolls into small dice and put in a bowl. Heat the milk in a pan, pour over the diced roll and mix well together. Now stir in the diced bacon and onion mixture and leave to cool.

5 Stir in the eggs and parsley and season the mixture with salt. Peel the apple, cut in half, remove the core, grate and stir into the mixture. Stuff the goose with the mixture. Close the cavity by sewing the skin with cooking string or by securing it with wooden skewers. Rub the outside of the goose all over with salt, pepper and marjoram.

6 Place a roasting tin on a shelf in the bottom third of the oven and put 125 ml/4 fl oz (½ cup) hot water in it. Place the goose, breast side down, on a grid, then place this grid with the goose on top above the roasting tin in the preheated oven. Cook the goose for about 90 minutes. Prick the goose several times in the underside of the wings and legs so that the fat can drain out easily.

7 As soon as the cooking residues begin to brown, add hot water until the water is about 1 cm/⅜ in deep in the roasting tin. Baste the goose regularly with the cooking juices. Replace the evaporated liquid by more hot water when necessary.

8 Meanwhile peel the celery and carrots, rinse and leave to drain. Prepare the leeks, cut in half lengthways, wash them thoroughly and leave to drain. Cut the soup vegetables into pieces.

9 After about 90 minutes, turn the goose over. Add the soup vegetables to the roasting tin and continue cooking for about another 3 hours.

10 Stir ½ teaspoon salt into 50 ml/1½ fl oz (3 tablespoons) cold water. About 10 minutes before the end of the cooking time brush this all over the goose and increase the temperature by about 20 °C/35 °F so that the skin becomes beautifully crisp. Remove the goose from the oven, cover and leave to rest for 5–10 minutes.

11 Scrape the cooking residues from the bottom of the drip pan, adding a little water. Pour through a sieve, top up with water to make 600 ml/21 oz (2½ cups) and transfer into a saucepan. Bring to the boil. Stir the flour into 50 ml/1½ fl oz (3 table-

spoons) water until smooth and whisk into the hot liquid, using a whisk. Make sure no lumps are formed. Bring the sauce to the boil and simmer gently without a lid for about 5 minutes over low heat, stirring occasionally. Season the sauce with salt, pepper and marjoram. Carve the goose into individual servings, arrange on a prewarmed serving dish and serve with the sauce.

Serve with: potato dumplings (p. 170) and red cabbage (p. 120).

TIP » If you are preparing a larger goose, increase the cooking time by about 30 minutes per 1 kg/2¼ lb.

Recipe variation: For goose with apricot and pear stuffing, peel and finely chop 2 onions. Peel the pears, cut into quarters, core and dice. Finely chop 200 g/7 oz dried apricots. Stir together 100 g/3½ oz cream and 4 tablespoons Poire William liqueur. Add 200 g/7 oz toasted bread cut into dice and leave to soak. Gently fry (sauté)

the pears, apricots and onions in 2 tablespoons cooking oil, then add 125 g/4½ oz chopped goose liver and continue frying. Leave the mixture to cool. Squeeze the soaked toast to remove the liquid and add to the pear mixture. Add 1 medium egg, then season generously with ground cinnamon, salt and pepper and mix all the ingredients thoroughly. Stuff the goose with this mixture and roast as described in the recipe.

Game

Since game animals live in their natural habitat, free to roam and living naturally off the land, their meat has a very special, unmistakable flavour. Moreover, it is lean and rich in important proteins, B-vitamins, iron and potassium. Game is sold by breeders and is also sold as a frozen product so that it is no longer only available during the hunting season.

Classification of the types of game
Game is divided into furred game and feathered game. Furred game includes:
» Roe deer with its particularly tender and lean meat. The best parts are the saddle and leg of venison. To ensure that this highly aromatic meat does not dry out during the cooking process, it is often covered with slices of bacon.
» Red deer has very tender dark-coloured meat with fine fibres.
» Fallow deer has more tender meat than red deer and is more often streaked with veins of fat. It is very similar in taste to roe deer.
» Game boar makes delicious tender roasts, steaks and ragouts. Only the meat of young animals should be used because the meat of older boars is not only tough but also fatter and more difficult to digest; many people dislike the intense gamey flavour of older game boars.
» Hare has very tender, reddish-brown meat until the age of

8 months. But the quality of the meat depends not only on the age of the animal but also on its natural habitat.
» Game rabbit has very tender, lean meat which is easy to digest. The white rabbit meat is rich in protein but low in fat and cholesterol.

Feathered game includes:
» Pheasants: these are available oven-ready and are about the size of a chicken. The meat of young birds is particularly tender.
» Partridges: these are the size of a pigeon. The meat of younger birds is very tender with a particularly fine flavour.

Game should only be eaten when thoroughly cooked through.

Game seasons
The shooting season and closed season of game depend on the life cycles of the creatures concerned and are determined according to the region.

Buying game and venison
Game and venison can be bought either fresh or frozen. It is available directly from shoots, suppliers on the internet, butchers (it maybe necessary to order in advance) and supermarkets. However fresh game and venison will only be available during the relevant shooting season. When buying game and venison you must always check the colour and smell of the meat.

Skinning game and venison
(photograph 1)
To do this you need a very sharp, pointed knife. Slide it under the sinewy skin with the sharp side of the blade upwards. Then pull up the end of the skin slightly and free more it by moving the knife further under the skin, while continuing to pull on the skin. Detach the skin from the meat in broad strips.

Barding game and venison
(photographs 2+3)
Barding involves wrapping lean

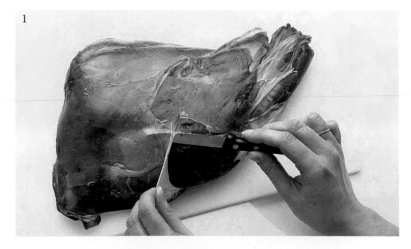

1

pieces of meat in slices of bacon. This will prevent the meat from drying out during the cooking process. Thus the meat is wrapped in slices of fatty or streaky bacon which are secured with cooking string. The bacon slices are then removed after cooking. The "spiking" of game and venison which was very popular in the past is no longer recommended today because the delicate fibres of the meat are damaged by the spiking needles and the opposite of what was actually intended is achieved: the meat juices escape and the meat becomes dry.

Marinating

The excellent refrigeration facilities used when hanging meat and venison day mean that it is no longer absolutely necessary to marinate game and venison. Hanging makes the meat more tender and allows it to develop its distinctive flavour. In the past, when game and venison were hung without refrigeration facilities, a strong taste and smell developed as the putrefaction

process began to set in (also known as "high", with a very pronounced "gamey" flavour). Marinating the meat in a buttermilk, vinegar or wine marinade reduced this gamey flavour and smell. Today game or venison is only marinated to obtain a particular aroma or to make older, tougher meat more tender.

For red wine marinade you will need:

2 carrots and 2 onions, prepared and coarsely chopped, 1 prepared, coarsely chopped head celery, 2 rinsed sprigs of thyme, 1 tablespoon crushed juniper berries, 1 tablespoon peppercorns, 4 cloves, 2 bay leaves and 1 litre/1¾ pints (4¼ cups) dry red wine. Stir together the chopped vegetables, the herbs and the spices and put in a bowl together with the meat. Pour the wine over the meat, cover with clingfilm (plastic wrap) and keep in the refrigerator to marinate for 12 to 24 hours. The meat must be completely covered by the marinade. Do not add salt to the marinade because this would dry out the meat.

Frozen game and venison

Frozen game and venison are available all year round in the shops. Freezing makes the meat more tender and mellow. When stored at -18 °C/-0 °F frozen game and venison can be keep for 8–10 months and game fowl up to 6 months. Being stored frozen for a longer time is not good for the meat which then dries and become straw-like, or in other words leathery.

If you want to freeze game and venison yourself, here are a few helpful tips:

» Skin furred game, removing any sinews, and cut into servings.
» Draw and truss game birds before freezing them.
» Carefully pack the pieces and write the contents, weight and date on the container.

Before preparing frozen game or venison, cover it and defrost it in the refrigerator, then throw away the defrosting water and prepare the meat immediately.

2

3

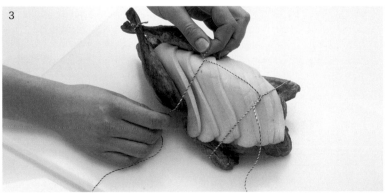

Marinated venison steaks

A LITTLE MORE LUXURIOUS

Preparation time:
about 30 minutes,
excluding marinating time

4 venison or wild boar steaks
(about 150 g/5 oz each)

For the marinade:
3 tablespoons lemon juice
5 tablespoons cooking oil,
e.g. sunflower or rapeseed
(canola) oil
10 crushed juniper berries
1 bay leaf in pieces
1 teaspoon dried chopped
thyme or rosemary
salt, pepper
125 g/4½ oz whipping cream
2 teaspoons blackberry or red
currant jelly
cayenne pepper (optional)

Per serving:
P: 32 g, F: 27 g, C: 4 g,
kJ: 1640, kcal: 392, CU: 0.5

1 Pat the steaks dry with a kitchen paper towel and, if necessary, remove any remaining skin.

2 To make the marinade, stir together the lemon juice, juniper berries, bay leaf and thyme or rosemary. Put the steaks in a bowl and pour the marinade over them. Cover with clingfilm (plastic wrap) and leave the steaks to marinade in the refrigerator for about 2 hours, turning the steaks over occasionally.

3 Heat a pan without any fat. Remove the meat from the marinade, leave to drain a little, put in the pan and sear on both sides. Then cook the steaks for about 10 minutes over medium heat, turning them once during this time. Season the steaks with salt and pepper, then put in a warm place.

4 Now add the rest of the marinade to the pan and loosen the cooking residues from the bottom of the pan. Add the cream and the jelly, then mix together well. Stir in the meat juices which come out of the steaks. Season the sauce with salt and pepper and cayenne pepper if liked. Serve the sauce with the steaks.

Serve with: boiled potatoes (p. 158), mixed leaf salad or lamb's lettuce (p. 146).

TIP » If you wish you can also thicken the sauce with dark gravy granules.

Recipe variation 1: To make venison steaks with blackberry sauce, take 250 g/9 oz fresh blackberries (or defrost 250 g/9 oz frozen blackberries). Melt 75 g/3 oz (⅓ cup) sugar in a pan over medium heat, stirring all the time with a wooden or metal spoon. Continue stirring until the sugar has melted into a pale brown, syrupy, caramelised mass. Stir in 165 ml/5½ fl oz (scant ¾ cup) blackcurrant juice, bring to the boil, then add the blackberries. Stir 1–2 teaspoons cornflour (cornstarch) into a little water, then add this to the sauce and bring to the boil. Season the sauce with salt and pepper. Garnish the steaks with a few basil leaves just before serving.

Recipe variation 2: To make venison steaks with cocktail-beer sauce, take 1 can of cocktail fruit (drained weight 250 g/9 oz) and reserve the juice. Chop up ½ prepared chilli pepper. Bring to the boil 1 bottle, 330 ml/11 fl oz (scant 1½ cups) grapefruit-flavoured wheat beer (or if not available, ordinary wheat beer) together with the chopped chilli pepper and the fruit juice. Stir 1–2 teaspoons cornflour (cornstarch) into a little water, then stir it into the sauce and bring to the boil. Season the sauce with salt, pepper and honey.

Recipe variation 3: To make venison stew, take 800 g/1¾ lb venison (without bones, for instance leg of deer, roe deer, wild boar), pat the meat dry with a kitchen paper towel, remove the skin and cut into 2.5 cm/1 in cubes. Peel and chop 2 onions. Heat 2 tablespoons oil in a pan and add the meat cut into cubes. Fry (sauté) briskly on all sides, season with salt and pepper. Add the chopped onion and fry with the meat. Stir in 125 ml/4 fl oz (½ cup) maracuja syrup and bring to the boil while stirring. Put 4 pieces of star anise, 3 cloves and 1 broken cinnamon stick in a tea ball or tea filter bag, seal well and add to the pan. Cover and cook the meat for about 55 minutes over medium heat. Gradually replace the evaporated liquid by another 125 ml/4 fl oz (½ cup) maracuja syrup. Meanwhile rinse 4 peaches, leave to drain, cut into cubes and add to the stew. Continue cooking for a further 5 minutes. Add 2 tablespoons peach liqueur and 1 tablespoon fruit vinegar. Stir 1–2 teaspoons cornflour (cornstarch) into a little water, then stir it into the stew and bring to the boil again. Rinse ½ bunch of basil, pat dry, remove the leaves and chop them. Remove the tea-filter of herbs from the stew. Season with salt and pepper, then sprinkle with the basil before serving.

Saddle of venison Baden style

WITH ALCOHOL

Preparation time:
about 30 minutes
Roasting time: 35–50 minutes

1 saddle of venison with
bones (about 1.6 kg/3½ lb)
salt, pepper
75 g/3 oz streaky bacon
in slices
1 onion
50 g/2 oz celery
100 g/3½ oz carrots
5 juniper berries
125 ml/4 fl oz (½ cup) dry red
wine or vegetable stock
2–3 pears, e.g. Williams Christ
200 ml/7 fl oz (⅞ cup)
sweet white wine
juice of 1 lemon
200 ml/7 fl oz (⅞ cup)
dry red wine
250 g/9 oz whipping cream
180 g/6½ oz cranberry
compote
dark sauce thickener
(optional)

Per serving:
P: 64 g, F: 28 g, C: 36 g,
kJ: 3002, kcal: 718, CU: 3.0

1 Preheat the oven
Top and bottom heat:
about 200 °C/400 °F (Gas mark 6)
Fan oven:
about 180 °C/350 °F (Gas mark 4)

2 Pat the meat dry with a kitchen
paper towel and remove the skin if
necessary. Rub the saddle with salt
and pepper and place in a roasting
tin, rinsed under cold water. Then
arrange the slices of bacon on top.

3 Peel the and finely chop the onion.
Prepare the celery and carrots, peel,
rinse, leave to drain and chop up.
Put the vegetables in the roasting
tin. Put the roasting tin without a
lid on the middle shelf in the preheated oven and roast the saddle
for 35–50 minutes. As soon as the
cooking juices begin to turn brown,
add the juniper berries and red
wine or vegetable stock.

4 Meanwhile wash the pears, cut in
half and remove the core (this is
best done with an apple corer). Add
the pear halves to the white wine
and lemon juice and bring to the
boil. Cover and cook over medium
heat for about 10 minutes. Remove
the pears from the liquid using a
skimming ladle, then leave to cool.

5 Take the saddle out of the roasting
tin, cover and leave to rest for about
10 minutes to let the meat juices
settle evenly. Scrape the cooking

residues off the bottom of the
roasting tin with red wine and rub
through a sieve together with the
vegetables. Bring to the boil and
stir in the cream. Add 2 tablespoons cranberry compote, bring
to the boil again and cook briskly
for 3–5 minutes so that it makes
bubbles. If you wish, add the meat
juices which have oozed out of the
resting saddle to the sauce. You can
also thicken the sauce with gravy
thickener and season it with more
herbs.

6 Remove the slices of bacon and
detach the meat from the bones.
Cut into slices, then arrange the
slices back on the bones. Arrange
the saddle on a pre-warmed
serving platter.

7 Stuff the pear halves with the rest
of the cranberry compote and
arrange them round the saddle.
Serve the sauce separately.

Serve with: Spätzle (p. 178) and
red cabbage (p. 120).

TIP » **Carving saddle of venison**
to serve: place the saddle with the
bones pointing downwards on a
carving board. With a sharp knife,
cut along the middle bone, then cut
the meat off the lower bones so that
it can be removed. Cut the meat
which you have just detached from
the bones into slices or pieces.

Haunch of venison
WITH ALCOHOL (ABOUT 6 SERVINGS)

Preparation time:
about 30 minutes,
excluding marinating time
Roasting time: 2–2½ hours

1.5 kg/3¼ lb leg of venison
on the bone
3 tablespoons cooking oil,
e.g. sunflower oil
1 teaspoon each dried
chopped marjoram and thyme
1 teaspoon dried chopped
rosemary
100 g/3½ oz streaky bacon,
thinly sliced
salt, pepper
about 150 ml/5 fl oz (⅝ cup)
hot game stock
1 onion
100 g/3½ oz carrots
150 g/5 oz leeks
2 tablespoons tomato purée

For the sauce:
125 ml/4 fl oz (½ cup) red wine
250 ml/8 fl oz (1 cup) game
stock, hot water or meat stock
100 g/3½ oz whipping cream
20 g/¾ oz (2 tablespoons)
cornflour (cornstarch)
3 tablespoons cold water
3 tablespoons cranberries
(from a jar)
a few prepared thyme leaves

Per serving:
P: 46 g, F: 14 g, C: 14 g,
kJ: 1605, kcal: 384, CU: 1.0

1 Pat the meat dry with a kitchen paper towel and if necessary remove the skin. Mix together the oil, marjoram, thyme and rosemary and brush this mixture over the haunch; cover with clingfilm (plastic wrap) and leave to marinate overnight in the refrigerator.

2 Preheat the oven:
Top and bottom heat:
about 200 °C/400 °F (Gas mark 6)
Fan oven:
about 180 °C/350 °F (Gas mark 4)

3 Place half the slices of bacon in a roasting tin, rinsed in water. Sprinkle the haunch of venison with salt and pepper and place on top of the slices of bacon in the roasting tin. Now arrange the remaining slices of bacon so that they cover the haunch. Put the roasting tin without a lid on a shelf in the bottom third of the preheated oven. Roast the haunch of venison for 2–2½ hours.

4 As soon as the cooking juices begin to brown, add the stock. Baste the haunch regularly with the cooking juices. Gradually replace the evaporated liquid with hot water or stock.

5 Meanwhile peel the onion. Prepare, peel and rinse the carrots, then leave to drain. Prepare the leeks, cut in half lengthways, wash thoroughly and leave to drain. Coarsely chop the vegetables. After 60 minutes, first add the tomato purée to the roasting tin and cook lightly, then add the vegetables and continue

roasting all the ingredients for a further 60–90 minutes.

6 Remove the meat from the roasting tin, cover and leave to rest for about 10 minutes.

7 Scrape the cooking residues from the bottom of the roasting, add red wine and venison stock and rub through a sieve with the vegetables. Top up the cooking juices with water or stock to make 400 ml/14 fl oz (1¾ cups); add the cream and bring to the boil. Mix together the cornflour (cornstarch) and water and stir into the boiling sauce, making sure there are no lumps. Simmer the sauce gently without a lid for about 5 minutes, stirring occasionally.

8 Now stir in the cranberries, thyme and, if you wish, the juices from the resting meat, into the sauce. Season the sauce with salt and pepper. Remove the bacon from the haunch. Cut the haunch into slices and serve with the sauce.

TIP » Instead of venison, wild boar may also be used, following the same recipe. Marinate the haunch overnight in 1 litre/1¾ pints (4¼ cups) of buttermilk. If you use a boneless haunch (about 1 kg/ 2¼ lb), cook for about 1½ hours. To ensure that the haunch does not fall apart, tie it together with cooking string.

Serve with: potato dumplings, (p. 170), red cabbage (p. 120).

Fish & seafood

Let us put fish on the table again! Sea fish, freshwater fish, shellfish and crustaceans – the choice offered by the oceans, rivers and lakes is wide. Fish and seafood will bring a pleasing variety to the menu and they are also highly recommended for their nutritional values, because they are rich in essential unsaturated fatty acids which contribute to maintaining a healthy heart and cardiovascular system. They also contains valuable protein, vitamins and iodine. Well prepared fish is "naturally" slimming because it contains little fat. Fish and seafood is a pleasure to which one should treat oneself at least once a week.

Sea fish (saltwater fish)
These include many kinds of shellfish, turbot, brill, halibut, plaice, coley, sole, Atlantic sole, tuna fish, mackerel, herring, gilthead sea bream, sea bass, silver bream, monkfish, red mullet, sardine, hake, red snapper, rosefish, cod, salmon.

Freshwater fish
Eel, pike, trout, salmon (when spawning), carp, whitefish, zander, tench, sea saibling, greyling, catfish, tilapia.

What to look for when buying fish
There are several criteria which will determine whether fish is fresh:
» clear, bright eyes with lenses curving outwards
» red, luminous gills (photograph 1)
» very shiny skin, covered with a clear epidermal mucus

Because the oceans have been overfished, fish farming – aquaculture – is providing an increasing proportion of fish for eating. Since stocks of rosefish, haddock, salmon, cod and sole are particularly at risk, it is preferable to use farmed fish or less endangered species of wild-caught fish, such as pollock or mackerel.

» firm scales
» fresh smell (in the case of sea fish, a smell of sea water or seaweed)

In prepared fish, look for the following signs of freshness:
» fillets with smooth, shiny flesh
» a fresh smell

How to store fish correctly
Fresh fish must be stored immediately in the refrigerator. Put it in a glass or china bowl at the bottom of which you have put a saucer turned upside down, so that any liquid from the fish can run away. Cover the fish with clingfilm (plastic wrap) and eat it the same day because fish goes bad very quickly.

Frozen fish
Frozen fish is processed and frozen on the boat as soon as it has been caught, as is farmed fish. Stored at -18° C/0 °F, frozen fish can be kept in the freezer for 2-5 months, depending on the fat content. To defrost the fish, take it out of the packaging. Put it in a bowl at the bottom of which you have put a saucer turned upside down and leave it to defrost overnight. In this way the water meting from the fish will run away and the fish will not come into contact with the defrosting liquid. Prepare the fish no later than the following day.

How to prepare fresh fish correctly
Most fresh fish is sold ready to be cooked. But if you have decided to buy a whole fish which has not been gutted, this is how you should proceed:
» Preparation: Wash the fish, leave to drain, open up the belly lengthways with a very sharp knife and gently pull the insides out.
» Scales: Hold the fish by the tail. Using a wide, flat knife or a fish scale remover remove the scales – preferably under running water – by scraping in the direction of the head.
» Skinning (for instance plaice): Make an incision near the tail fin with a sharp knife. Hold the tail fin with a cloth and pull the skin by tugging in the direction of the head.

Turn the fish over and proceed in the same way on the back. Cut off the head with a knife, then remove the tail fin and dorsal fin with kitchen scissors.

» Filleting: Cut open the skinned fish by running a sharp knife along the backbone from head to tail. Turn the knife over so that it lies flat and carefully separate the top and bottom fillet from the bones. Turn the fish over and separate the two fillets on the other side in the same way.

» Cleaning the fish: Rinse whole fish inside and out under cold running water and pat dry. Rinse fillets and dry in the same way.

» Seasoning with salt. Season with salt only just before cooking, otherwise the salt will draw out the water and the fish will become dry and lose flavour.

The fish is cooked when

» the fins and bones are easily detached.

» the eyes are bulging and look dark and cloudy.

» the skin comes off and is easily removed.

» the flesh separates into scales on being pressed with a fork (photograph 2).

Seafood includes

» Crustaceans: lobster, crab and shrimps, crayfish, spiny lobster

» Shellfish: mussels, oysters

» Cephalopods: cuttlefish, calamaries, octopus.

Crustaceans (photograph 3)

The range of seafood on offer with or without a protective shell is very large. The pinky-reddish colour only develops during the cooking process; before being cooked, crustaceans are grey. The varieties sold in the shops are often already cooked or frozen.

Removing crustaceans from their shell, for instance shrimps or prawns:

» Hold the cooked prawn or shrimp behind the head with one hand and the body section with the other hand.

» Twist the head and pull it off the body.

» From the underside, prise the shell slightly open from the head end and remove the meat.

» If dealing with king prawns, you must also remove the intestines which are just below the top part of the back and look like dark threads. They are easily removed with a knife: carefully cut the prawn open along the back and remove the black threads. Then rinse the prawn briefly under cold running water and pat dry. Today king prawns are available with the intestines already removed.

Bivalves (photograph 4)

There are thousands of kinds of bivalves, the best known and most popular of which include Jacobs mussels, comb mussels, cockles, Venus mussels, horse or common mussels and oysters. Bivalves are enclosed in two shells which are joined together on one side by a kind of hinge. The tender, protein-rich meat is very nourishing but unfortunately it goes bad very easily. This is why fresh oysters, mussels and the like are only available during the cold months of the year.

2

3

4

Deep-fried fish

FOR CHILDREN

Preparation time:
about 30 minutes
Cooking time:
about 10 minutes per serving

600 g/1¼ lb fish fillets, e.g.
tilapia, catfish or coley
salt
freshly ground pepper

For the batter:
100 g/3½ oz (1 cup) plain
(all purpose) flour
1 egg (medium)
salt
125 ml/4 fl oz (½ cup) milk
1 tablespoon cooking oil,
e.g. sunflower oil or
melted butter

oil for deep-frying,
e.g. sunflower oil

Per serving:
P: 27 g, F: 18 g, C: 10 g,
kJ: 1297, kcal: 309, CU: 1.0

1 Rinse the fish fillets under running cold water, pat dry and cut into individual servings. Sprinkle with salt and pepper.

2 For the batter, put the flour in a bowl and make a well in the middle. Whisk the egg into the milk and add a pinch of salt. Pour a little of this egg-milk mixture into the well. Starting in the middle, stir together the egg-milk mixture and flour. Then gradually add the rest of the egg-milk mixture and the oil or butter. Make sure that no lumps are formed.

3 Using a fork, dip the fish fillets in the batter (photograph 1) and deep-fry (sauté) several fish nuggets at a time (photograph 2) in the hot deep-frying oil for about 10 minutes until brown and crisp. Leave the fried nugget to drain on kitchen paper towels and keep warm until all the nuggets have been fried.

TIP ›› When deep-frying it is absolutely essential to choose a high-heat cooking oil with a neutral taste. If you use good quality deep-frying oil and follow the recommended temperatures, you can deep-fry chips, fish, vegetables, pastry and fruit one after the other without the taste of the oil being affected or being transferred from one food to the other. If you have no chip pan, you can deep-fry the fish in a high-sided sauté pan or in a saucepan filled with oil. Be very careful not to splash the hot oil.

Serve with: potato salad (p. 152) or serve as fish and chips.

Recipe variation: For fried fish fillets (at the front of photograph 3), rinse 4 pieces of fish fillet (for instance, tilapia or catfish fillets, about 200 g/7 oz each) under running cold water, pat dry and, if necessary, cut into servings. Sprinkle with salt and pepper. With a fork, whisk together 1 medium egg with 2 tablespoons cold water in a deep bowl. Coat the fillets first in 40 g/1½ oz (⅜ cup) plain (all purpose) flour, then in the egg and finally in 50-75 g/2-3 oz (¾–1 cup) breadcrumbs, gently shake off loose breadcrumbs. Heat about 75 ml/3 fl oz (⅜ cup) cooking oil in a pan. Add the fillets and fry (sauté) over medium heat for about 5 minutes on each side until golden brown, then leave to drain on kitchen paper towels. If you want to garnish the fish, thoroughly wash 1 organic lemon (untreated, unwaxed), wipe dry, cut into slices and place on the fish before serving.

EXTRA TIP ›› You can replace the breadcrumbs with sesame seeds or crumbled tortilla crisps and 1½ teaspoons chilli flakes.

Herring fillets home style

IDEAL FOR PREPARING IN ADVANCE (PHOTOGRAPH)

Preparation time:
about 30 minutes
Marinating time: about 12 hours

8 herring fillets (about
600 g/1¼ lb)
250 ml/8 fl oz (1 cup) water
salt
3 onions
400 g/14 oz apples
150 g/5 oz gherkins (from a jar)
200 g/7 oz whipping cream
1 carton (150 g/5 oz)
crème fraîche
3 tablespoons lemon juice
pepper, sugar

1 Rinse the herring fillets under running cold water and pat dry. Remove any remaining bones and cut the fillets into 2 cm/¾ in chunks.

2 Bring the water to the boil in a pan and add ¼ teaspoon salt. Peel the onions and cut in half, then cut into slices. Blanch the onion slices briefly in the salted boiling water, then leave to drain.

3 Peel the apple, cut into quarters and core. Leave the gherkins to drain. Cut the apple and gherkins into slices.

4 Stir together the cream, crème fraîche and lemon juice, then season with salt, pepper and sugar. Stir in the sliced onions, sliced apples and sliced gherkins. Now add the pieces of herring to the sauce, mix well, cover with clingfilm (plastic wrap) and put in the refrigerator for about 12 hours for the herring to absorb the flavours of the sauce.

Serve with: boiled potatoes (p. 158) and caramelised onion rings, green (snap) beans (p. 119).

Per serving: P: 30 g, F: 51 g, C: 16 g, kJ: 2686, kcal: 643, CU: 1.0

Smoked fish mousse

FOR GUESTS

Preparation time:
about 15 minutes
Cooling time: about 60 minutes

2 smoked trout fillets (about
125 g/4½ oz each)
30 g/1 oz soft butter
1–2 tablespoons sour cream
1–1½ tablespoons lemon juice
salt, pepper
some lamb's lettuce
½ teaspoon red peppercorns

1 Coarsely chop up the trout fillets and remove any remaining bones. Purée the fillets with butter, sour cream and lemon juice.

2 Season the mixture with salt and pepper, cover with clingfilm (plastic wrap) and put in the refrigerator for about 60 minutes.

3 Prepare the lamb's lettuce, wash thoroughly, dry in a salad spinner and arrange on 4 plates.

4 Using 2 tablespoons, previously dipped in hot water, form fish mousse balls and arrange them on the lamb's lettuce. Sprinkle with peppercorns before serving.

Serve with: ciabatta, brown bread or coarse rye bread.

TIP » Serve the smoked fish mousse as a starter.

Per serving: P: 14 g, F: 10 g, C: 1 g, kJ: 620, kcal: 148, CU: 0.0

Salmon trout with leaf spinach

FOR GUESTS

Preparation time:
25–30 minutes
Cooking time: small trout
about 35 minutes,
large trout about 55 minutes

1.5 kg/3¼ lb leaf spinach
200 g/7 oz shallots
2 cloves garlic
300 g/10 oz mushrooms
150 g/5 oz tomatoes
2 tablespoons butter or
margarine
salt
freshly ground pepper
ground nutmeg
1 large salmon trout
(about 1.3 kg/2¾ lb)
or 2 small salmon trout
(about 600 g/1¼ lb each)
75 g/3 oz smoked streaky
bacon
1 bunch parsley
1 organic lemon (untreated,
unwaxed)

6 thin slices streaky bacon

Per serving:
P: 42 g, F: 18 g, C: 4 g,
kJ: 1468, kcal: 351, CU: 0.0

1 Prepare the spinach and remove all tough stems. Wash the spinach thoroughly and leave to drain. Peel the shallots and cloves of garlic. Take half the shallots and cut each one into eight pieces. Finely chop the rest of the shallots and the garlic.

2 Prepare the mushrooms and rub clean with a kitchen paper towel. Slice half the mushrooms. Finely chop the remaining mushrooms. Wash the tomatoes, wipe dry, cut in half, remove the seeds and cut out the stalks and base. Cut the tomatoes into cubes.

3 Melt the butter or margarine in a pan. Add the shallots cut into eighths, the garlic and the sliced mushrooms and fry (sauté) briefly. Now add the spinach and fry while stirring (until the spinach "collapses"). Season with salt, pepper and nutmeg. Now stir in the chopped tomatoes.

4 Preheat the oven:
Top and bottom heat:
about 200 °C/400 °F (Gas mark 6)
Fan oven:
about 180 °C/350 °F (Gas mark 4)

5 Rinse the salmon trout inside and out under running cold water, then pat dry. Rub inside and out with salt and pepper. Chop the bacon finely. Rinse the parsley, pat dry, pull the leaves off the stems and chop them finely.

6 Wash the lemon in hot water and grate off the yellow rind. Cut the lemon in half and squeeze out the juice. Now stir in the diced bacon, chopped mushrooms, chopped shallots, parsley, lemon rind and juice. Stuff the mixture inside the belly cavity of the salmon trout.

7 Put the spinach in a large casserole or roasting tin. Place the salmon trout on top and arrange any remaining stuffing around it. Put the slices of bacon on top of the fish. Put the casserole or roasting tin without a lid on a shelf in the bottom third of the preheated oven. Cook small salmon trout for about 35 minutes and large salmon trout for about 55 minutes.

Serve with: boiled potatoes (p. 158) or rice.

Recipe variation: For **trout meunière**, take 4 ready-to-cook trout (each about 200 g/7 oz) and prepare as described in step 5. Turn the trout over in 40 g/1½ oz (⅜ cup) plain (all purpose) flour, gently shaking off any excess. Heat 3 tablespoons cooking oil in a pan. Add the trout and fry (sauté) on both sides over medium heat. Add 40 g/1½ oz (3 tablespoons) butter and melt it. Continue frying the trout for about 10 minutes, turning them over several times and regularly basting them with the butter. Wash 1–2 organic lemons (untreated and unwaxed) with hot water, wipe dry and cut into slices. Garnish the trout with the slices of lemon before serving.

Pollack cooked in foil

SOPHISTICATED

Preparation time:
about 25 minutes
Cooking time: 20–25 minutes

**4 slices pollack fillet
(about 180 g/6½ oz each)**
salt
freshly ground pepper
2 small leeks
2 tablespoons cooking oil, e.g.
rapeseed (canola) oil
4 tomatoes
½ bunch flat-leaved parsley
3 tablespoons roasted onion
(from a jar)

Also:
**4 sheets foil
(about 20 x 30 cm/8 x 12 in
each)**

Per serving:
P: 35 g, F: 10 g, C: 7 g,
kJ: 1093, kcal: 260, CU: 0.5

1 Preheat the oven:
Top and bottom heat:
about 200 °C/400 °F (Gas mark 6)
Fan oven:
about 180 °C/350 °F (Gas mark 4)

2 Rinse the fish under running cold water and pat dry. Sprinkle both sides with salt and pepper.

3 Prepare the leeks, cut in half lengthways, wash them thoroughly and leave to drain; then cut into thin strips. Heat the oil in a pan, add the strips of leaks and fry (sauté) for about 3 minutes while stirring. Season with salt and pepper.

4 Spread four sheets of foil on a work surface and place 1 slice of pollack on top.

5 Wash the tomatoes, wipe dry and cut out the stalks. Chop the tomatoes into small cubes. Rinse the parsley, pat dry and pull the leaves from the stems. Coarsely chop the leaves. Mix together the tomatoes, parsley and roast onions and arrange on the slices of pollack (photograph 1).

6 Wrap up each piece of fish and one quarter of the vegetables in foil, seal well (photograph 2) and place on a baking sheet. Put the baking sheet on the middle shelf in the preheated oven. Cook the fish and vegetables for 20–25 minutes.

7 Place 1 pollack parcel on each plate, open up the aluminium parcel and serve immediately.

Serve with: potatoes in their skins (p. 158).

TIP: » Instead of foil you can also use non-stick baking paper.

Recipe variation: To make **fried fish medallions on a bed of vegetable pasta**, take 250 g/9 oz frozen zander fillet and 250 g/9 oz salmon fillet and defrost following the instructions on the packages. Prepare 500 g/18 oz vegetables (for instance carrots, leeks) and peel if necessary, then wash, leave to drain and cut into fine strips or small cubes. Cook 250 g/9 oz spaghetti in plenty of salted water; you should use about 1 teaspoon salt per 1 litre/1¾ pints (4¼ cups) water, following the instructions on the package. Then pour into a colander, rinse under hot water and leave to drain. Rinse the defrosted fish fillets under running cold water, pat dry and cut into six pieces. Put 200 ml/7 fl oz (⅞ cup) white wine, salt, pepper, sugar and 1 bay leaf in a pan and heat up. Add the fish fillets and cook over low heat for about 8 minutes. Heat 2 tablespoons olive oil in a pan. Add the prepared vegetables and fry (sauté), then season with salt and pepper. Add the pasta and mix well. Arrange the fish medallions on the vegetable pasta and if desired garnish with a few basil leaves.

Salmon steaks with lemon foam

QUICK

Preparation time:
about 30 minutes

In advance:
125 g/4½ oz butter

4 salmon steaks (about
200 g/7 oz each)
salt
3 tablespoons cooking oil,
e.g. sunflower oil
20 g/¾ oz (1½ tablespoons)
butter or margarine

For the lemon foam:
3 egg yolks (medium)
5 tablespoons lemon juice
2 teaspoons medium
strong mustard
salt
freshly ground pepper
1 pinch sugar
2 teaspoons chopped dill
(optional)

Per serving:
P: 39 g, F: 46 g, C: 1 g,
kJ: 2433, kcal: 582, CU: 0.0

1 Melt the butter in a pan and leave to cool.

2 Rinse the salmon fillets under running cold water, pat dry and sprinkle with salt. Heat the oil in a pan, add the butter or margarine and melt. Add the steaks and fry (sauté) and on each side for 3–4 minutes. Take the salmon steaks out of the pan, put them on a pre-warmed dish and keep warm.

3 To make the lemon foam, stir together the egg yolk and lemon juice in a small pan, using a whisk. Continue stirring over low heat until the mixture becomes foamy (photograph 1).

4 Then put the pan immediately on a cold, wet cloth. Now slowly stir the cooled but still liquid melted butter into the egg yolk mixture (photograph 2). Season with mustard, salt, pepper and sugar. If liked, also stir in some dill. Serve the lemon foam with the salmon steaks.

Serve with: roast potatoes or rice (p. 182) and a green salad.

TIP » For a richer dish, you can add 2–3 tablespoons whipped cream to the lemon foam.

Recipe variation 1: To make salmon steaks with mustard sauce, bring 400 g/14 oz whipping cream to the boil and simmer gently without a lid until the mixture becomes creamy. Stir in 3–4 tablespoons tarragon mustard and 1 teaspoon chopped tarragon leaves into the sauce. Season the sauce with salt, pepper, 1 pinch of sugar and a dash of lemon juice. Serve the mustard with the salmon steaks.

Recipe variation 2: To make salmon steaks with lemon butter, wash 1–2 organic lemons (untreated and unwaxed) under hot water and wipe dry. Using a knife, peel the lemon, removing a very thin layer of rind, and cut this zest into thin strips. Mix together the strips of lemon zest and 125 g/4½ oz (⅝ cup) softened butter. Roll the butter into a cylinder about 3 cm/1¼ in in diameter on a piece of clingfilm (plastic wrap). Wrap it in the clingfilm and put it in the refrigerator. Shortly before serving, cut the butter into slices about 5 mm/³⁄₁₆ in thick and garnish the steaks with them. Lemon butter can also be frozen.

Plaice with diced bacon

FOR GUESTS

Preparation time:
about 20 minutes
Cooking time: about 15 minutes
per serving

**4 oven-ready plaice (about
300 g/10 oz each)
salt
freshly ground pepper
40 g/1½ oz (⅜ cup) plain (all
purpose) flour
about 150 g/5 oz streaky bacon
1 organic lemon (untreated,
unwaxed)
3–4 tablespoons cooking oil,
e.g. sunflower oil
a few sprigs dill**

Per serving:
P: 47 g, F: 15 g, C: 6 g,
kJ: 1455, kcal: 349, CU: 0.5

1 Rinse the plaice under cold running water, pat dry and rub in salt and pepper. Coat the plaice in flour, gently shaking off any excess, and dice the bacon. Wash the lemon in hot water and cut into eight segments.

2 Heat the oil in a large pan, add the diced bacon and fry (sauté) so that the fat runs out. Remove the bacon pieces from the pan and keep warm.

3 Depending on the size of the pan, fry the plaice one after the other in the bacon fat for about 15 minutes on both sides until golden brown; if there is not enough fat, add a little oil. Arrange the plaice on a pre-warmed dish and keep warm until all the plaice have been fried.

4 Rinse the dill and pat dry. Sprinkle the diced bacon over the plaice, garnish with the lemon segments and sprigs of dill and serve.

Serve with: boiled potatoes (p. 158) and lamb's lettuce (p. 146).

TIP » In addition, you can also fry some crab meat in the bacon fat and arrange on the plaice.

Mussels in a wine-based stock

WITH ALCOHOL

Preparation time:
about 60 minutes
Cooking time: about 10 minutes

2 kg/4½ lb mussels
2 onions
1 bunch soup vegetables
(celery, carrots, leeks)
50 g/2 oz (4 tablespoons)
butter or margarine
500 ml/17 fl oz (2¼ cups) dry
white wine
salt
freshly ground pepper

Per serving:
P: 9 g, F: 12 g, C: 3 g,
kJ: 1022, kcal: 244, CU: 0.5

1 Carefully wash the mussels in plenty of cold water. Brush each mussel separately (photograph 1) until every trace of sand has been removed (mussels which open while being washed must not be eaten). If necessary remove the threads (photograph 2).

2 Peel the onions, cut into slices and then separate into rings. Peel the celery. Prepare the carrots and peel. Wash the celery and carrots and leave to drain. Prepare the leeks, cut in half lengthways, wash them thoroughly and leave to drain, then cut into rings. Coarsely chop the carrots and celery.

3 Melt the butter or margarine in a pan. Add the onions and other vegetables and fry (sauté) briefly while stirring. Add the white wine, bring to the boil and season with salt and pepper. Add the mussels, cover and heat (but do not boil) for about 10 minutes, stirring occasionally, until the mussels open up (mussels which do not open after cooking must not be eaten).

4 Take the mussels out of the cooking liquid using a skimming ladle and put in a pre-warmed bowl. Pour the cooking liquid through a sieve, adjust the seasoning if necessary and serve with the mussels.

Serve with: brown bread and butter.

Recipe variation: For mussels "alla Livornese", prepare the mussels as described in step 1. Wash 6 tomatoes, leave to drain, make a cross-shaped cut at the bottom, plunge briefly in boiling water, then in cold water. Then peel the tomatoes, cut in half and cut out the stalks. Chop up the tomatoes. Peel and finely chop 2 onions. Peel 2 cloves of garlic and push through a garlic press. Leave 2 chillies (from a jar) to drain and chop finely. Heat 8 tablespoons olive oil in a pan. Add the onions, garlic and peppers and fry while stirring. Add the chopped tomatoes and 200 ml/ 7 fl oz (⅞ cup) vegetable stock or white wine and bring to the boil. Add the mussels, cover and cook for about 10 minutes, stirring occasionally. Season with salt and pepper. If desired, garnish with lemon segments before serving.

TIP » How to buy fresh mussels. Only buy mussels with shells which are still firmly closed. Throw away any mussel which is already open because it will be bad. Fresh mussels have a fresh sea smell.

Brown beef stock (bouillon)

GOOD TO PREPARE IN ADVANCE

Preparation time:
about 20 minutes
Cooking time: about 2½ hours

Quantities to make about
1 litre/1¾ pints (4¼ cups)
1 kg/2¼ lb meat bones, e.g.
from veal (from the butcher,
chopped into small pieces)
2 onions
1 bunch soup vegetables
(celery, carrots, leeks)
2 tablespoons cooking oil,
e.g. sunflower or rapeseed
(canola) oil
1 tablespoon tomato purée
about 3 litres/6½ pints
(12 cups) water or red wine
2 sprigs thyme
2 sprigs rosemary
1 bay leaf
salt

In total:
P: 28 g, F: 23 g, C: 40 g,
kJ: 3191, kcal: 761, CU: 2.0

1 Rinse the bones under running cold water and leave to drain. Peel and coarsely chop the onions. Peel the celery. Prepare and peel the carrots. Wash the celery and carrots and leave to drain. Prepare the leeks, cut in half lengthways, wash them thoroughly and leave to drain. Coarsely chop up all the vegetables.

2 Heat the oil in pan or roasting tin. Then add the bones and fry (sauté) them (photograph 1). Add the prepared vegetables and fry with the bones. Now add the tomato purée (photograph 2) and fry briefly (photograph 3).

3 Add enough water or red wine to cover the bottom of the pan or roasting tin. Allow the liquid to boil away. Repeat this process twice more, but make sure that the bones and vegetables do not burn.

4 Now add the rest of the water or red wine, bring to the boil again and skim the foam off the surface. Rinse the herbs and add together with the bay leaf. Simmer the liquid over low heat without a lid for about 2½ hours, reducing it slowly until only 1 litre/1¾ pints (4¼ cups) of liquid remains.

5 Pour the stock through a fine sieve and season with salt.

Uses: Brown beef stock (bouillon) can be used to make dark gravy and sauces to accompany roasts.

TIP » Beef broth is useful to have in reserve. Prepare double the quantity, freeze or pour when still hot into well-washed and rinsed jars with screw-top lids. When frozen the stock will keep for about 3 months and when stored in jars in the refrigerator for about 2 weeks.

Recipe variation: To make light-coloured chicken stock, take 1 kg/2¼ lb chicken bones or chicken wings and giblets and rinse under running cold water, then leave to drain. Prepare 1 bunch of soup vegetables as described in step 1 of the recipe. Peel 1 onion and stud with 1 clove and 1 bay leaf. Put all the ingredients together with 125 ml/4 fl oz (½ cup) white wine, 2 litres/3½ pints (8½ cups) water and 2 teaspoons salt in a pan and bring to the boil over medium heat without a lid. Keep removing the foam while it is cooking, using a skimming ladle. Then reduce the stock over low heat without a lid for about 2½ hours until only 1 litre/ 1¾ pints (4¼ cups) of stock remains. Strain the stock through a sieve.

Uses: Light-coloured chicken stock is used as a base for chicken-flavoured sauces, chicken ragout, cream soups, risotto and fish dishes.

Light-coloured basic sauce

QUICK (TOP RIGHT IN THE PHOTOGRAPH)

Preparation time:
about 10 minutes
Cooking time: about 5 minutes

25 g/1 oz (2 tablespoons)
butter or margarine
20 g/¾ oz (3 tablepsoons) plain
(all purpose) flour
375 ml/13 fl oz (1⅝ cups) stock
(bouillon), e.g. vegetable stock
salt
freshly ground pepper

Per serving:
P: 1 g, F: 5 g, C: 4 g,
kJ: 279, kcal: 67, CU: 0.5

1 Melt the butter or margarine in a pan. Stir in the flour and continue cooking until the mixture turns pale yellow.

2 Add the stock (bouillon) and stir well, using a whisk; make sure that there are no small lumps left.

3 Bring the sauce to the boil and simmer lightly over low heat without a lid for about 5 minutes, stirring occasionally. Season the sauce with salt and pepper.

Uses: Light-coloured basic sauce is used as a base for herb-flavoured and cheese sauces. Serve the sauce with braised vegetables, fish or flash-fried meat.

Recipe variation 1: For horseradish sauce, make the light-coloured basic sauce with 125 ml/4 fl oz (½ cup) vegetable stock, 125 ml/4 fl oz (½ cup) milk and 125 g/4 oz (½ cup) whipping cream instead of the stock. Finally stir in 2 tablespoons grated horseradish (freshly grated or from a jar) and season the sauce with salt, white pepper, sugar and lemon juice.

Recipe variation 2: To make a herb sauce (bottom left in the photo-graph), make the light-coloured basic sauce with 250 ml/8 fl oz (1 cup) milk and 125 ml/4 fl oz (½ cup) vegetable stock instead of the stock. Finally stir in 3 table-spoons chopped herbs (for instance parsley, chervil or dill) and 2 table-

spoons crème fraîche. Season the sauce with salt, pepper and grated nutmeg.

Recipe variation 3: To make a dark basic sauce (bottom right in the photograph), heat the flour and melted butter, as described in step 1, until the mixture turns to a medium dark brown. Then continue as described in the recipe.

Recipe variation 4: To make béchamel sauce with ham (top left in the photograph), peel and finely chop 1 onion. Cut 40 g/1½ oz uncooked ham into small cubes. Melt 30 g/1 oz (2 tablespoons) butter or margarine in a pan. Add the diced ham and fry (sauté). Then add the chopped onion and 25 g/1 oz (4 tablespoons) plain (all purpose) flour and continue frying until the flour mixture has become pale yellow. Pour in 125 ml/4 fl oz (½ cup) vegetable stock, 250 ml/ 8 fl oz (1 cup) milk or 250 g/9 oz (1 cup) whipping cream and stir briskly with a whisk. Make sure that there are no lumps. Now simmer the sauce without a lid for about 5 minutes over low heat, stirring occasionally. Season the sauce with salt, pepper and grated nutmeg.

TIP » Serve the béchamel sauce with vegetables such as cauliflower (p. 118), asparagus (p. 122), carrots (p. 118), kohlrabi (p. 118) or poached eggs. For a vegetarian version, leave out the ham.

Sauce hollandaise

CLASSIC · WITH ALCOHOL

Preparation time:
about 15 minutes,
excluding cooling time

150 g/5 oz butter
2 egg yolk (medium)
2 tablespoons white wine
a few drops lemon juice
salt
freshly ground pepper

Per serving:
P: 2 g, F: 34, C: 0 g,
kJ: 1343, kcal: 321, CU: 0.0

1 Melt the butter, leave to cool a little and remove the foam with a skimming ladle (photograph 1).

2 Whisk the egg yolk with white wine in a stainless steel bowl. Place the bowl over a bain-marie but do not allow the water to boil. Whisk the egg yolk mixture, using a whisk, until the mixture is foamy (photograph 2).

3 Carefully whisk the melted butter into the egg yolk mixture (photograph 3). Season the sauce with salt, pepper and lemon juice.

Advice: Only use very fresh eggs which are not more than 5 days old – check the date when the eggs were laid!

TIP » Whipped sauces should only be kept warm for a short time in a bain-marie. After a while, the sauce separates into fat and egg yolk, in other words it curdles. This is why the sauce should only be made just before serving. A curdled sauce can be "rescued" by whisking again with a hand-held mixer or by gradually stirring 1 egg yolk and 1 tablespoon cold water into the curdled sauce in a bain-marie.

EXTRA TIP » Whisking. Whisk the ingredients for sauces and creams uninterruptedly with a whisk, slowly warming them until you obtain a thick mixture.

Recipe variation 1: To make sauce béarnaise, replace the white wine with a herb-flavoured stock as follows. Peel and finely chop 1 onion and put in a pan. Add 1 teaspoon chopped tarragon, 1 teaspoon chopped chervil, 2 teaspoons white wine vinegar, 2 tablespoons water and bring to the boil. Remove the pan from the heat and leave the herb-flavoured stock to stand with the lid on for 5 minutes. Then pour the stock through a fine sieve. Stir 1–2 teaspoons chopped chervil and chopped tarragon into the sauce. Finally season the sauce with salt, pepper and lemon juice.

Recipe variation 2: To make sauce maltaise, replace the white wine with 2 tablespoons freshly squeezed blood orange juice, 2 teaspoons warm water and 1 tablespoon lemon juice. Season the sauce with salt and sugar and sprinkle the grated rind of a quarter of an organic orange (untreated, unwaxed) on top.

Recipe variation 3: To make a quick hollandaise sauce (without a bain-marie), melt the butter. Whisk together the egg yolk and only ½ tablespoon lemon juice or white wine in a bowl using a hand-held whisk. Slowly add the hot melted butter and continue whisking to thicken. If the sauce becomes too thick, thin with ½ tablespoon hot water. Season the sauce again.

Mayonnaise

QUICK (IN THE MIDDLE IN THE PHOTOGRAPH)

Preparation time:
about 10 minutes

1 egg yolk (medium)
1–2 teaspoons white wine
vinegar or lemon juice
salt
½–1 teaspoon medium strong
mustard
125 ml/4 fl oz (½ cup)
cooking oil, e.g. sunflower oil

Per serving:
P: 1 g, F: 33 g, C: 0 g,
kJ: 1234, kcal: 295, CU: 0.0

1 Mix together the egg yolk with vinegar or lemon juice, salt and mustard in a bowl, using a whisk (photograph 1) until the mixture becomes foamy.

2 Pour in the oil slowly and steadily as you continue stirring (photograph 2). It is not necessary to add the oil drop by drop since the seasoning which has been added to the egg yolk will prevent the mayonnaise from curdling.

Uses: Mayonnaise is an excellent base for cold sauces and dips, on its own with a fondue or as a filling in sandwiches.

TIPS » All the ingredients used in mayonnaise must be the same temperature to ensure they bind properly together.
» If the mayonnaise should curdle, mix together another egg yolk and vinegar or lemon juice and slowly stir into the curdled mayonnaise.

Advice: **Only use very fresh eggs which are not more than 5 days old – check the date when the eggs were laid!** When you have finished the mayonnaise, keep in the refrigerator and consume within 24 hours.

Recipe variation 1: For a light mayonnaise, follow the instructions in the recipe but use only 5 tablespoons oil. Then mix 4 tablespoons low-fat quark curd cheese with 1 tablespoon whipping cream and stir into the mayonnaise. If you wish, season with ½ peeled, pressed clove of garlic.

Recipe variation 2: To make a cold curry sauce (bottom in the photograph), follow the instructions in the recipe, then stir in 1–2 teaspoons curry powder and 150 g/5 oz yoghurt (3.5 % fat) or soured milk. To make a sweet curry sauce, add 1–2 tablespoons apricot jam (jelly) which has been rubbed through a sieve.

Recipe variation 3: To make a remoulade sauce, (at the top in the photograph) shell 2 hard-boiled (hard-cooked) eggs. Push the egg yolk through a sieve and chop the white. Mix the crushed hard-boiled egg and 1 raw egg yolk and make a mayonnaise as described in the recipe. Finally stir in 1 medium, finely chopped gherkin, 2 tablespoons chopped herbs (for instance parsley, chives, dill, chervil, cress), 1 teaspoon drained chopped capers and the chopped egg white. Season with salt, pepper and sugar.

Recipe variation 4: To make sauce tartare, peel and finely chop 4 shallots or small onions. Stir into the mayonnaise with 2 teaspoons drained chopped capers and 2 tablespoons chopped herbs, such as parsley. Then season the sauce with salt.

Frankfurt green sauce

CLASSIC (PHOTOGRAPH)

Preparation time:
about 20 minutes

about 150 g/5 oz fresh herbs
for Frankfurt green sauce
1 carton (150 g/5 oz) crème
fraîche or sour cream
1 small onion
150 g/5 oz yoghurt (3.5 % fat)
1–2 tablespoons olive oil
1 teaspoon medium strong
mustard
1 drop lemon juice
½ teaspoon sugar
salt, pepper

Per serving:
P: 4 g, F: 13 g, C: 7 g,
kJ: 677, kcal: 162, CU: 0.5

1 Rinse the herbs, pat dry and remove the leaves from the stems. Chop the leaves coarsely and purée together with 2 tablespoons crème fraîche or sour cream in a bowl; alternatively chop the herbs very finely and stir together with the crème fraîche or the sour cream. Peel and finely chop the onions.

2 Stir the rest of the crème fraîche or sour cream, yoghurt, chopped onions, oil and mustard into the herb-crème fraîche mixture or mix with the herbs. Season the sauce with lemon juice, sugar, salt and pepper and refrigerate until ready to serve.

Uses: Frankfurt green sauce is delicious served with new potatoes and hard-boiled (hard-cooked) eggs or with boiled beef.

TIP » The "authentic" Frankfurt green sauce is made with 7 fresh herbs. But depending on the season the composition can vary. In some place bags of ready-to-use mixed herbs (about 150 g/5 oz) for making Frankfurt green sauce are available. If these are not available you can use a bunch of mixed herbs such as parsley, chives, chervil, burnet, borage, lemon balm and cress or sorrel. You can also use frozen herbs.

Mushroom sauce

SOPHISTICATED

Preparation time:
about 20 minutes

1 small onion
1 cloves garlic
250 g/9 oz fresh mushrooms,
e.g. champignons, chanterelles,
oyster mushrooms
30 g/1 oz (2 tablespoons) butter
15 g/½ oz (2½ tablespoons)
plain (all purpose) flour
250 ml/8 fl oz (1 cup)
vegetable stock
1 carton (150 g/5 oz) crème
fraîche
salt, pepper, some thyme
1 tablespoon chopped parsley

1 Peel and finely chop the onion and clove of garlic.

2 Prepare the mushrooms, rub with a kitchen paper towel and slice the mushrooms.

3 Melt the butter in a pan, add the chopped onion and clove of garlic and fry (sauté) briefly while stirring. Now add the sliced mushrooms and fry with the onion and garlic. Sprinkle the flour on top and continue frying while still stirring until the mixture has turned pale

yellow. Now gradually stir in the vegetable stock, making sure that there are no lumps. Bring everything to the boil, then simmer for about 5 minutes without a lid over low heat, stirring occasionally.

4 Stir in the crème fraîche. Season the sauce with salt, pepper and thyme. Stir in the parsley.

Uses: Mushrooms sauce is a perfect accompaniment to steaks, schnitzel and fried fish.

Per serving: P: 3 g, F: 18 g, C: 5 g, kJ: 807, kcal: 194, CU: 0.5

Tomato sauce

VEGETARIAN (PHOTOGRAPH AT THE BOTTOM)

Preparation time:
about 10 minutes
Cooking time: about 15 minutes

1 kg/2¼ lb ripe tomatoes
1 onion
1 cloves garlic
2–3 tablespoons olive oil,
to taste
2 tablespoons tomato purée
salt
freshly ground pepper
about 1 teaspoon sugar
1 drop white wine vinegar
1 tablespoon chopped oregano

Per serving:
P: 2 g, F: 7 g, C: 8 g,
kJ: 438, kcal: 104, CU: 0.0

1 Wash the tomatoes, leave to drain, then cut out the stalks and base (photograph 1). Make a cross-shaped cut in the non-stalk end (photograph 2), plunge briefly in boiling water, then in cold water. Peel the tomatoes, cut in half and chop up into cubes. Peel and finely chop the onion and clove of garlic.

2 Heat the oil in a pan. Add the chopped onion and garlic and fry (sauté). Now add the chopped tomatoes as well as tomato purée if wished. Season with salt and pepper. Bring the tomato mixture to the boil, cover and simmer gently over low heat for about 15 minutes, stirring occasionally.

3 If you like the sauce can be puréed (photograph 3) and seasoned with salt, pepper, sugar, vinegar and oregano.

TIP » If the finished sauce is still too liquid, reduce it a little further by boiling over medium heat, or thicken the sauce with light gravy thickener. Instead of fresh tomatoes you can also used tinned peeled tomatoes (800 g/1¾ lb) as well as the juice. The addition of tomato purée will make the sauce creamier and give it an intense tomato flavour.

Recipe variation 1: To make a tomato and vegetable sauce (in the centre in the photograph), prepare 1 bunch of soup vegetables, wash, leave to drain, then chop into small cubes or chunks. Put 1 tablespoon of chopped soup vegetables to one side for the garnish. Fry (sauté) the rest of the soup vegetables with 1 peeled, chopped onion and 1 peeled chopped clove of garlic in 2–3 tablespoons olive oil. Add 1 bay leaf and 125 ml/4 fl oz (½ cup) vegetable stock. Cover and simmer the sauce over low heat for about 15 minutes. Add 1 can of peeled chopped tomatoes (800 g/1¾ lb) with the juice and cook for another 5 minutes. Remove the bay leaf. Purée the sauce, season with salt, pepper and sugar. Before serving garnish the sauce with the chopped soup vegetables put aside earlier.

Recipe variation 2: To make a Bolognese sauce (at the top in the photograph), peel 1 onion and 1 clove of garlic. Prepare and peel 100 g/3½ oz carrots. Peel 50 g/2 oz celery. Wash the carrots and celery and leave to drain. Finely chop all the vegetables. Heat 2 tablespoons cooking oil in a pan. Add the chopped vegetables and fry (sauté) over medium heat. Add 250 g/9 oz minced (ground) beef and fry, stirring all the time, crushing any clumps that may form with a fork. Take 1 can (800 g/1¾ lb) of peeled tomatoes and chop them up. Now add the tomatoes together with the juice and 2 tablespoons tomato purée to the minced beef. Season with salt, pepper, oregano and sugar. Bring the sauce to the boil and simmer over low heat without a lid for about 15 minutes. Adjust the seasoning with a little more salt and pepper and 2–3 tablespoons red wine.

1

2

3

Marinade for grilled (broiled) meat

EASY (LEFT IN THE PHOTOGRAPH)

Preparation time:
about 10 minutes,
excluding cooling time

125 ml/4 fl oz (½ cup) maple
syrup
2 tablespoons brown sugar
2 tablespoons tomato ketchup
1 teaspoon medium strong
mustard or ½ teaspoon
powdered mustard
1–2 tablespoons fruit vinegar
1 tablespoon Worcestershire
sauce
½ teaspoon salt
freshly ground pepper

In total:
P: 4 g, F: 0 g, C: 46 g,
kJ: 1632, kcal: 389, CU: 4.0

1 Stir together maple syrup, sugar, ketchup, mustard or mustard powder, vinegar, Worcestershire sauce, salt and pepper in a pan. Bring to the boil, simmer over low heat without a lid for about 2 minutes, then leave to cool.

2 Brush the marinade over the meat and put in the refrigerator. Marinate small pieces of meat for 2–3 hours and large pieces for at least 8 hours. Turn the pieces of meat over from time to time.

Uses: This quantity is enough for 1 kg/2¼ lb spareribs or 800 g/ 1¾ lb steak.

Recipe variation 1: To make a marinade with sour cream (at the top in the photograph), stir together 150 g/5 oz (⅝ cup) sour cream, 1 tablespoon lemon juice, 1 peeled and crushed clove of garlic, 1 tablespoon diced onion, ½–1 teaspoon hot paprika, 1 pinch salt and 1 teaspoon Worcestershire sauce. Use for lamb cutlets or chicken legs.

Recipe variation 2: For an oriental marinade (on the right in the photograph), stir together 4 table-spoons soy sauce, 2 tablespoons liquid honey, 4 tablespoons sherry, 1 peeled and crushed clove of garlic, 1 teaspoon ground cinnamon, freshly ground pepper, 1 pinch of ground cloves and 4 tablespoons cold black tea. This marinade can be used for lamb, pork or beef.

Beetroot sauce with aniseed

WITH ALCOHOL

Preparation time:
about 15 minutes

1 jar sliced beetroot (beet)
(drained weight 220 g/8 oz)
250 ml/8 fl oz (1 cup) red wine
1–2 pieces star anise
1 packet vanilla sugar
2 tablespoons aniseed brandy,
pastis or ouzo
salt
freshly ground pepper
1 tablespoon red currant jelly

1 Put the beetroot (beet) slices in a sieve and leave to drain. Put the red wine, star-anise, vanilla sugar and aniseed brandy in a small pan and bring to the boil. Purée the beetroot.

2 Remove the star anise. Stir in the puréed beetroot. Heat up again. Season with salt, pepper and red currant jelly.

TIP » Use the sauce to marinate venison steaks or haunch of venison (p. 86).

Per serving: P: 1 g, F: 0 g, C: 12 g, kJ: 408, kcal: 97, CU: 1.0

Carrots

FOR CHILDREN

Preparation time:
about 20 minutes
Cooking time: 5–10 minutes

1 kg/2¼ lb carrots
50 g/2 oz (4 tablespoons) butter
100 ml/3½ fl oz (½ cup) vegetable stock
salt
1 level teaspoon sugar
1–2 tablespoons chopped parsley

Per serving:
P: 2 g, F: 11 g, C: 11 g,
kJ: 640, kcal: 153, CU: 0.0

1 Prepare the carrots, then peel, wash and leave to drain. Cut into slices or sticks.

2 Melt the butter in a pan. Add the carrots and fry (sauté) briefly. Now add the vegetable stock, cover and cook the carrots over low heat for 5–10 minutes.

3 Season the carrots with salt and sugar and sprinkle with parsley before serving.

Recipe variation 1: Instead of carrots you can also use 1 kg/2¼ lb Kohlrabi, following the instructions in the recipe above.

Season the kohlrabi with nutmeg instead of sugar.

Recipe variation 2: To make glazed carrots, prepare 1 kg/2¼ lb baby carrots, leaving some of the green leaves. Peel the carrots, wash and leave to drain. Melt 50 g/2 oz (4 tablespoons) butter, add the carrots and fry (sauté) briefly. Stir in 4 tablespoons sugar and add 100 ml/31/2 fl oz (½ cup) vegetable stock. Cover and braise the carrots for 10–15 minutes over low heat, season with salt. Sprinkle with 1 tablespoon chopped mint or basil just before serving.

Cauliflower

CLASSIC (4–6 SERVINGS)

Preparation time:
about 20 minutes
Cooking time: about 20 minutes

750 ml/1¼ pints (3½ cups) water
2–3 slices organic lemon (untreated, unwaxed)
1 larger cauliflower (about 1.2 kg/4½ lb)
2 teaspoons salt
60 g/2 oz butter
2–3 tablespoons breadcrumbs
ground nutmeg

Per serving:
P: 4 g, F: 11 g, C: 9 g,
kJ: 635, kcal: 152, CU: 0.5

1 Bring the water to the boil with the slices of lemon. Remove the leaves and any bad parts of the cauliflower, then cut out the stalk but do not throw it away. Rinse the cauliflower thoroughly.

2 Add the cauliflower together with the stalk to the boiling water. Season with salt and bring to the boil again. Cover and cook over low heat for about 20 minutes.

3 Melt the butter in a small pan. Add the breadcrumbs and fry (sauté) until light brown, stirring all the time. If liked you can also season with nutmeg. Take the cauliflower out of the water with a skimming ladle, leave to drain and put in a pre-warmed bowl. Sprinkle the butter and breadcrumbs mixture over the cauliflower.

TIP » Cauliflower cheese, browned under the grill, makes a delicious main meal. The cauliflower will cook more quickly if you divide it into florets. This will reduce the cooking time by about 10 minutes.

Green (snap) beans

EASY

1 Bring water to the boil in a pan. Top and tail the beans and remove the strings. Wash the beans, leave to drain and cut into pieces. Rinse the savory. Add the beans, savory and 2 teaspoons salt to the boiling water. Bring to the boil again. Cover and cook the beans for 8–10 minutes.

2 Meanwhile peel and chop the onion. Melt the butter or margarine. Add the chopped onion and fry (sauté) briefly while stirring.

3 Drain the cooked beans in a colander and remove the savory. Stir the fried chopped onion into the beans. Season with salt, pepper and nutmeg. Sprinkle with parsley before serving.

TIP » Green beans are delicious served with meat dishes of all kinds or as an accompaniment to soused herring.

EXTRA TIPS » You can prepare yellow beans in the same way.
» Bush beans or Kenya beans are particularly tender (cooking time 5–7 minutes).
» Rinse the cooked beans in cold water to preserve their green colour.

Recipe variation: To make green beans with bacon, chop up 70 g/ 3 oz streaky bacon and sweat out the fat in a pan. Add the butter or margarine. Then add the chopped onion and fry briefly. Toss the cooked beans in the pan with the onions. Green beans with diced bacon are delicious with lamb.

Preparation time: about 15 minutes
Cooking time: 8–12 minutes

2 l/3½ pints (9 cups) water
750 g/1½ lb green (snap) beans
3–4 sprigs summer savory
salt
1 onion
40 g/1½ oz (3 tablespoons) butter or margarine
freshly ground pepper
ground nutmeg
1 tablespoon chopped parsley

Per serving:
P: 4 g, F: 9 g, C: 6 g,
kJ: 522, kcal: 124, CU: 0.5

Petits pois

FOR CHILDREN

1 Melt the butter in a pan. Add the frozen peas and fry (sauté) briefly while stirring. Add the vegetable stock, salt, pepper, nutmeg and sugar. Cover and cook the peas over low heat for about 8 minutes, stirring occasionally.

2 Season the peas with salt and sugar, then sprinkle with parsley before serving.

TIPS » Peas are delicious served with meat and chicken dishes or as part of a mixed vegetable platter.
» You will need 2 kg/4½ lb of unshelled peas (in the pod) to get 750 g/1½ lb peas. Shell the peas, wash, leave to drain and cook as described in the recipe.

Preparation time: about 5 minutes
Cooking time: about 8 minutes

35 g/1 oz (2 tablespoons) butter
750 g/1½ lb frozen peas
100 ml/3½ fl oz (½ cup) vegetable stock
salt, pepper, nutmeg, pinch sugar
1 tablespoon chopped parsley

Per serving:
P: 13 g, F: 8 g, C: 25 g,
kJ: 971, kcal: 232, CU: 2.0

Red cabbage

SUITABLE FOR FREEZING (PHOTOGRAPH)

Preparation time:
about 35 minutes
Cooking time: 45–60 minutes

1 kg/2¼ lb red cabbage
375 g/13 oz sharp apples, e.g.
Cox's Orange or Boskop
2 onions
5 tablespoons cooking oil or 50 g/
2 oz (4 tablespoons) goose fat
1 bay leaf
3 cloves
3 juniper berries
5 allspice
salt, pepper, sugar
2 sticks cinnamon
2 tablespoons red wine vinegar
3 tablespoons red currant jelly
125 ml/4 fl oz (½ cup) water

Per serving:
P: 4 g, F: 13 g, C: 32 g,
kJ: 1116, kcal: 268, CU: 2.0

1 Remove the outer, wilted leaves of the red cabbage. Cut into quarters, rinse, leave to drain and cut out the stalk (photograph 1). Cut the cabbage into very thin strips or grate it (photograph 2). Peel the apple, cut into quarters, remove the core and cut into small pieces. Peel and chop the onions.

2 Heat the oil or fat in a pan. Add the chopped onions and fry (sauté) briefly while stirring. Add the red cabbage cut into strips and the pieces of apple and fry with the onions.

3 Now add the bay leaf, cloves, juniper berries, allspice grains, salt, pepper, sugar, cinnamon, vinegar, red currant jelly and water (photograph 3). Cover and cook the cabbage over low heat for 45–60 minutes, stirring occasionally. Season the cabbage with salt and sugar.

TIPS » It is worth preparing the red cabbage in a large quantity and freezing it in small servings. If intended for freezing the red cabbage should still have some "bite", in other words it should not be completely cooked through. » Red cabbage may also be braised in the same amount of red or white wine instead of water, and 2 tablespoons cranberry compote can be used instead of the red currant jelly.

Brussels sprouts

EASY

Preparation time:
about 15 minutes
Cooking time: 10–15 minutes

2 l/3½ pints (9 cups) water
1 kg/2¼ lb Brussels sprouts
2 teaspoons salt
40 g/1½ oz (3 tablespoons)
butter
nutmeg, pepper

Per serving:
P: 9 g, F: 9 g, C: 7 g,
kJ: 615, kcal: 146, CU: 0.0

1 Bring water to the boil in a pan. Meanwhile remove the wilted outer leaves and cut off part of the stalk. Make a cross-shaped incision across the stalk end. Wash the sprouts and leave to drain.

2 Add salt to the boiling water followed by the Brussels sprouts. Bring to the boil again. Cover and cook over low heat for 10–15 minutes.

3 Transfer the Brussels sprouts to a colander and leave to drain. Melt the butter and toss the Brussels sprouts in it. Season with salt, pepper and nutmeg.

TIP » Serve Brussels sprouts with substantial roasts, such as venison, pork, goose or beef. If you use frozen Brussels sprouts, you will need 800–900 g/1¾–2 lb for 4 servings. Cook the frozen sprouts as described in the recipe.

Black salsify in cream sauce

CLASSIC (PHOTOGRAPH)

Preparation time:
about 30 minutes
Cooking time: 10–15 minutes

1.4 l/2½ pints (6 cups) water
4 tablespoons white wine
vinegar
1 kg/2¼ lb black salsify
(scorzonera)
1 teaspoon salt

For the cream sauce:
30 g/1 oz (2 tablespoons)
butter or margarine
25 g/1 oz (4 tablespoons) plain
(all purpose) flour
125 g/4½ oz (½ cup)
whipping cream
cooking liquid (see step 2)
1 egg yolk (medium)
2 tablespoons cold water
salt, white pepper
1–2 tablespoons chopped parsley

Per serving:
P: 4 g, F: 18 g, C: 8 g,
kJ: 900, kcal: 214, CU: 0.5

1 Pour 1 litre/1¾ pints (4¼ cups) water and half the vinegar into a bowl. Brush the black salsify thoroughly, clean under running cold water (it is advisable to wear rubber gloves since black salsify stains badly). Peel the salsify thinly, rinse and leave to drain. Put the salsify in the water-vinegar for about a minute so that the stems will remain white, then leave to drain and cut into pieces 3 cm/1¼ in long.

2 Bring the rest of the water and the remaining vinegar to the boil with the salt. Add the black salsify, cover and cook over low heat for 10–15 minutes. Then remove the salsify from the water with a skimming ladle and arrange in a pre-warmed bowl, keeping it warm. Reserve 250 ml/8 fl oz (1 cup) of the cooking liquid.

3 To make the cream sauce, melt the butter or margarine in a pan. Add the flour and continue stirring until the mixture turns pale yellow (photograph 1). Little by little add the cooking liquid you have put aside (photograph 2) and the cream (photograph 3). Stir thoroughly with a whisk, making sure that there are no lumps. Simmer the sauce for about 5 minutes over low heat without a lid, stirring occasionally.

4 Whisk together the egg yolk and water in a small bowl, stir in 4 tablespoons of the sauce, then stir the egg yolk mixture into the sauce (do not let the sauce come to the boil again because the egg yolk would curdle). Season the sauce with salt and pepper, then stir in the parsley. Pour the sauce over the black salsify and mix well.

TIP » Serve the black salsify with ham and boiled potatoes or as an accompaniment to steak, sausages (p. 41) or chicken legs (p. 68).

Asparagus

A LITTLE MORE EXPENSIVE

Preparation time:
about 45 minutes
Cooking time: 10–15 minutes

2 kg/4½ lb white asparagus
2 l/3½ pints (9 cups) water
1–2 teaspoons salt
½ teaspoon sugar
70 g/3 oz (6 tablespoons) butter

1 Peel the asparagus very thinly from the top down to bottom, making sure that all the skin has been removed but without damaging the heads. Cut off the lower part. Wash and leave to drain.

2 Bring the water to the boil. Season with salt and pepper, add 10g/⅜ oz (2 teaspoons) butter and the asparagus. Bring to the boil again, cover and cook for 10–15 minutes depending on the stems' thickness.

3 Remove the asparagus from the pan with a skimming ladle and place on a serving platter. Keep it in a warm place.

4 Melt the rest of the butter, let it colour slightly if liked and pour over the asparagus.

TIP » Serve the asparagus with uncooked or cooked ham, veal or turkey schnitzel and parsley potatoes. Instead of melted butter you can also serve the asparagus with a sauce hollandaise (p. 108) or sauce béarnaise (p. 108), sprinkled with parsley.

Variation: Instead of white asparagus, green asparagus can be used. Wash the asparagus, leave to drain. Peel the lower third of the stems thinly and cut off the woody ends. Cook the green asparagus as described in the recipe (7–10 minutes).

Per serving:
P: 7 g, F: 13 g, C: 8 g,
kJ: 745, kcal: 179, CU: 0.0

Braised beetroot (beet) with cream

INEXPENSIVE (PHOTOGRAPH OPPOSITE)

Preparation time:
about 20 minutes
Cooking time: about 35 minutes

750 g/1½ lb beetroot (beet)
40 g/1½ oz (3 tablespoons)
butter or margarine
salt
freshly ground pepper
250 ml/8 fl oz (1 cup)
vegetable stock
about 400 g/14 oz Spanish
onions
50–75 g/3 oz streaky bacon
1 carton (150 g/5 oz) crème
fraîche or sour cream
2 tablespoons chopped chives

Per serving:
P: 7 g, F: 21 g, C: 18 g,
kJ: 1221, kcal: 293, CU: 1.0

1 Brush the beetroot (beet) thoroughly clean under running cold water (photograph 1), peel (but wear rubber gloves because beetroot stains terribly), rinse and cut into thin slices (photograph 2). Cut any very large slices into half or quarters.

2 Melt the butter or margarine in a pan. Add the slices of beetroot and fry (sauté) briefly while stirring. Season with salt and pepper. Add the vegetable stock, cover and cook the beetroot over low heat for about 20 minutes, stirring occasionally.

3 Meanwhile peel the onions and cut into slices. Add the sliced onions to the beetroot, cover again and continue braising for about another 15 minutes, stirring occasionally.

4 Dice the bacon and sweat the fat out in a pan without added oil or butter. Add this to the cooked beetroot. Arrange the vegetables on a serving dish. Garnish with the crème fraîche or sour cream and sprinkle chopped chives on top before serving.

TIPS ›› Serve braised beetroot with roast pork (p.48), steak, baked and deep-fried fish (p. 90).
›› You can also use peeled, vacuum-packed beetroot. In this case the entire cooking time will only be 15 minutes.

Recipe variation: To make baked beetroot (6–8 servings), preheat the oven: top and bottom heat: about 200 °C/400 °F (Gas mark 6), fan oven: about 180 °C/350 °F (Gas mark 4). Cut off the roots and leaves of 8 beetroot (about 1.2 kg/ 2½ lb). Brush the bulbs under cold water, then wrap each beetroot in greased foil. Place the beetroot parcels on a baking sheet and bake on a shelf in the lower third of the preheated oven. Bake for about 90 minutes. Serve with herb-flavoured or horseradish quark.

Braised cucumber

QUICK (PHOTOGRAPH 3 OPPOSITE)

1 Peel the cucumber, cut off the ends and cut in half. Remove the seeds with a spoon. Cut the cucumber into strips 1 cm/⅜ in thick.

2 Heat the butter, margarine or oil in a pan. Add the strips of cucumber, cover and cook over low heat for about 5 minutes, stirring now and again. Season with salt and pepper. Sprinkle with herbs before serving.

TIPS » Serve braised cucumber with fish dishes or meatballs (p. 40).
» For a richer dish, stir in 2 tablespoons crème fraîche.

» In late summer you can serve braised cucumber instead of cucumber salad because the flavour is even more intense then.

Recipe variation: For braised curried cucumber, peel and chop 1 onion, add to the oil in the pan with the cucumber. Sprinkle 1 tablespoon curry powder in the pan and continue cooking as described in the recipe. Finally stir in 4 tablespoons whipping cream and heat up again. Season with lemon juice and 1 pinch sugar. Sprinkle with chopped herbs before serving.

Preparation time:
about 20 minutes
Cooking time: about 5 minutes

1 kg/2¼ lb cucumbers
30 g/1 oz (2 tablespoons) butter or margarine or
3 tablespoons cooking oil
salt
freshly ground pepper
1 tablespoon chopped herbs, e.g. dill, parsley or coriander

Per serving:
P: 1 g, F: 7 g, C: 3 g,
kJ: 350, kcal: 84, CU: 0.0

Braised squash

QUICK (ABOUT 8 SERVINGS, PHOTOGRAPH)

Preparation time:
about 25 minutes
Cooking time: about 8 minutes

1.2 kg/2½ lb squash
30 g/1 oz (2 tablespoons)
butter or margarine
125 ml/4 fl oz (½ cup)
vegetable stock
salt
freshly ground pepper
some sugar
1 tablespoon white wine
vinegar
2 tablespoons chopped dill
2 tablespoons chopped parsley

Per serving:
P: 2 g, F: 3 g, C: 5 g,
kJ: 248, kcal: 59, CU: 0.5

1 Cut the squash in half, then remove the seeds and fibres from the centre. Cut into segments, peel and cut the flesh into sticks or cubes.

2 Melt the butter or margarine. Add the squash and fry (sauté) briefly while stirring. Add the vegetable stock. Cover and cook the squash over low heat for about 8 minutes, stirring occasionally.

3 Season the squash with salt, pepper, sugar and vinegar. Fold in the dill and parsley.

Recipe variation: To make **roast squash segments**, wash 1.2 kg/ 2½ lb Hokkaido or other similar squash. Cut in half without peeling (photograph 1), cut further into quarters, then remove the seeds and the fibres inside (photograph 2). Now cut each quarter into segments 2.5 cm/1 in thick. Peel and finely chop 1 clove garlic. Stir in 2 teaspoons orange zest (from a washed, untreated, unwaxed orange), ½ teaspoon chilli flakes, ½ teaspoon ground pepper, ½ teaspoon cumin, 1 teaspoon herbes de Provence and garlic into 5 tablespoons olive oil. Marinate the squash segments for at least 30 minutes in the herb and spice marinade. While the squash is marinating, preheat the oven: top and bottom heat: about 200 °C/ 400 °F (Gas mark 6), fan oven: about 180 °C/350 °F (Gas mark 4). Arrange the squash segments on a greased baking sheet. skin side down. Put the baking sheet on a shelf in the bottom third of the preheated oven. Roast for about 30 minutes. Season with a little salt.

Leeks

EASY

Preparation time:
about 25 minutes
Cooking time: 5–8 minutes

1.2 kg/2½ lb leeks
30 g/1 oz (2 tablespoons)
butter or margarine
100 ml/3½ fl oz (½ cup)
vegetable stock
salt, pepper, nutmeg, parsley

Per serving:
P: 4 g, F: 8 g, C: 6 g,
kJ: 453, kcal: 109, CU: 0.0

1 Prepare the leeks, cut in half lengthways, wash them thoroughly and leave to drain. Then cut them into pieces 6 cm/2½ in long.

2 Melt the butter or margarine in a pan. Add the leeks, fry (sauté) briefly, add the vegetable stock, cover and cook over low heat for 5–8 minutes.

3 Season the leeks with salt, pepper and nutmeg. Chop the parsley and sprinkle on the leeks before serving.

TIPS » Leeks are delicious served with beef roulade (p. 52), braised beef (p. 58), braised pork (p. 48), steak or schnitzel (p. 42).
» You can also garnish the leeks with 2 chopped hard-boiled (hard-cooked) eggs sprinkled on top.

Fennel

EASY

Preparation time:
about 20 minutes
Cooking time: 15–20 minutes

250 ml/8 fl oz (1 cup) water
600 g/1¼ lb fennel bulbs
¼ teaspoon salt
40 g/1½ oz (3 tablespoons)
butter

Per serving:
P: 3 g, F: 9 g, C: 4 g,
kJ: 458, kcal: 110, CU: 0.0

1 Bring the water to the boil in a pan. Cut off the stems close to the top of the fennel bulbs. Cut away any brown spots as well as the leaves. Put the leaves to one side and keep for the garnish. Cut off the roots, wash the fennel bulbs, leave to drain and cut each one in half.

2 Add salt to water, bring to the boil and add the fennel halves. Cover and cook over low heat for about 15–20 minutes. Turn the fennel over once during the cooking.

3 Meanwhile rinse, pat dry and chop the leaves. Take the fennel out of the water using a skimming ladle, arrange on a pre-warmed platter and put in a warm place. Melt the butter and pour over the fennel. Sprinkle the chopped fennel leaves on top before serving.

Recipe variation: To make baked fennel in tomato sauce (photograph), prepare the fennel according to the recipe but cut into quarters instead of halves. Cook the fennel for about 10 minutes in salted water, drain and reserve the cooking liquid. Fry (sauté) 1 chopped onion in 30 g/1 oz (2 tablespoons) butter. Add 400 g/14 oz tinned chopped tomatoes and 100 ml/3½ fl oz (½ cup) of the tomato juice. Season with salt, 1 teaspoon herbes de Provence, pepper and sugar. Fry for about 5 minutes. Preheat the oven: top and bottom heat: about 200 °C/400 °F (Gas mark 6), fan oven: about 180 °C/350 °F (Gas mark 4). Put the fennel in a greased gratin dish. Pour the tomato sauce over the fennel and sprinkle 100 g/3½ oz (1 cup) grated cheese on top. Put the dish on a shelf in the bottom third of the preheated oven.

Sauerkraut

CLASSIC

Preparation time:
about 20 minutes
Cooking time: 25–30 minutes

4 onions
1 apple, e.g. Cox's Orange
3 tablespoons cooking oil, e.g.
sunflower oil
750 g/1½ lb sauerkraut
125 ml/4 fl oz (½ cup) water,
white wine or cider
1 bay leaf
4 juniper berries

1 Peel and chop the onions. Peel the apple, cut into quarters and cut out the core. Cut the apple into slices.

2 Heat the oil in a pan. Add the onions and fry (sauté). Separate the sauerkraut a little and add to the pan together with the water, white wine or cider. Place the slices of apple on top of the sauerkraut.

3 Add the bay leaf, juniper berries and peppercorns and season with salt. Cover and cook over low heat for 25–30 minutes, stirring occasionally. If necessary, add a little liquid. Season the sauerkraut with salt, sugar and pepper.

TIPS » Serve sauerkraut with cured, smoked pork (p. 46) and mashed potatoes (p. 166).

» Sauerkraut will acquire a creamier consistency if you add 1 grated raw potato in the last 10 minutes of cooking. This will also reduce the sharpness of the sauerkraut.

» If you like you can replace the apple by 150 g/5 oz pineapple chunks (from a can; keep the juice). Then pour the pineapple juice into the sauerkraut.

6 peppercorns
salt, sugar, pepper

Per serving:
P: 4 g, F: 8 g, C: 8 g,
kJ: 590, kcal: 142, CU: 0.5

Swiss chard

INEXPENSIVE (PHOTOGRAPH)

Preparation time:
about 40 minutes

2–3 cloves garlic
2 red onions
1 kg/2¼ lb Swiss chard
1–2 teaspoons lemon juice
3 tablespoons cooking oil,
e.g. sunflower oil
125 ml/4 fl oz (½ cup)
vegetable stock
salt
freshly ground pepper
ground nutmeg
200 g/7 oz (¾ cup) sour cream

Per serving:
P: 6 g, F: 20 g, C: 10 g,
kJ: 1049, kcal: 252, CU: 0.0

1 Peel and finely chop the garlic and onions. Prepare the Swiss chard and wash thoroughly. Cut off the leaves from the white stems. Now cut the leaves and stems into 1 cm/⅜ in strips. Stir the lemon juice into the Swiss chard.

2 Heat the oil in a large pan. Add the stems of Swiss chard, garlic and chopped onion and fry (sauté) briefly while stirring. Add the vegetable stock, cover and continue braising over low heat for 3–4 minutes. Then add the strips of chard leaves and braise for about another 5 minutes.

3 Season with salt, pepper and nutmeg. Stir the sour cream until smooth and pour over the vegetables shortly before serving.

TIP » Serve Swiss chard with steak, schnitzel or chicken legs (p. 68).

Recipe variation: For Swiss chard in a curry sauce, cook the Swiss chard as instructed in the recipe, season and leave to drain in a colander but keep the cooking liquid. Make a light-coloured basic sauce (p. 106) with the cooking liquid, topped up with vegetable stock to 250 ml/8 fl oz (1 cup), and 125 g/4½ oz (½ cup) whipping cream. Season the sauce with 1–2 teaspoons curry powder, a little lemon juice and sugar. Stir into the Swiss chard and adjust the seasoning again if necessary.

Leaf spinach

QUICK

Preparation time:
about 25 minutes

1 kg/2¼ lb leaf spinach
2 onions
40 g/1½ oz butter or
4 tablespoons olive oil
salt
freshly ground pepper
ground nutmeg

Per serving:
P: 6 g, F: 10 g, C: 3 g,
kJ: 534, kcal: 128, CU: 0.0

1 Prepare the spinach and remove the thicker stems. Wash the spinach thoroughly and leave to drain in a sieve. Peel and chop the onions. Heat the butter or oil in a large pan. Add the chopped onions and fry (sauté) briefly.

2 Add the spinach, then season with salt, pepper and nutmeg. Cover and cook over low heat for about 5 minutes. Carefully stir the spinach and adjust the seasoning, adding more salt, pepper and ground nutmeg if necessary.

TIPS » Serve the spinach with poached eggs (p.192), fried eggs (p. 190), braised fish or flash-fried meat.
» You can also stir 2 peeled, crushed cloves of garlic, fried together with the onions, into the spinach; or stir in some finely diced mozzarella or Gorgonzola (or other blue cheese) .
» Instead of fresh spinach you can use frozen leaf spinach. 1 kg/2¼ lb fresh spinach is equivalent to about 600 g/1¼ lb frozen spinach. Cook about 5 minutes longer (follow the instructions on the package).

Savoy cabbage

INEXPENSIVE

Preparation time:
about 55 minutes
Cooking time: 15–20 minutes

1 kg/2¼ lb Savoy cabbage
1 onion
40 g/1½ oz (3 tablespoons)
butter or margarine
about 125 ml/4 fl oz (½ cup)
vegetable stock
salt
freshly ground pepper
1 pinch sugar
1 pinch grated zest of organic
lemon (untreated, unwaxed)
1–2 tablespoons lemon juice
or white wine

Per serving:
P: 6 g, F: 9 g, C: 6 g,
kJ: 548, kcal: 132, CU: 0.0

1 Remove any wilted outer leaves from the Savoy cabbage. Cut the Savoy cabbage into eighths, rinse and leave to drain. Cut out the stalk. Cut the cabbage into thin strips. Peel and chop the onion.

2 Melt the butter or margarine in a pan. Add the chopped onion and fry (sauté) briefly. Now add the Savoy cabbage strips and continue sweating. Then add the vegetable stock, salt and pepper. Then cover and braise over low heat for 15–20 minutes.

3 Adjust the seasoning by adding more salt, pepper, sugar, lemon rind, lemon juice or wine.

TIP » Serve Savoy cabbage with meat-based dishes.

EXTRA TIP » Enhance the seasoning with the addition of pounded or ground caraway seeds, aniseed or fennel seeds. This will make the cabbage easier to digest.

Recipe variation 1: Instead of Savoy cabbage you can also use Chinese cabbage or sweetheart (pointed) cabbage. The cooking time for both these kinds of cabbages is 10–15 minutes.

Recipe variation 2: To make Savoy cabbage and carrots, only use 800 g/1¾ lb of Savoy cabbage prepared as described in the recipe. Then prepare 250 g/9 oz carrots, peel, wash, leave to drain and cut into strips. Peel and slice 1–2 cloves of garlic and slice. Now braise the carrots, garlic and Savoy cabbage as described in the recipe.

Recipe variation 3: To make Savoy cabbage in a cream sauce (photograph), take a Savoy cabbage of 1 kg/2¼ lb and remove the tough outer leaves. Cut the cabbage into quarters and cut out the stalk. Cut the cabbage into strips, wash and leave to drain. Melt 1 tablespoon butter in a pan. Add the strips of cabbage, fry (sauté) briefly, season with salt and pepper. Add 125 ml/ 4 fl oz (½ cup) vegetable stock and braise the cabbage for 15–20 minutes. Stir in 75 g/3 oz (5 tablespoons) whipping cream or 2 tablespoons crème fraîche and heat up again briefly. Sprinkle with 1 tablespoon chopped chives before serving.

Ceps

A LITTLE MORE EXPENSIVE

Preparation time:
about 30 minutes
Roasting time: 5–7 minutes

500 g/18 oz ceps
1 clove garlic
150 g/5 oz tomatoes
5 tablespoons olive oil
salt
freshly ground pepper
1 tablespoon chopped parsley

Per serving:
P: 4 g, F: 13 g, C: 2 g,
kJ: 574, kcal: 137, CU: 0.0

1 Prepare the ceps (photograph 1), rub clean with a kitchen paper towel (photograph 2) or use a brush to clean the ceps (photograph 3). Cut the ceps into slices. Peel and finely chop the clove of garlic. Rinse the tomatoes, leave to drain, make a cross-shaped cut in the non-stalk end, plunge briefly in boiling water, then dip in cold water. Peel the tomatoes, cut in half, cut out the stalks and chop up into cubes.

2 Heat half the oil in a pan. Add half the ceps and fry (sauté) over medium heat for 5–7 minutes, season with salt and pepper, then take out of the pan. Put the ceps in a pre-warmed serving dish and keep warm. Cook the rest of the ceps in the same way.

3 Fry (sauté) the garlic in the remaining cooking fat. Add the chopped tomatoes and heat up. Stir in the parsley, season with salt and pepper and pour over the ceps.

Mushrooms in a cream sauce

CLASSIC

Preparation time:
about 35 minutes
Cooking time: 8–10 minutes

800 g/1¾ lb mushrooms,
e.g. champignon, oyster
mushrooms, chanterelles
2 onions
1 bunch spring onions
(scallions)
30 g/1 oz (2 tablespoons) butter
100 ml/3½ fl oz (½ cup)
vegetable stock
salt, pepper
1 carton (150 g/5 oz) crème
fraîche
1 pinch cayenne pepper
Worcestershire sauce
about 1 teaspoon lemon juice
some sugar
2 tablespoons chopped parsley

1 Prepare the mushrooms, rub clean with a kitchen paper towel or use a brush. Cut the white mushrooms into slices and the oyster mushrooms into strips. If necessary, cut the chanterelles in half. Peel and chop the onions. Prepare the spring onions, wash, leave to drain and cut into slices.

2 Melt the butter in a large pan. Add the chopped onion and fry (sauté) briefly while stirring. Add the mushrooms and continue frying. Pour in the vegetable stock and braise the mushrooms over low heat without a lid for 6–8 minutes, stirring all the time. Season with salt and pepper.

3 Add the chopped spring onions and fry for 1–2 minutes. Stir in the crème fraîche and heat up again. Season with cayenne pepper, Worcestershire sauce, lemon juice and sugar, then sprinkle with parsley.

TIPS » Serve the mushrooms in a cream sauce with steak, schnitzel (p. 42) or white bread dumplings (p. 172). Instead of vegetable stock, you can also use white wine.
» Wild mushrooms can be prepared in the same way.

Per serving: P: 7 g, F: 18 g, C: 8 g, kJ: 936, kcal: 225, CU: 0.0

Green cabbage
SUITABLE FOR FREEZING

Preparation time:
about 30 minutes
Cooking time: about 60 minutes

4 l/7 pints (17 cups) water
4 teaspoons salt
1.5 kg/3¼ lb kale
2 onions
3 tablespoons cooking oil, e.g.
sunflower oil or 30 g/1 oz
(2 tablespoons) goose fat
375 ml/13 fl oz (1⅝ cups)
vegetable stock
freshly ground pepper
about 2 teaspoons medium
strong mustard
500 g/18 oz smoked pork
shoulder (with bones)
2 smoked Mettwürstsausages
(about 150 g/5 oz each)
2 fresh or smoked Kohlwürst
sausages (about 150 g/5 oz each)
1 pinch sugar
20 g/¾ oz soft oatmeal

Per serving:
P: 55 g, F: 58 g, C: 13 g,
kJ: 3294, kcal: 789, CU: 0.5

1 Bring the water to the boil in a large pan and add the salt. Meanwhile remove any wilted outer leaves from the cabbage and cut out the leaf veins. Wash the cabbage thoroughly, leave to drain and chop finely. Put the cabbage in the boiling water a small amount at a time and bring to the boil again. Blanch for 1–2 minutes. Then plunge briefly in cold water and leave to drain in a colander.

2 Peel and chop the onions. Heat the oil or fat in a pan. Add the chopped onion and fry (sauté), stirring all the time. Add the cabbage and vegetable stock, then season with salt and pepper. Stir in 2 teaspoons mustard. Bring to the boil, cover and cook over low heat for about 30 minutes, stirring occasionally.

3 Meanwhile pat the smoked, cured pork dry with a kitchen paper towel and take out the bone. Put the meat and the bones in the pan with the cabbage, cover and cook for about 15 minutes.

4 Add the sausages to the cabbage, cover and cook gently over low heat for about 15 minutes.

5 Remove the meat, bones and sausages, cover and put in a warm place. Season the cabbage with salt, pepper, mustard and sugar. Stir in the oat flakes and bring to the boil again. Cut the meat into slices and arrange with the sausages and cabbage on a large serving dish.

Serve with: boiled potatoes or potatoes, fried in butter and sugar.

TIPS » Green cabbage can easily be prepared in large quantities and frozen in small servings. It can also be blanched and chopped, then frozen for use later.
» Green cabbage is very delicious when reheated.

Stuffed bell peppers

POPULAR

Preparation time:
about 40 minutes
Cooking time: about 50 minutes

4 peppers (about 150 g/5 oz
each)
250 g/9 oz Spanish onions
500 g/18 oz tomatoes
6 tablespoons olive oil
400 g/14 oz minced (ground)
meat (half beef, half pork)
2 tablespoons tomato purée
salt
freshly ground pepper
about 375 ml/13 fl oz
(1⅝ cups) vegetable stock
15 g/½ oz (2 tablespoons) plain
(all purpose) flour
6 tablespoons whipping cream
dried chopped oregano
some sugar

Per serving:
P: 24 g, F: 37 g, C: 17 g,
kJ: 2073, kcal: 495, CU: 0.5

1 Cut off the stalk end of the bell peppers to make a "lid". Remove the seeds and white membranes. Rinse the peppers inside and out, then leave to drain. Peel the onions, cut in half and finely chop. Wash the tomatoes, wipe dry, cut in half, remove the seeds and cut out the stalks. Chop half the tomatoes.

2 Heat 2 tablespoons oil in a pan. Add half the chopped onions and fry (sauté) briefly. Add the minced (ground) meat and fry, stirring all the time, squashing any small lumps of meat with a fork.

3 Stir in the chopped tomatoes and half the tomato purée, then season with salt and pepper. Leave to cool a little. Then stuff the peppers with the minced meat mixture. Put the "lids" back on top of the peppers.

4 Coarsely chop the rest of the tomatoes. Heat the rest of the oil in a large pan. Add the rest of the chopped onions and fry briefly. Put the stuffed peppers next to each other in the pan. Add the chopped tomatoes and 375 ml/13 fl oz (1⅝ cups) vegetable stock, cover and braise the peppers over low heat for about 50 minutes. Then take the peppers out of the pan, arrange on a pre-warmed dish and keep warm.

5 To make the sauce, rub the cooking liquid with the chopped tomatoes and onions through a sieve. Put aside 375 ml/13 fl oz (1⅝ cups) of

the liquid, topping up with vegetable stock if necessary. Stir in the rest of the tomato purée. Bring the sauce to the boil. Stir the flour into the cream until smooth, then stir this mixture little by little into the boiling sauce. Simmer the sauce gently for about 10 minutes, stirring occasionally.

6 Season the sauce with salt, pepper, oregano and sugar. Serve with the stuffed peppers.

Serve with: rice, boiled potatoes or potatoes in their skins and a mixed leaf salad.

Recipe variation 1: To make peppers stuffed with chicken or turkey, replace the minced meat with 400 g/14 oz chicken breast or turkey breast fillet. Rinse the fillets under running cold water, pat dry and cut into very small cubes, then cook as described in the recipe from step 2 onwards. Flavour the sauce with 2 tablespoons chopped parsley instead of oregano.

Recipe variation 2: To make stuffed courgettes (zucchini), wash 4 courgettes (about 1 kg/2¼ lb), wipe dry and cut off the ends. Cut the courgettes in half lengthways and hollow out with a spoon but leaving an edge all round. Stuff the courgettes as described in the recipe and cook in a roasting tin for about 30 minutes.

Recipe variation 3: To make **stuffed kohlrabi**, peel 6 kohlrabi and cut off the tops to make "lids". Hollow out the kohlrabi with a melon baller or spoon (use the kohlrabi flesh in the sauce). Stuff the kohlrabi as described in the recipe and cook for about 50 minutes.

Salads

In recent years salads have gradually blossomed from being a simple side dish into a popular and often sophisticated main dish which frequently includes the most varied ingredients such as cheese, ham, nuts, seafood and egg. Salad dishes are further enhanced by a series of delicious dressings and sauces, ranging from sweet and spicy to bitter and aromatic; these transform salad dishes into a pleasure for the palate as well as for the eyes. These pleasurable aspects of salad dishes almost make one forget that (leaf) salads are also very healthy because they contains many important vitamins, minerals and trace elements while being more or less fat-free.

Buying the right kind of salad and storing it correctly

» Always use locally grown fresh produce when preparing raw vegetable, leaf or green salads.
» Make sure you do not squash the heads of lettuce while bringing the shopping home.
» Store fresh leaf salads in a cool, dark place immediately after returning home. It is helpful to wrap leaf salad in a moist cloth and put it in large plastic bag with a little air in it before sealing it tightly. Then store the plastic bag in the vegetable drawer in the refrigerator.
» Leaf salads should be eaten as soon as possible because they soon lose their flavour and nutrients.

The right way to prepare leaf salad

» Remove the wilted outer leaves.
» Separate the head of lettuce into individual leaves and remove any bad parts. Alternatively, halve or quarter the lettuce and cut out the stalk.
» Wash the individual leaves carefully but thoroughly. Make sure you do not squash the leaves. It also important not to allow the leaves to remain too long in the water because it would make them soggy and many important nutrients would be lost.
» Pat the leaves completely dry or use a salad spinner to dry them. This will ensure that the dressing adheres better to the leaves.
» Cut out any coarse stems and hard veins in the middle. The tear the leaves into bite-size pieces.

Dressing

A good dressing enhances the flavour of the ingredients in a salad and can add a special touch. Dressings may be mild, spicy or hot, and creamy or liquid. The classic vinaigrette dressing is based on an oil and vinegar mixture which usually consists of 2 parts of oil to 1 part of vinegar. Depending on the recipe it is seasoned with salt, herbs and spices.

Oil and vinegar (photograph 1)

» How good your dressing or vinaigrette tastes depends on the oil and vinegar you choose. Particularly recommended are high quality, cold-pressed, so-called "native" edible oils. They are very healthy because they are rich in unsaturated fatty acids and liposoluble vitamins. Unlike olive oil and nut oils, sunflower , rapeseed (colza) and corn oils have a neutral taste.

Olive oil

Sunflower oil

Pumpkin seed oil

White wine vinegar

Balsamic vinegar

» Vinegar is the result of the fermentation of alcoholic liquids or juices, for instance apple juice makes cider vinegar. Wine and fruit vinegars are fairly mild in taste but just as versatile as herb-flavoured vinegars. Balsamic vinegar – a dark, aromatic vinegar from Italy – is also very popular. It is made from pure grape must and must be matured for several years.

Pot herbs, chopped nuts, seeds and croutons (photograph 2)

It is ingredients like these that give your salad a special touch.

» Pot herbs enhance the flavour of a salad and give it an attractive appearance. Use fresh or frozen herbs since they are more aromatic than dried herbs.

» Nuts, squash seeds and other seeds give the salad a pleasant bite, in addition to the valuable mono or polyunsaturated fatty acids they contain, not to mention their vitamins and minerals. Roasted in a pan without fat, they are aromatic.

» Croutons are small cubes of bread fried in butter or cooking oil, which are often included in a salad to add a crispy touch. Black bread or brown bread croutons, fried in garlic-flavoured or lemon oil are particularly delicious.

Vegetables – the main ingredients in many salads

Most kinds of vegetables contain few calories, very little sugar and a lot of water. For these reasons alone vegetables are ideal to provide a healthy, low-calorie diet which is rich in fibre at the same time. When vegetables are used in salads, they are mostly used raw or briefly braised to ensure they retain their valuable nutrients.

General tips about vegetables

» Many vegetables are available all year round. Whenever possible choose seasonal, fresh, locally produced, crisp vegetables because they will not only taste better but they will also be less expensive.

» In the case of leaf vegetables, always favour those grown outdoors rather than in the greenhouse – the leaves will be firmer, containing more nutrients and fewer nitrates.

» Vegetables with wilting stems and leaves are no longer fresh. Lettuces where the cut surface at the base is dark or blotchy are not fresh either.

» Whenever possible use vegetables the day they were harvested or bought because they will e at their crispiest and will still have all their valuable nutrients.

» Vegetables are best stored in the vegetable drawer of your refrigerator or in a cool cellar or larder.

2

Tomato and onion salad

FOR GUESTS (4–6 SERVINGS)

Preparation time:
about 35 minutes

500 g/18 oz tomatoes
250 g/9 oz onions
1 tablespoon chopped
flat-leaved parsley
salt
freshly ground pepper

For the salad dressing:
2 tablespoons herb dressing
2 tablespoons orange juice
1 teaspoon orange or
fig mustard
1 tablespoon runny honey
6 tablespoons olive oil
salt, pepper
chopped flat-leaved parsley
(optional)

Per serving:
P: 2 g, F: 12 g, C: 8 g,
kJ: 637, kcal: 152, CU: 0.5

1 Wash the tomatoes, wipe them dry and cut out the stalks. Peel the onions, cut into slices and then separate into rings. Slice the tomatoes and put in a salad bowl with the onion rings and parsley. Mix carefully and season the tomatoes with salt and pepper.

2 To make the dressing, stir together the vinegar, orange juice, mustard and honey. Whisk in the oil little by little. Season the dressing with salt and pepper.

3 Pour the dressing over all the ingredients in the salad and put the salad in a cool place until ready to serve it. Sprinkle with parsley if liked.

TIP » Serve the tomato and onion salad with steak or grilled (broiled) meat or fish, with ham or as part of a party buffet.

Recipe variation 1: To make a tomato salad with an oil and vinegar dressing, whisk together 4 tablespoons olive oil with 2 tablespoons white vinegar. Season the sauce with salt, pepper and sugar.

Recipe variation 2: To make a tomato and leek salad, use leeks instead of onions. Prepare the leeks, cut in half lengthways, wash thoroughly and leave to drain. Cut the leeks into slices. Blanch the leeks in boiling salted water, then leave to drain and arrange with the tomatoes instead of the onions.

Recipe variation 3: To make a Corsican salad, prepare 800 g/ 1¾ lb beef tomatoes as described in step 1. Slice the tomatoes and arrange in a serving dish. Peel and finely chop 2 onions and 4 cloves of garlic. Take 1 bunch of flat-leaved parsley, chop and sprinkle over the salad with 3 tablespoons capers, 10 black olives and the finely chopped onions and garlic. Then sprinkle with 4 tablespoons olive oil. Season the salad with salt and pepper.

Green (snap) bean salad

Preparation time:
about 35 minutes
Standing time: about 30 minutes

750 g/1½ lb green (snap) beans
250 ml/8 fl oz (1 cup) water
¼ teaspoon salt

For the dressing:
1 onion
2–3 tablespoons vinegar,
e.g. herb vinegar
salt, pepper, sugar
3 tablespoons cooking oil,
e.g. sunflower or olive oil
1 tablespoon chopped herbs,
e.g. parsley, dill, summer
savory

Per serving:
P: 4 g, F: 6 g, C: 6 g,
kJ: 395, kcal: 94, CU: 0.0

1 Top and tail the green (snap) beans, and remove the tough strings along the sides. Wash, leave to drain and cut into pieces. Bring the water to the boil. Add the salt and beans, cover and cook over medium heat for about 10 minutes.

2 Transfer the cooked beans into a colander, pour cold water over them and leave to drain.

3 To make the dressing, peel and finely chop the onion. Stir together the vinegar, salt, pepper and sugar. Whisk in the oil. Now stir in the chopped onion and herbs. Pour the dressing over the still warm beans, mix well and leave for about 30 minutes for the flavours to develop.

4 Adjust the seasoning once more with salt, pepper and sugar just before serving.

Recipe variation 1: To make a bean salad with sheep's cheese, stir in 100 g/3½ oz diced sheep's cheese into the bean salad and garnish the salad with 2–4 tablespoons chopped basil leaves.

Recipe variation 2: To make a bean salad with a honey vinaigrette, stir together 3 tablespoons cooking oil, 2 tablespoons white wine vinegar, 1 tablespoon honey, some salt, pepper, sweet paprika powder and 1 teaspoon savory. Bring briefly to the boil and stir in the beans, adjust the seasoning again and arrange in a bowl.

TIP » If you are in a rush you can use tinned green beans (2 cans, drained weight 350 g/12 oz each).

White cabbage salad

Preparation time:
about 30 minutes
Standing time: about 60 minutes

1–1.5 kg/2¼ lb–3¼ lb white
cabbage
300 g/10 oz Spanish onions
1 teaspoon caraway seeds
5 tablespoons cooking oil,
e.g. sunflower or rapeseed
(canola) oil
150 g/5 oz diced bacon

1 Remove any outer wilted leaves of the white cabbage. Cut into quarters, rinse and leave to drain. Cut out the stalk and cut or grate the cabbage into thin strips (photograph 1). Peel the onions and cut into fine strips. Put the cabbage and onion strips in a large bowl. Chop up the caraway seeds coarsely with a few drops of oil on a chopping board (photograph 2: the oil is used to prevent the caraway seeds from jumping away when being chopped).

2 Heat 1 tablespoon oil in a pan. Add the diced bacon and fry (sauté) until crisp. Remove the bacon from the pan and leave to drain on a kitchen paper towel.

3 To make the marinade, put the rest of the oil, spices, sugar and horseradish in a pan and bring to the boil.

4 Pour the hot marinade on the white cabbage salad, mix well and leave the salad to stand for about 60 minutes for the flavours to develop.

5 Adjust the seasoning with salt, pepper, horseradish and sugar just before serving. Sprinkle the diced bacon on top.

TIP » Alternatively you can garnish the salad with crisp fried bacon slices. The salad can be prepared the day before it is required. Before leaving it to stand, turn the white cabbage salad over with your hands so that the flavours are well distributed.

Recipe variation: To make a vegetarian white cabbage salad, leave out the bacon. Instead roast sunflower seeds in a pan without fat and sprinkle on the salad.

5 tablespoons white wine vinegar
1 teaspoon celery salt
1 teaspoon salt
½ teaspoon pepper
1–2 tablespoons sugar
1–2 teaspoons ground horseradish (from a jar)

Per serving:
P: 4 g, F: 10 g, C: 8 g,
kJ: 576, kcal: 137, CU: 0.0

Rocket with Parmesan

A LITTLE MORE EXPENSIVE (PHOTOGRAPH)

Preparation time:
about 25 minutes,
excluding cooling time

30 g/1 oz pine kernels
125 g/4½ oz rocket
200 g/7 oz cherry tomatoes
30 g/1 oz Parmesan cheese

For the dressing:
2–3 tablespoons balsamic
vinegar
½ teaspoon runny honey
salt, pepper
5 tablespoons olive oil

1 Roast the pine nuts in a pan without fat until golden brown, then transfer onto a plate and leave to cool.

2 Prepare the rocket, removing the tough stems. Wash, dry in a salad spinner or pat dry with a kitchen paper towel and cut the larger leaves in half.

3 Wash the cocktail tomatoes, wipe dry, then cut into halves or quarters. Grate the Parmesan.

4 To make the dressing, stir together the vinegar, honey, salt and pepper. Add the oil and whisk to incorporate. Arrange the rocket in a shallow bowl, drizzle the dressing over it and sprinkle the pine nuts and grated Parmesan on top.

TIPS » Serve the salad as a starter, as an accompaniment to grilled (broiled) dishes or flash-fried meat. » Instead of pine nuts you can use coarsely chopped walnut kernels.

Per serving: P: 5 g, F: 19 g, C: 3 g, kJ: 849, kcal: 203, CU: 0.0

Lamb's lettuce

EASY (4–6 SERVINGS)

Preparation time:
about 25 minutes

250 g/9 oz lamb's lettuce
(mache or corn salad)
2 slices white bread
(about 20 g/¾ oz each)
20 g/¾ oz (1½ tablespoons)
butter
1 hard-boiled (hard-cooked) egg

For the dressing:
1 tablespoon vinegar,
e.g. balsamic or sherry vinegar
salt, pepper, sugar
3 tablespoons cooking oil,
e.g. walnut oil
1 tablespoon chopped herbs,
e.g. parsley, chives

1 Prepare the lamb's lettuce, cutting off the stems. Wash it thoroughly and spin dry.

2 Remove the crusts and cut the slices of white bread into small cubes. Melt the butter in a pan. Then add the diced bread and fry (sauté) until crisp. Shell and finely chop the egg.

3 To make the dressing, stir together the vinegar, salt, pepper and sugar. Whisk in the oil. Stir in the herbs. Stir the dressing into the salad just before serving. Sprinkle the fried croutons and chopped egg on top.

TIPS » Serve the lamb's lettuce as a starter, as an accompaniment to roast potatoes or boiled potatoes or

prepared without egg as an accompaniment to egg-based dishes.
» You can also replace the lamb's lettuce with 400–500 g/14–18 oz young spinach (the quantity depending on the kind). Wash the spinach thoroughly because spinach grown in the open is often very sandy.

Recipe variation 1: To make lamb's lettuce with walnut kernels, chop 1 small, peeled and cored pear very finely and add to the dressing. Coarsely chop 50 g/2 oz walnut kernels and sprinkle on top of the salad instead of the egg.

Recipe variation 2: Instead of the dressing described above you can make a potato vinaigrette (about

Per serving: P: 3 g, F: 11 g, C: 4 g, kJ: 521, kcal: 124, CU: 0.5

10 servings). Boil 200 g/7 oz potatoes with a bay leaf for about 25 minutes. Drain the potatoes, leave to cool a little, peel and coarsely chop. Peel and coarsely chop 1–2 cloves of garlic. In a bowl purée 2 tablespoons white wine or herb-flavoured vinegar, 1 tablespoon honey, the garlic and potatoes. Add 200–300 ml/ 7–10 fl oz (⅞–1¼ cups) water or meat stock and 3 tablespoons olive or rapeseed (canola) oil. Continue puréeing the dressing. Season with salt and pepper and leave to stand for 30 minutes for the flavours to develop. The dressing will keep in the refrigerator for about 3 days.

Crisp vegetable salad

FOR GUESTS (PHOTOGRAPH)

Preparation time:
about 30 minutes

about 600 g/1¼ lb mixed
vegetables, e.g. fennel, carrots,
celery, kohlrabi, squash
50 g/2 oz sprouts, e.g. beetroot
(beet) or soya sprouts

For the dressing:
1 carton (150 g/5 oz) crème
fraîche
2 tablespoons whipping cream
or milk
1–2 tablespoons vinegar,
e.g. sherry vinegar
salt, pepper, 1 pinch sugar
2 tablespoons chopped herbs,
e.g. chervil, tarragon, basil

1 Prepare all the vegetables except for the sprouts, peel where necessary, wash and leave to drain.

2 Cut the vegetables such as the carrots lengthways into thin strips. Cut the vegetables such as fennel and squash into thin slices. Rinse the sprouts and pat dry.

3 To make the dressing, stir together the crème fraîche with the cream or milk and vinegar. Season with salt, pepper and sugar. Stir in the herbs.

4 Arrange the various vegetables, cut in strips or slices, on a serving dish. Pour the sauce over the top. Garnish with the sprouts.

TIPS » Serve the salad with grilled (broiled) or flash-fried meat or as a snack with a baguette or pitta bread.
» To reduce the calories, you can replace the crème fraîche with yoghurt (3.5% fat).

Variation: In the asparagus season you can also use white asparagus. In this case, peel the asparagus thinly, starting from the top, and cut off the woody ends. Rinse the asparagus in cold water, leave to drain and cut at an angle into very thin slices.

Per serving: P: 4 g, F: 13 g, C: 7 g, kJ: 663, kcal: 160, CU: 0.0

Chinese cabbage salad with fromage frais

FOR CHILDREN

Preparation time:
about 25 minutes

600 g/1¼ lb Chinese cabbage
1 can mandarin oranges
(drained weight 175 g/3 oz)
100 g/3½ oz cooked ham

For the dressing:
100 g/3½ oz herb cream cheese
4 tablespoons whipping cream
4 tablespoons mandarin
orange juice (from the can)
1–2 tablespoons white wine
vinegar
salt, sugar, pepper

1 Remove the wilted outer leaves of the cabbage, cut in half and cut out the stalk. Rinse the cabbage and leave to drain in a sieve. Pat dry and cut into thin strips.

2 Drain the mandarin oranges in a sieve, put the juice aside and reserve 4 tablespoons. For the dressing. Cut the ham into strips.

3 To make the sauce, stir together the fromage frais, cream and mandarin juice. Season with vinegar, salt, sugar and pepper. Pour the dressing over the salad, mix well and serve immediately.

TIPS » Serve the Chinese cabbage with bread or rice as a light meal.
» The dish is also suitable as part of a salad buffet, but in that case serve the salad and the dressing separately.
» You can also use iceberg lettuce instead of Chinese cabbage.

Per serving: P: 9 g, F: 10 g, C: 13 g, kJ: 777, kcal: 186, CU: 1.0

Carrot and apple salad

QUICK

Preparation time:
about 20 minutes

500 g/18 oz carrots
250 g/9 oz sharp apples,
e.g. Elstar, Cox's Orange

For the dressing:
3 tablespoons lemon juice
3 tablespoons orange juice
1–2 teaspoons sugar or honey
salt
1 teaspoon cooking oil,
e.g. sunflower oil

1 Prepare the carrots, peel, wash and leave to drain. Peel the apples, cut into quarters and remove the cores. Grate both the carrots and apples on a hand grater.

2 To make the sauce, stir together the lemon and orange juice and season with sugar or honey and salt. Whisk in the oil. Stir the grated carrots and grated apples into the sauce. Season the salad with sugar.

TIPS » If the apples have not been sprayed, you only need to wash the apple; it can be grated with the skin on.
» You can also season the sauce with 1 pinch of ground ginger.

Per serving: P: 1 g, F: 1 g, C: 14 g, kJ: 314, kcal: 75, CU: 1.0

Bean sprout and avocado salad

VEGETARIAN (PHOTOGRAPH)

Preparation time:
about 30 minutes

150 g/5 oz lamb's lettuce
250 g/9 oz tomatoes
1 ripe avocado
150 g/5 oz soya, radish
or pea sprouts

For the dressing:
2–3 tablespoons vinegar,
e.g. herb dressing
2 tablespoons water, salt, pepper
1 pinch sugar
1 teaspoon medium mustard
4 tablespoons oil, e.g. walnut oil

1 Prepare the lamb's lettuce and cut off any stems which still hold the leaves together (photograph 1). Remove any bad leaves, wash the lamb's lettuce thoroughly and spin dry or leave to drain in a colander or sieve.

2 Wash the tomatoes and wipe dry, then cut out the stalk and base. Cut the tomatoes into segments. Cut the avocado in half lengthways, remove the stone (photograph 2), peel the avocado and cut each half into segments lengthways. Rinse the bean sprouts and pat dry.

3 To make the dressing, stir together the vinegar, water, salt, pepper, sugar and mustard, Whisk in the oil. Arrange the salad ingredients in a shallow bowl and pour the dressing over the top. Put the bean sprouts on top of the salad.

TIP » Serve the bean sprouts and avocado salad with bread as a light meal or as an accompaniment to white meat or fish. You can also sprinkle 50 g/2 oz chopped walnut kernels on the salad as a garnish.

Per serving: P: 4 g, F: 24 g, C: 4 g, kJ: 1045, kcal: 249, CU: 0.0

Potato salad with mayonnaise

CLASSIC (IN THE MIDDLE IN THE PHOTOGRAPH)

Preparation time:
about 45 minutes,
excluding cooling time
Standing time: about 30 minutes

800 g/1¾ lb waxy potatoes
2 onions
100 g/3½ oz gherkins
(from a jar)
3 hard-boiled (hard-cooked) eggs

For the dressing:
6 tablespoons mayonnaise
3 tablespoons gherkin liquid
1 tablespoon medium strong
mustard
salt, pepper

Per serving:
P: 10 g, F: 25 g, C: 31 g,
kJ: 1630, kcal: 389, CU: 2.5

1 Wash the potatoes thoroughly, put in a pan filled with water, cover and boil over medium heat for 20–25 minutes.

2 Pour off the water when the potatoes are boiled, leave to drain and cool a little, then peel. Cut the potatoes into slices and put them in a large bowl.

3 Peel and finely chop the onions. Cut the gherkins and shelled eggs into slices.

4 To make the dressing, stir together the mayonnaise, gherkin liquid and mustard. Mix together the onions, gherkins, egg slices, cooled sliced potatoes and dressing. Leave the potato salad to stand for at least 30 minutes for the flavours to develop.

TIP ›› Serve potato salad with grilled (broiled) meat or fish, sausages, meat loaf, ham roast or meatballs (p. 40).

Recipe variation 1: For a **potato salad with pork sausage**, add 1 peeled, cored apple, cut into small cubes to the salad. Also take 250 g/9 oz pork sausage, remove the skin and cut into small cubes. Add to the salad and mix well.

Recipe variation 2: To make a **potato salad with pumpkin**, use pickled pumpkin (in a jar – drained weight 200 g/7 oz) instead of the gherkins. Leave the pumpkin to drain in a sieve, reserving 3 tablespoons of the liquid for the dressing (use it instead of the gherkin liquid). Cut the pumpkin pieces smaller if necessary.

South German potato salad

GOOD TO PREPARE AHEAD (AT THE TOP IN PHOTOGRAPH)

Preparation time:
about 50 minutes,
excluding standing time

1 kg/2¼ lb waxy potatoes
1 bay leaf

For the dressing:
2 onions
50 g/2 oz diced streaky bacon

1 Wash the potatoes thoroughly, put in a pan filled with water and 1 bay leaf, cover and bring to the boil. Cook over low heat for 20–25 minutes but do not overcook; the potatoes should still be firm.

2 Meanwhile, peel and chop the onions. Add 1 tablespoon oil in a pan, add the diced bacon and fry (sauté). Now add the chopped onions, then pour in the vinegar

and stock. Leave to stand for about 3 minutes, then season the dressing with salt and pepper.

3 Pour off the water from the potatoes. Drain, then peel while still hot. Cut the potatoes into slices and arrange in an oven-proof dish. Carefully fold the dressing into the sliced potatoes, then gradually add the rest of the oil. Leave the salad for a few hours for the flavours to develop.

4 Preheat the oven:
Top and bottom heat:
about 150 °C/300 °F (Gas mark 2)
Fan oven:
about 130 °C/270 °F (Gas mark ½)

5 Adjust the seasoning again, adding more salt, pepper and vinegar. Place the dish with the salad in the preheated oven. Leave the salad to warm for 15–20 minutes, mixing carefully from time to time. Stir in the chives. Serve the salad warm.

TIP ›› Boil the potatoes over low heat to ensure that they do not get too soft.

Recipe variation: To make a **South German potato salad with pumpkin seeds** (at the bottom in the photograph), roast 70 g/3 oz pumpkin seeds in a pan without fat but omit the diced bacon. Stir the roast pumpkin seeds into the salad. If available, drizzle a little pumpkin seed oil on the salad.

about 100 ml/3½ fl oz (½ cup) cooking oil, e.g. rapeseed (canola) oil
4–5 tablespoons herb dressing
125 ml/4 fl oz (½ cup) hot vegetable stock
salt, pepper
2 tablespoons chopped chives

Per serving:
P: 7 g, F: 29 g, C: 35 g,
kJ: 1803, kcal: 430, CU: 3.0

Sausage and cheese salad

EASY (PHOTOGRAPH)

Preparation time:
about 35 minutes
Standing time: about 1 hour

250 g/9 oz onions
250 g/9 oz Emmental cheese
350 g/12 oz pork sausage
75 g/3 oz gherkins

For the dressing:
2 tablespoons white wine
vinegar
2 tablespoons water
1 teaspoon medium mustard
salt, pepper, sugar
4 tablespoons cooking oil,
e.g. sunflower oil
1 tablespoon chopped chives

1 Peel the onions, cut first into slices, then separate into rings. Put the onion rings in boiling water for about 2 minutes, then transfer to a sieve and leave to drain.

2 Cut the rind off the Emmental and cut into strips. Remove the skin from the sausages. Now cut the skinless sausages and gherkins into slices.

3 To make the dressing, mix together the vinegar, water, mustard, salt, pepper and sugar. Whisk in the oil. Mix together the ingredients of the salad and the dressing. Leave to stand for about 60 minutes to allow the flavours to develop. Sprinkle with chopped chives just before serving.

TIP ›› Sausage and cheese salad can be served as a light meal with a salted roll or pretzel or as part of a party salad buffet. You can also prepare the salad with poultry sausage or cured smoked pork.

Per serving: P: 29 g, F: 48 g, C: 4 g, kJ: 2357, kcal: 563, CU: 0.0

Egg salad with leeks

FOR GUESTS (4–6 SERVINGS)

Preparation time:
about 30 minutes

300 g/10 oz leeks
300 g/10 oz carrots
½ head iceberg lettuce
(about 150 g/5 oz)
6 hard-boiled (hard-cooked)
eggs

For the dressing:
100 g/3½ oz mayonnaise
150 g/5 oz yoghurt (3.5 % fat)
2 tablespoons lemon juice
salt, pepper, sugar
1 tablespoon chopped chives

1 Prepare the leeks, cut in half lengthways, wash them thoroughly and leave to drain. Cut into very thin strips. Prepare the carrots, peel, wash, leave to drain and grate coarsely.

2 Remove the outer wilted leaves of the iceberg lettuce. Cut the salad into thin strips, wash and spin dry. Shell the eggs and cut each one into six segments.

3 To make the dressing, stir together the mayonnaise, yoghurt and lemon juice; season with salt, pepper and sugar. Put all the salad ingredients you have just prepared (except the eggs) in a bowl and stir in the dressing; adjust the seasoning if necessary. Garnish with the egg segments and sprinkle the chopped chives on top.

TIP ›› Serve the salad with bread as a light meal.

Per serving: P: 11 g, F: 19 g, C: 7 g, kJ: 1034, kcal: 247, CU: 0.5

Potatoes, rice & pasta

Potatoes

Potatoes are not only a valuable basic food which plays an important part in our diet but their versatility is almost unlimited. In addition, this humble vegetable is also a veritable "vitamin bomb": besides being an important source of vitamins C and A and vitamins of the B-group, potatoes also contain minerals and trace elements such as sodium, potassium, calcium and iron. In addition, of all vegetable sources of protein, potatoes have the highest proportion of vegetable protein which can be converted by the body.

Among the numerous varieties of potatoes are the following:
» Waxy potatoes: such Charlotte, Pink Fir Apple, Red or Norland and Nicola. Waxy potatoes are recommended for use in salads, gratins, boiled potatoes, potatoes in their skins and roast potatoes.
» Firm potatoes: such as Desiree, Russet, Yukon Gold. Firm potatoes are particularly suitable for boiled potatoes, potatoes in the skin, fried potatoes, potatoes "en papillotte" (wrapped in foil) and soups.
» Floury potatoes: such as Maris Piper, King Edward, Desiree, Russet, Bintje and Idaho. Floury potatoes make delicious soups, stews, dumplings and potato pancakes.

Storing potatoes correctly

Potatoes soon germinate if stored in a warm, light place and they will also turn green, so it is advisable that potatoes should be stored in cool (4–12 °C/40–55 °F), airy, dry conditions. If you do not have the right conditions for storing potatoes, buy only small amounts and put them in a linen, jute or netting bag because potatoes will go bad very quickly if they are left in a plastic bag. If you have a cellar at home you can store larger quantities. Never store potatoes together with apples or pears because these fruits exude a gas (ethylene) which accelerates ripening, thus causing the potatoes to go bad more quickly.

Dumplings

For connoisseurs, dumplings are more than a mere accompaniment. The different kinds of basic dough alone give us an idea of their incredible versatility. There are the kinds made predominantly from raw or cooked potatoes or bread rolls and there are also the kinds made with yeast dough or semolina. It is easy to make excellent dumplings at home so long as you stick to the following five rules:
» Dumplings like to be well-mixed! Mix all the ingredients thoroughly until the dough is completely homogenous.
» Dumplings need space! Choose a large pan to cook the dumplings.
» Dumplings like to move (but not too much!). Shake them now and again while they are cooking so that the dumplings that are ready will rise to the surface.

» Dumplings need checking! When the dumplings are cooked, open up one of the dumplings with two forks. If the dumpling is dry inside it means that it is done but if it is still moist inside they must be cooked a little longer.
» Dumplings hate wet feet! Remove the dumplings from the pan with a skimming ladle and leave to drain thoroughly before serving.

Fresh gnocchi

Fresh ravioli

Dried spaghetti

Fresh ribbon noodles

Dried fusilli

Pasta

Pasta is a very popular and versatile food which can be served as an accompaniment to other dishes, in soups or as a main meal. It comes in many shapes and colours, with or without a filling, dried or fresh, from the frozen food or refrigerated section of the store. They are easy to store (dry pasta in particular will keep for a long time). There are two basic kinds: pasta made with eggs and pasta made without.

Buying the right kind of pasta

Pasta should always be cooked in plenty of water. At least 1 litre/

1¾ pints (4¼ cups) of water per 100 g/3½ oz – (if the quantity of pasta exceeds 400–500 g/14–18 oz, it is best to use two pans). Salt enhances the taste of pasta – use 1 teaspoon salt per 1 litre/1¾ pints (4¼ cups) of water. Do not add the salt to the cold water; add it to the boiling water at the same time as the pasta. Cook the pasta over medium heat without a lid, following the instructions on the packet (home-made pasta only needs a few minutes).

Stir briefly now and again to prevent the pasta from sticking. When the pasta is cooked, pour it into a colander, rinse in hot water and leave to drain.

Rice

Whether you prefer long-grain, round-grain, Patna or wild rice, it is always full of vitamins and minerals, low in calories and very digestible.

Wild rice mixture

Parboiled rice

Basmati rice

Brown rice

Risotto rice

Preparing rice correctly

While cooking, rice increases in volume three times: in other words 1 cup of uncooked rice will produce three cups of cooked rice. White rice is cooked after about 15 to 20 minutes but brown rice takes about 35 to 40 minutes, while (it is important to follow the instructions on the packet). There are two ways to prepare rice: boiling it in plenty of salted water and then draining it, or frying (sautéing) it first in a little oil and cooking it in a precise amount of water (1 cup of rice to 2 cups of water), which it will absorb completely. When boiling rice in plenty of water, many of its nutrients are lost when the excess water is poured away. But by cooking it in a small amount of liquid, the rice absorbs all the liquid, so all the nutrients are preserved.

Tips

» Cooked rice will remain as individual grains if, after cooking, you put a clean cotton cloth, for instance a tea-cloth, over the saucepan under the lid.
» To warm up rice, put it in a greased oven-proof dish, cover and warm it up in the oven preheated (top and bottom heat) to about 150 °C/300 °F (Gas mark 2).
» Left-over rice can be packed and frozen; when needed, place the rice in a sieve and defrost above steam before warming it.
» Rice is also delicious in soups. Cook it in a separate pan until "al dente" and add to the soup shortly before serving. In this way, it will continue cooking in the hot soup but will not become too soft.

Prepared cereals

Cereals is the general term for dry-processed cereal-based food. Cereals include pearl barley, sago, semolina, custard powder, breakfast cereals and soups and sauces in powder form.
» Cereals such as rye, barley, oats, millet or buckwheat should be included in the diet because they contain important vitamins, minerals, trace elements and fibre. Cereals can be bought in several forms such as whole grains, coarsely or finely shredded or ground, as flakes, or more or less finely milled.

Boiled potatoes

EASY

Preparation time:
about 10 minutes
Cooking time: 20–25 minutes

750 g/1½ lb potatoes
1 teaspoon salt

Per serving:
P: 3 g, F: 0 g, C: 22 g,
kJ: 447, kcal: 107, CU: 2.0

1 Peel the potatoes thinly with a knife or potato peeler. Cut out any dark eyes, bad or green parts.

2 Rinse the potatoes, leave to drain and cut the larger potatoes in half or into quarters. Put them in a saucepan, sprinkle salt in the pan and add enough water to cover the potatoes. Cover and bring to the boil. Cook for 20–25 minutes.

3 Pour away the cooking water and leave the potatoes to dry off in the saucepan without a lid, lightly shaking the pan. You can also dry the potatoes by placing a tea-towel or a kitchen paper towel between the saucepan and the lid.

TIP » Boiled potatoes are delicious with most meat, fish, and vegetable dishes prepared in a sauce.

Recipe variation 1: To make **parsley potatoes**, prepare the potatoes as described in the recipe and toss in 20–30 g/ ¾–1 oz (1½–2 tablespoons) melted butter and 2 table-spoons chopped parsley.

Recipe variation 2: To make **potatoes in their skins**, wash 1 kg/2¼ lb potatoes thoroughly or brush clean under water. Put in a pan with water and bring to the boil. Cover and cook for 20–25 minutes. When the potatoes are cooked, pour the water away, then plunge in cold water, leave to drain and peel immediately. Serve boiled potatoes as an accompaniment or as a main dish with herb quark low fat curd cheese or béchamel sauce and salad.

Potatoes "en papillotte"

EASY (AT THE BACK IN THE PHOTOGRAPH)

Preparation time:
about 20 minutes
Cooking time: 45–60 minutes

8 floury potatoes (about
1 kg/2¼ lb)
salt

For the sauce:
1 carton (150 g/5 oz) crème
fraîche
1 tablespoon chopped parsley
salt, pepper

1 Preheat the oven:
Top and bottom heat:
about 200 °C/400 °F (Gas mark 6)
Fan oven:
about 180 °C/350 °F (Gas mark 4)

2 Wash the potatoes thoroughly, if necessary using a brush (photo-graph 1), wipe dry and make lengthways incisions 1 cm/⅜ in deep (photograph 2). Sprinkle salt in the cuts. Wrap the potatoes individually in greased foil (photo-graph 3) and put them on a shelf in the bottom third of the preheated oven. Bake the potatoes for 45 to 60 minutes depending on their size.

3 Meanwhile, for the sauce, stir together the crème fraîche and parsley, then season with salt and pepper. Add some caraway if liked.

4 When the potatoes are cooked, open the foil parcels. Open up the potatoes using 2 forks and spoon the sauce into the hollow.

TIPS » Serve baked potatoes in foil with grilled (broiled) meat or vegetables, with steak or as a snack.
» Baking potatoes can be very large (about 250 g/9 oz each), when 1 potato per person will be enough).

Recipe variation 1: To make **potatoes baked in foil with salmon** (in the front of the main photograph), cut 100 g/3½ oz smoked salmon into very thin strips. Spoon the crème fraîche and strips of salmon into the hollow in the baked potatoes.

Recipe variation 2: To make **potatoes baked in foil with horseradish**, use a sauce made of 200 g/ 7 oz quark (20 % fat) mixed with 1–2 tablespoons milk and 1–2 tablespoons grated horseradish, seasoned with salt. Cut 100 g/3½ oz ham into small cubes and fold into the sauce. Stuff the quark and ham into the hot potatoes.

a few caraway seeds (optional)

Also:
foil
some fat

Per serving:
P: 6 g, F: 12 g, C: 38 g,
kJ: 1207, kcal: 289, CU: 3.0

Potato gratin

FOR GUESTS

Preparation time:
about 30 minutes
Baking time: about 45 minutes

1 clove garlic
800 g/1¾ lb waxy potatoes
salt
freshly ground pepper
grated nutmeg
125 ml/4 fl oz (½ cup) milk
125 g/4½ oz whipping cream
2 tablespoons grated
Parmesan cheese

Also:
fat for the baking dish

Per serving:
P: 7 g, F: 15 g, C: 26 g,
kJ: 1148, kcal: 274, CU: 2.0

1 Preheat the oven.
Top and bottom heat:
about 180 °C/350 °F (Gas mark 4)
Fan oven:
about 160 °C/325 °F (Gas mark 3)

2 Peel the clove of garlic, cut in half and rub the greased surfaces of a shallow gratin dish with it (photograph 1).

3 Peel the potatoes, rinse and pat dry. Cut into thin slices. Arrange the slices in circles in the greased gratin dish in such a way that they overlap (photograph 2). Season the potatoes with salt, pepper and nutmeg.

4 Stir together the milk and the cream and pour over the potatoes (photograph 3). Sprinkle Parmesan on top. Put the gratin on the middle shelf in the preheated oven and bake for about 45 minutes until golden brown.

TIP ›› Serve the potato gratin with meat, fish or vegetable-based dishes which have not been prepared in sauce.

Variation: Instead of milk and cream you can mix together 250 ml/8 fl oz (1 cup) vegetable stock with 2 tablespoons white wine or crème fraîche. Pour over the potatoes and sprinkle with Parmesan and bake in the oven as described in the recipe.

Recipe variation 1: To make a **potato gratin with ceps**, put 20 g/¾ oz dried ceps in a sieve, rinse in cold water, bring to the boil in 250 ml/8 fl oz (1 cup) vegetable stock and leave to cool in the pan with the lid on. Put the ceps on top of the sliced potatoes instead of the milk and cream, sprinkle Parmesan on top, dot with 40 g/1½ oz (3 tablespoons) flakes of butter all over the gratin and bake as described in the recipe.

Recipe variation 2: To make a **potato-carrot gratin**, replace 300 g/10 oz of the potatoes with thinly sliced carrots. Arrange the sliced carrots in the gratin dish with the sliced potatoes and sprinkle with 1 tablespoon thyme.

Baked potatoes with herb-flavoured quark

EASY (ABOUT 8 SERVINGS)

Preparation time:
about 20 minutes,
excluding standing time
Cooking time: about 40 minutes

1.2 kg/4½ lb medium
waxy potatoes
2 cloves garlic
4 sprigs thyme
2 sprigs rosemary
5 tablespoons olive oil
salt
freshly ground pepper
1 pinch chilli flakes

For the herb-quark:
500 g/18 oz quark (low fat
curd cheese)
1 carton (150 g/5 oz) crème
fraîche
2 teaspoons each chopped
chervil, parsley and dill
2 teaspoons chopped chives
salt
freshly ground pepper
½ teaspoon ground caraway
seed

Also:
fat for the baking sheet

Per serving:
P: 12 g, F: 12 g, C: 25 g,
kJ: 1105, kcal: 265, CU: 2.0

1 Preheat the oven:
Top and bottom heat:
about 200 °C/400 °F (Gas mark 6)
Fan oven:
about 180 °C/350 °F (Gas mark 4)

2 Wash the potatoes thoroughly under running cold water, using a brush if necessary, and wipe dry. Peel and chop the cloves of garlic. Rinse the thyme and rosemary, then pat dry. Pull the leaves off the stems and chop up coarsely.

3 To make the marinade, stir together the chopped herbs, garlic, salt, pepper and chilli flakes. Cut the potatoes – not peeled – lengthways in half, put in the marinade, mix well and leave to stand for at least 30 minutes for the flavours to develop.

4 Place the potatoes with their cut surfaces facing upwards on a greased baking sheet. Sprinkle the rest of the marinade over the potatoes. Put the baking sheet on the middle shelf in the pre-heated oven and bake for about 40 minutes.

5 Meanwhile, make the herb-quark. Mix the quark with the crème fraîche and herbs. Season with salt, pepper and caraway. Serve with the baked potatoes.

TIP ›› Serve the baked potatoes with vegetables or a leaf salad as a main meal or as a party dish. You can also serve the baked potatoes with tzatziki or herb butter.

EXTRA TIP ›› To reduce the cooking time, peel the potatoes, do not cut them and parboil for about 10 minutes. Pour off the water, mix together the marinade and potatoes and leave to stand for the flavours to develop. After this they will only need about 20 minutes in the oven. Turn over the potatoes over after about 10 minutes.

Potato fritters
(potato pancakes)

Preparation time:
about 45 minutes
Frying (sautéing) time:
6–8 minutes

1 kg/2¼ lb waxy potatoes
1 onion
3 eggs (medium)
1 level teaspoon salt
40 g/1½ oz (⅜ cup) plain (all purpose) flour
100 ml/3½ fl oz (½ cup) cooking oil, e.g. sunflower oil

To taste:

a few red pepper dice
chopped chives
some coarsely chopped parsley

Per serving:
P: 11 g, F: 25 g, C: 38 g,
kJ: 1758, kcal: 419, CU: 3.0

1 Peel the potatoes, rinse and leave to drain. Peel the onion. Grate the potatoes and onion finely. Add the eggs, salt and flour.

2 Heat a little of the oil in the pan. Add the dough in small amounts and press flat immediately. Fry (sauté) the potato pancakes on both sides over medium heat for 6-8 minutes until crispy brown.

3 Take the pancakes out of the pan and pat away any excess fat with a kitchen paper towel. Serve immediately or keep warm.

4 Make the rest of the pancakes in the same way. You may also garnish them with diced peppers, chopped chives and small sprigs of parsley before serving.

TIPS » Serve the potato pancakes with apple sauce (p. 210), herb-quark or smoked salmon with herb-crème fraîche.

EXTRA TIP » Replace half the flour with 2–3 tablespoons oatmeal for even crispier potato pancakes.

Recipe variation: **Potato pancakes with tomato and mozzarella cheese. Preheat the oven: top and bottom heat: about 220 °C/425 °F (Gas mark 7), fan oven: about 200 °C/400 °F (Gas mark 6). Place the finished fried potato pancakes on a baking sheet covered with non-stick baking paper. Top with 1–2 tomato slices and 1 slice of mozzarella cheese, sprinkle with pepper and bake in the oven until the cheese has melted. Sprinkle the potato pancakes with chopped basil.**

Rösti

Preparation time:
15–20 minutes, excl. cooling time
Cooking time for the potatoes:
about 20 minutes
Frying (sautéing) time for the Rösti: about 10 minutes

500 g/18 oz waxy potatoes
salt, pepper, 6 tablespoons cooking oil

Per serving:
P: 2 g, F: 15 g, C: 17 g,
kJ: 889, kcal: 212, CU: 1.5

1 Wash the potatoes thoroughly, put in a pan with plenty of water, cover and bring to the boil. Cook for about 20 minutes, then drain and rinse under cold water. Peel the potatoes, cover and refrigerate for at least 4 hours or overnight.

2 Grate the potatoes coarsely (photograph 1). Season with salt and pepper. Heat the oil in a non-stick pan with a diameter of 24 cm/9½ in. Put the grated potatoes in the pan and press them slightly flat (photograph 2). Then fry (sauté) over low heat for about 10 minutes, turning them over once, until brown and crisp.

3 Cut the rösti into four when serving.

TIP » To turn over the rösti, slide it out of the pan onto a saucepan lid (photograph 3) and return it to the pan to fry the other side.

Mashed potatoes
(potato purée)

Preparation time:
about 15 minutes
Cooking time for the potatoes:
about 15 minutes

1 kg/2¼ lb floury potatoes
salt
50 g/2 oz (4 tablespoons)
butter or margarine
about 250 ml/8 fl oz (1 cup)
milk
ground nutmeg

Per serving:
P: 6 g, F: 13 g, C: 32 g,
kJ: 1164, kcal: 278, CU: 2.5

1 Peel the potatoes, rinse, leave to drain and cut into pieces. Put the potatoes in a saucepan, sprinkle 1 teaspoon salt on the potatoes, add enough water to cover them and bring to the boil. Cover and cook for about 15 minutes. Then drain and put immediately through a potato press (photograph 1) or mash with a potato masher. Add butter or margarine.

2 Bring the milk to the boil and stir little by little into the mashed potatoes, using a wooden spoon or whisk (photograph 2). The amount of milk needed may vary depending on the texture of the potatoes.

3 Whisk the mashed potatoes over low heat until they have formed a homogenous mass with a light and airy texture. Season with salt and nutmeg.

Important: Do not use a hand mixer or stick blender because this would make the mashed potatoes gluey!

TIP » Serve mashed potatoes as an accompaniment, for instance with roasts, meatballs (p. 40) or fish. For variety you can garnish the mashed potatoes with onion rings browned in butter.

Variation: You can replace the milk with whipping cream but in this case leave out the butter. Alternatively omit the butter and dice

100 g/3½ oz streaky bacon, fry (sauté) to sweat out the fat and stir into the mashed potatoes before serving.

Recipe variation 1: To make mashed potatoes with garlic and herbs, peel and chop 1–2 more cloves of garlic and chop up. Melt the butter, add the chopped garlic and fry for about 5 minutes over low heat. Just before serving, stir the garlic butter with 2 tablespoons chopped parsley and 1 tablespoon chopped chives into the mashed potatoes.

Recipe variation 2: To make mashed potatoes with cheese, stir 4 tablespoons grated Gouda or Emmental cheese into the mashed potatoes just before serving and sprinkle with 1 tablespoon chopped parsley or chervil.

Recipe variation 3: To make mashed potatoes with pesto stir 100 g/3½ oz red or green pesto from a jar into the finished mashed potatoes. Pesto-flavoured mashed potatoes are delicious served with lamb (p. 62).

Recipe variation 4: To make mashed potatoes with olive oil, replace the butter with 50–75 ml/ 1½–3 fl oz (3–4½ tablespoons) olive oil. Also add 100 g/3½ oz finely chopped, drained, stoned black or green olives. Then season with pepper.

Fried potatoes

INEXPENSIVE

Preparation time:
about 20 minutes,
excluding cooling time
Cooking time for the potatoes:
20–25 minutes
Frying (sautéing) time for the
potaotes:
about 15 minutes

1 kg/2¼ lb waxy potatoes
5–7 tablespoons cooking oil,
e.g. rapeseed (canola) or
sunflower oil
salt
freshly ground pepper
2 large onions
1 tablespoon chopped chives

Per serving:
P: 5 g, F: 15 g, C: 35 g,
kJ: 1252, kcal: 299, CU: 3.0

1 Wash the potatoes thoroughly, then bring to the boil in a pan with plenty of water. Cover and cook for 20–25 minutes. Drain the potatoes, leave them to cool a little, then peel them and finally let them cool completely. Then cut them into slices.

2 Heat the oil in a large pan. Add the sliced potatoes and season with salt and pepper. Fry (sauté) the potatoes over low to medium heat for about 15 minutes until golden brown, turning them over occasionally.

3 Meanwhile peel and finely chop the onions. Add the chopped onions to the potatoes and continue frying for another 2 minutes, turning them over occasionally. Season the fried potatoes with salt and pepper and sprinkle with chopped chives.

TIPS » Serve fried potatoes with fried egg (p.190) or scrambled eggs (p. 188), with vegetables in aspic or meat in aspic, salads, sausages or roast beef with remoulade sauce. You can also season the fried potatoes with sweet paprika powder or 1–2 teaspoons dried herbs (for instance marjoram, thyme or rosemary). » Fried potatoes are also an excellent way to serve up left-over boiled potatoes or potatoes in their skins.

Recipe variation 1: To make a **bacon and potato omelette**, peel and chop 1 more onion. Also chop up 75 g/3 oz streaky bacon. Add the chopped onion and diced bacon to the fried potatoes about 5 minutes before the end of the cooking time and continue frying. Stir together 3 eggs with 3 tablespoons milk, a little salt, pepper, sweet paprika powder and grated nutmeg and pour over the fried potatoes in the pan. Allow the egg-mixture to thicken over low heat for about 5 minutes, perhaps turning the potatoes once. Serve the with pickled gherkins.

Recipe variation 2: For **oven-roasted potatoes**, preheat the oven: top and bottom heat: about 220 °C/425 °F (Gas mark 7), fan oven: about 200 °C/400 °F (Gas mark 6). Peel 1 kg/2¼ lb potatoes, wash, wipe dry and cut into slices 3 mm/⅛ in thick (you can use a knife, grater or slicing machine). Pat the potatoes dry again, then peel and finely chop 2 onions. Put the sliced potatoes and chopped onions in a bowl with 5–7 tablespoons cooking oil and stir to cover with the oil. Season with salt and pepper. Spread the sliced potatoes on a baking sheet lined with non-stick baking paper and put on the middle shelf in the preheated oven. Cook for about 25 minutes, turning them over halfway through the cooking time. The potatoes should be golden yellow and crisp. If you are using new potatoes, there is no need to peel them, just wash and brush them clean.

Boiled potato dumplings

Preparation time:
about 40 minutes (over 2 days),
excluding cooling time
Cooking time for the potatoes:
20–25 minutes
Cooking time for the dumplings:
about 20 minutes

750 g/1½ lb floury potatoes
50 g/2 oz (¾ cup) breadcrumbs
20 g/¾ oz (3 tablespoons) plain
(all purpose) flour
2 eggs (medium)
salt
ground nutmeg
salted water
(1 litre/1¾ pints (4½ cups)
water with 1 teaspoon salt)

Per serving:
P: 9 g, F: 4 g, C: 38 g,
kJ: 944, kcal: 225, CU: 3.0

1 Wash the potatoes thoroughly, bring to the boil in a pan with plenty of water, cover and cook for about 20–25 minutes. Drain the potatoes, rinse in cold water and leave to drain again. Peel the potatoes, then push them through a potato press (photograph 1) or mash with a potato masher, leave to cool, cover and refrigerate until the next day.

2 Knead together the breadcrumbs, flour and eggs with a hand mixer fitted with a kneading hook, or with a wooden spoon, then incorporate this mixture in the mashed potatoes. Season with salt and nutmeg. Now cover your hands with flour and shape 12 dumplings (photograph 2).

3 Fill a large pan with enough salted water for the dumplings to "swim" in the water (photograph 3). Put the dumplings in the boiling water, bring to the boil again and simmer without a lid for about 20 minutes (the water should only move very slightly). Remove the dumplings from the water with a skimming ladle and drain thoroughly.

TIP » Potato dumplings are delicious served with marinated beef (p. 44) or pork roast and red cabbage (p. 120) or broccoli. If you like, sprinkle with nutmeg before serving.

Recipe variation 1: To make potato dumplings with bacon and parsley, chop up 100 g/3½ oz streaky bacon and fry (sauté) over medium heat to sweat out the fat. Add 1 tablespoon chopped parsley and leave to cool. Stir the bacon and parsley mixture into the mashed potatoes. Then make the dumplings as described in the recipe.

Recipe variation 2: To make sweet potato dumplings, wash 8–12 apricots or plums (the quantity depends on the size of the fruit), pat dry, make a cut lengthways in each one, take out the stone and fill the hollow with a sugar cube. Prepare the mashed potatoes without the nutmeg and divide into 8–12 servings of equal size. Put a piece of fruit in each serving, shape into a dumpling and cook as described in the recipe. Melt 70 g/3 oz (5 tablespoons) butter, add 1–2 tablespoons breadcrumbs and 1 tablespoon sugar, fry until brown, then pour over the dumplings.

Recipe variation 3: To make raw potato dumplings (in the right on the photograph), peel 1.5 kg/3¼ lb floury potatoes, rinse, leave to drain, then grate in a bowl with cold water. Line a sieve with a tea-towel and pour the grated potato mixture in it. Now gather the tea-towel together and squeeze the grated potatoes inside it to get all the water out. Put the potatoes in a large bowl. Bring 250 ml/8 fl oz (1 cup) milk to the boil in a pan with 40 g/1½ oz (3 tablespoons) butter or margarine and 2 teaspoons salt. Sprinkle 150 g/5 oz durum wheat semolina, stir well and bring to the boil. Then immediately add the pressed grated potatoes and knead with a hand-mixer with a hook attachment until you have a smooth, homogenous mixture. Adjust the seasoning again by adding a little salt. Cut 1 bread roll into small cubes. Melt 30 g/1 oz (2 tablespoons) butter or margarine in a pan, add the cubed roll and fry (sauté) until golden brown, stirring from time to time. Make 12 dumplings from the mixture and press a few croutons in each dumpling. Now cook the dumplings as described in the recipe. Dumplings are delicious as an accompaniment to meat dishes, served with a sauce.

Recipe variation 4: To make "half and half" potato dumplings (at the top in the photograph), wash 750 g/1½ lb floury potatoes thoroughly, put in a pan filled with sufficient water to cover the potatoes, cover and bring to the boil. Cook for 20–25 minutes. Then drain and rinse the potatoes under cold water. Peel and immediately press the potatoes through a potato press or mash with a potato masher. Leave to potatoes to cool, cover and refrigerate overnight. Now wash another 500 g/ 18 oz floury potatoes, peel and

rinse them. Then grate them into a bowl filled with cold water. Put the potatoes in a sieve lined with a tea-towel, gather it together and squeeze out the water, then add to the mashed boiled potatoes. Knead 1 medium egg, 65 g/2 oz (⅝ cup) plain (all purpose) flour and 1 teaspoon salt into the potato mixture. With floury hands make 12 dumplings and cook as described in the recipe. Serve with melted butter as an accompaniment to meat dishes served a sauce, for instance roast pork or beef roulade (p. 52).

Bread dumplings

CLASSIC (12 PIECES)

Preparation time:
about 30 minutes,
excluding cooling time
Cooking time: about 20 minutes

50 g/2 oz streaky bacon
2 onions
1 tablespoon cooking oil,
e.g. sunflower oil
300 g/10 oz (about 8) bread
rolls (2 or 3 days old)
300 ml/10 fl oz (1¼ cups) milk
30 g/1 oz (2 tablespoons)
butter
4 eggs (medium)
2 tablespoons chopped parsley
salt
salted water
(1 litre/1¾ pints (4½ cups)
water with 1 teaspoon salt)

Per serving:
P: 17 g, F: 22 g, C: 43 g,
kJ: 1869, kcal: 447, CU: 3.5

1 Cut the bacon into cubes. Peel and finely chop the onions. Heat the oil in a pan. Add the diced bacon and fry (sauté) until crisp. Add the chopped onions and sweat over low heat while stirring until transparent.

2 Cut the bread rolls into small cubes and put in a bowl. Heat the butter with the milk, pour over the rolls cut into cubes and stir well. Pour the bacon-onion mixture together with the frying fat into the milk and diced roll mixture. Mix well and leave to cool.

3 Whisk the eggs with the parsley, stir into the cooled mixture, mix well and season with salt. With floury hands make 12 dumplings. Put sufficient water in a large pan for the dumplings to "swim" in and season with salt. Bring to the boil, add the dumplings to the boiling salted water, bring to the boil again and cook for about 20 minutes (the water must only simmer very lightly). Remove the dumplings from the water with a skimming ladle and leave to drain thoroughly.

TIP » Bread dumplings are delicious served with roasts or with mushrooms in a cream sauce (p.134). Leave the rolls for 2 to 3 days before using them to make bread dumplings so that they are stale.

Variation: To make pretzel dumplings, replace the rolls with salted pretzels and add 1 tablespoon chopped chives to the dumpling mixture.

Yeast dumplings

FOR CHILDREN (8 PIECES)

Preparation time:
about 20 minutes,
excluding rising time
Cooking time: 20–25 minutes

125 ml/4 fl oz (½ cup) milk
50 g/2 oz (4 tablespoons)
butter or margarine
300 g/10 oz (3 cups) plain
(all purpose) flour
1 packet easy-blend dried
yeast
50 g/2 oz (¼ cup) sugar
1 packet vanilla sugar
1 level teaspoon salt
1 egg (medium)

Per serving:
P: 12 g, F: 14 g, C: 77 g,
kJ: 2033, kcal: 486, CU: 6.5

1 Heat the milk in a pan and melt the butter or margarine in it. Put the flour in a mixing bowl, stir in the dried yeast and mix well. Now add the sugar, vanilla sugar, salt, egg and milk-butter or margarine mixture. Mix all the ingredients with a hand-mixer using the hook attachment, starting very briefly on the lowest setting, then using the highest setting for about 5 minutes until you have a smooth, homogenous dough. Cover the bowl and put it in a warm place until the dough has visibly increased in volume (about 40 minutes).

2 Sprinkle a little flour on the dough, then remove it from the bowl. Then sprinkle some flour on the work surface and knead briefly. Shape the dough into a cylinder, then cut it into 8 pieces. With floury hands, shape these pieces into dumplings and place on a floured board. Cover the dumplings and put in a warm place until they have visibly increased in volume (about 15 minutes).

3 Stretch a cloth tautly over a wide pan filled with boiling water. Secure the cloth round the pan with string (photograph 1), sprinkle flour on top and place the dumplings on the cloth (photograph 2). Then place an inverted heat-resistant bowl over the dumplings as a lid. But be careful: the bowl can become very hot. Cook the dumplings over medium heat for 20–25 minutes (to check whether they are done, stick a wooden skewer in the dumplings; it should come out dry without any dough sticking to it).

TIP » Serve the yeast dumplings with melted, browned sugar, cinnamon sugar or fruit compote.

Recipe variation 1: To make Bavarian dumplings, prepare the dough as described in the recipe. Make 8 large dumplings and leave on the work surface on which you have sprinkled a little flour. Cover the dumplings and leave to rise for about 30 minutes. Heat 30 g/1 oz (2 tablespoons) butter, 100 g/3½ oz (6 tablespoons) whipping cream and 100 ml/3½ fl oz (½ cup) milk in a wide pan (if you do not have one, you can use 2 small ones). Put the dumplings in the liquid, cover and cook over medium heat for 20–25 minutes. Serve the dumplings with the cooking liquid.

Recipe variation 2: To make stuffed dumplings, preheat the oven: top and bottom heat: about 180 °C/350 °F (Gas mark 4), fan oven: about 160 °C/325 °F (Gas mark 3). Make the dough as in the recipe but add only 1 pinch of salt. Shape into a cylinder and cut into 12 pieces. Put 1 teaspoon stewed plums on each piece and press the dough together to form a parcel. Put 40–50 g/1½–2 oz (3–4 tablespoons) melted butter in an ovenproof dish (about 20 x 30 cm/8 x 12 in). Place the dumplings in the dish with the sealed surface downward. Leave to rise in a warm place until they have visibly increased in size. Place on the middle shelf in the preheated oven and bake for about 25–30 minutes. Serve hot.

Finger dumplings

FOR GUESTS (36 PIECES)

Preparation time:
about 25 minutes,
excluding cooling time
Cooking time for the potatoes:
about 20 minutes
Cooking time for the dumplings:
6–8 minutes

300 g/10 oz floury potatoes
salt
1 egg (medium)
100 g/3½ oz (1 cup) plain
(all purpose) flour
freshly ground pepper
ground nutmeg
salted water
(1 litre/1¾ pints (4½ cups)
water with 1 teaspoon salt)
30 g/1 oz (2 tablespoons)
butter

Per serving:
P: 5 g, F: 8 g, C: 27 g,
kJ: 861, kcal: 206, CU: 2.0

1 Peel the potatoes, rinse and leave to drain. Put the potatoes in a pan, add ½ teaspoon salt, pour just enough water into the pan to cover the potatoes and bring to the boil. Cover the potatoes and cook for about 20 minutes. Pour away the water, dry the potatoes and push through a potato press or mash with a potato masher and leave to cool.

2 Knead the potatoes together with the egg, flour, salt, pepper and nutmeg in a mixing bowl using a hand-mixer with the hook attachment. Then transfer onto a work surface on which you have first sprinkled a little flour and knead into a smooth dough (photograph 1). With flour-covered hands, make finger-thick rolls about 5 cm/2 in long, then roll the ends to make them slightly thinner (photograph 2).

3 Bring enough salted water to the boil to enable the finger dumplings to "swim". Put the dumplings in the boiling salted water, bring to the boil again and cook without a lid over low heat for 3–4 minutes (the water must only move very slightly).

4 Remove the finger dumplings from the water with a skimming ladle and leave to drain thoroughly. Melt the butter. Add the finger dumplings and fry (sauté) for 3–4 minutes, stirring occasionally.

TIP » Serve finger dumplings with braised roast beef (p. 58), goulash (p. 54), meat cut into strips or sauerkraut (p. 128).

Recipe variation: To make gnocchi, do not make pointed ends but press the finger dumplings onto the tines of a fork (photograph 3) to create the distinctive grooved pattern. Dip the fork in the flour now and again. Serve the gnocchi in tomato sauce (p. 114).

Macaroni or spaghetti

QUICK

Preparation time:
about 25 minutes

2.5 litres/4¼ pints (11 cups)
water
2 ½ teaspoons salt
250 g/9 oz dried macaroni,
spaghetti or other dried pasta

Per serving:
P: 8 g, F: 1 g, C: 44 g,
kJ: 909, kcal: 218, CU: 3.5

1 Bring water to the boil in a large pan with a lid. Then add salt and the macaroni or spaghetti. Cook without a lid over medium heat, following the instructions on the packet until "al dente", stirring 4–5 times while the pasta is cooking.

2 Pour the pasta into a colander, rinse under hot water and leave to drain.

TIPS » 250 g/9 oz dried pasta will make 4 servings if served as an accompaniment but served as a main meal you will need 400–500 g/14–18 oz for 4 servings.
» 1 litre/1¾ pints (4¼ cups) water is needed per 100 g/3½ oz pasta and you should add 1 teaspoon salt per 1 litre/1¾ pints (4¼ cups) water. If you are preparing more than 500 g/18 oz pasta, it is best to use 2 pans.
» For a main meal you will need 500 g/18 oz fresh pasta or gnocchi for 2 servings.

EXTRA TIP » Macaroni is delicious served with goulash while spaghetti is excellent served with pesto or tossed in 20 g/¾ oz (1½ tablespoons) butter; serve grated Parmesan on top.

Recipe variation: To make spaghetti or macaroni carbonara, cook 400 g/14 oz spaghetti or macaroni as described in the recipe and leave to drain. Cut 150 g/5 oz streaky bacon into small cubes, heat 1 tablespoon oil in a large saucepan, add the diced bacon and fry (sauté) over medium heat to sweat out the fat. Beat together 4 eggs and 50 g/2 oz (⅜ cup) grated Parmesan. Season with salt and pepper and stir in 6 tablespoons whipping cream. Add 50 g/2 oz (4 tablespoons) butter to the pan with the bacon and melt. Now add the egg mixture and pasta and stir well with a fork until the egg mixture has thickened. Serve with a mixed leaf salad or lamb's lettuce.

Spätzle

INEXPENSIVE

Preparation time:
about 30 minutes
Cooking time: 3–5 minutes

250 g/9 oz (2½ cups) plain
(all purpose) flour
3 eggs (medium)
½ level teaspoon salt
1 pinch ground nutmeg

1 Put the flour in a mixing bowl. Add the eggs, salt, nutmeg and water or milk. Stir all the ingredients with a wooden spoon, making sure that there are no lumps. Continue stirring until the dough has acquired a thick, semi-liquid consistency and makes bubbles (photograph 1).

2 Put water in a large pan with a lid and bring to the boil. Add salt. Push the dough in small servings through a spätzle cutter (photograph 2 and 3) or spätzle press above the pan so that the spätzle fall into the boiling salted water. Cook for 3–5 minutes (they are cooked when they float to the surface).

3 Remove the spätzle from the water with a skimming ladle, transfer them into a sieve or colander, rinse under cold water and leave to drain. Brown the butter in a pan and toss the spätzle in it.

TIP » Serve with braised beef (p. 58) or goulash (p. 54).

Recipe variation 1: To make spätzle in melted butter, melt 30 g/ 1 oz (2 tablespoons) butter, stir in 2 tablespoons breadcrumbs and pour over the spätzle.

Recipe variation 2: To make cheese spätzle (photograph), peel 3 onions, cut first into slices and then into rings. Brown the onion rings in the melted butter or margarine. Preheat the oven: top and bottom heat: about 200 °C/ 400 °F (Gas mark 6), fan oven: about 180 °C/350 °F (Gas mark 4). Prepare the spätzle as described in the recipe and arrange in a greased gratin dish, alternating layers of spätzle and 200 g/7 oz grated Emmental, ending with a layer of cheese on top. Bake on the middle shelf in the preheated oven for about 20 minutes. Sprinkle the browned onion rings and chopped chives on the cheese spätzle before serving. Serve as a main dish with a mixed salad.

about 100 ml/3½ fl oz (½ cup) water or milk
3 litres/5¼ pints (12 cups) water
3 teaspoons salt
40 g/1½ oz (3 tablespoons) butter

Per serving:
P: 12 g, F: 14 g, C: 45 g,
kJ: 1501, kcal: 359, CU: 4.0

Ravioli with spinach filling

SUITABLE FOR FREEZING (24 PIECES)

Preparation time:
about 75 minutes,
excluding defrosting and
rising time
Cooking time: about 15 minutes

In advance:
600 g/1¼ lb frozen leaf spinach

For the dough:
300 g/10 oz (3 cups) plain
(all purpose) flour
3 eggs (medium)
1 tablespoon cooking oil,
e.g. sunflower oil
½ teaspoon salt
some water (optional)

For the spinach filling:
2 onions
2 cloves garlic
2 tablespoons cooking oil,
e.g. sunflower or olive oil
salt
freshly ground pepper
ground nutmeg
1 egg yolk (medium)
1 egg white (medium)
about 3 litres/5¼ pints
(12 cups) vegetable or
meat stock

Per serving:
P: 19 g, F: 15 g, C: 58 g,
kJ: 1892, kcal: 452, CU: 4.5

1 To make the spinach filling, defrost the frozen spinach following the instructions on the packet.

2 For the dough, put the flour in a mixing bowl. Add the eggs, oil and salt. Mix all the ingredients with a hand-mixer with the hook attachment, first briefly on the lowest setting, then on the highest setting for about 3 minutes until the dough is completely smooth and homogenous, adding a little water if necessary. Cover the dough with a cloth and leave to rise for about 40 minutes.

3 Meanwhile make the spinach filling. Squeeze out all the water from the thawed spinach and chop up coarsely. Peel and chop the onions and cloves of garlic.

4 Heat the oil in a pan. Add the chopped onions and cloves of garlic and fry (sauté) while stirring. Now add the chopped spinach. Cover and continue frying over low heat for about 3 minutes. Season with salt, pepper and nutmeg, leave to cool slightly. Finally stir in the egg yolk.

5 Roll out the dough thinly on a well floured work surface to make a rectangle of at least 40 x 60 cm/ 16 x 24 in (photograph 1). With a pastry wheel cut out squares 10 x 10 cm/4 x 4 in. Put a portion of filling on each square. Beat the egg white with a fork and brush along

the edges of the squares (photograph 2). Fold the squares to make triangles and press the edges together to seal them (photograph 3).

6 Heat the vegetable or meat stock in a large pan. Add the ravioli in small amounts and cook without a lid over low to medium heat for about 15 minutes. When they are cooked, take them out of the stock with a skimming ladle and keep in a warm place. Continue cooking the remaining ravioli in the same way.

7 Serve the ravioli in soup bowls with a little stock.

TIPS » Drain the ravioli thoroughly and fry on both sides in melted butter. Then before serving sprinkle with breadcrumbs fried in butter and onion rings fried in clarified butter or oil.
» You can also roll out the pasta dough with a pasta machine.

Recipe variation 1: To make ravioli filled with minced (ground) beef and pork, peel and finely chop 1 onion. Heat 1 tablespoon oil in a pan. Add the chopped onion and fry over medium heat. Now stir in 300 g/10 oz minced (ground) meat (half beef, half pork), 1 medium egg, 1 medium egg yolk and 2 tablespoons chopped parsley. Season with salt and pepper. Now fill the dough squares with this mixture and continue as described in the recipe.

Recipe variation 2: To make **ravioli with a herb filling**, prepare 1 sweetheart cabbage (about 700 g/1½ lb), cut into thin strips, rinse and leave to drain. Peel and finely chop 2 onions. Heat 2 tablespoons oil in a pan, add the chopped onions and fry. Then add the cabbage cut into strips, cover and cook over low heat for about 3 minutes. Season the vegetables with grated nutmeg, salt and pepper and cook over medium heat for about 5 minutes. Leave the vegetables to drain in a colander and to cool a little. Then transfer to a bowl and stir in 50 g/2 oz (½ cup) chopped pistachio kernels, 125 g/4½ oz (½ cup) whipping cream and 1 yolk from a medium egg. Adjust the seasoning if necessary. Put small amounts on the dough squares and continue as described in the recipe.

TIP ›› Cooked ravioli can also be frozen.

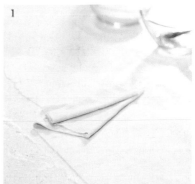

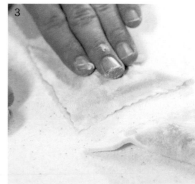

Fried rice

EASY

Preparation time:
about 5 minutes
Cooking time: 15–20 minutes

1 onion
20 g/¾ oz (1½ tablespoons)
butter or margarine
200 g/7 oz long grain rice
400 ml/14 fl oz (1¾ cups)
vegetable stock
salt (optional)

Per serving:
P: 4 g, F: 5 g, C: 40 g,
kJ: 916, kcal: 219, CU: 3.5

1 Peel and finely chop the onion. Melt the butter or margarine in a pan. Add the chopped onion and rice and fry (sauté) briefly while stirring.

2 Add the vegetable stock, bring to the boil, cover and cook the rice over low heat for 15–20 minutes. Season with a little salt if liked.

TIPS » Serve fried rice as an accompaniment to meat and vegetable-based dishes or as a base in rice salads.
» Instead of white rice you can use long grain brown rice. It has a brownish colour because the husk (which contains many vitamins and minerals) has not been removed. Brown rice should be cooked for 30–40 minutes (follow the instructions on the packet).

Recipe variation 1: To make **curried rice** (at the top in the photograph), fry the onion and rice as described in the recipe. Stir in 1 tablespoon curry powder and fry briefly. Then add the stock and cook as described in the recipe.

Recipe variation 2: To make **herb-flavoured rice**, stir 2 tablespoons chopped parsley, dill or peppermint into the cooked rice.

Recipe variation 3: To make **multi-coloured rice** (in the middle in the photograph), take 150 g/5 oz pork sausage, remove the skin, cut in half lengthways and then slice.

Prepare 200 g/7 oz carrots and 3 spring onions, wash them, leave to drain, then cut into slices. Drain a small can of sweetcorn (corn) in a colander (drained weight 140 g/ 5 oz). Melt 20 g/¾ oz (1½ tablespoons) butter in a pan, add the sliced vegetables and slices of sausage and fry. Now add 200 g/ 7 oz rice and 400 ml/14 fl oz (1¾ cups) vegetable stock. Bring to the boil, cover and cook over low heat for 15–20 minutes, stirring occasionally. Season the rice with a little salt.

Recipe variation 4: To make **spicy rice** (at the bottom in the photograph), peel and finely chop 1 clove garlic. Peel and finely chop 20 g/¾ oz fresh ginger. Cut 1 chilli in half lengthways, remove the stalk and seeds, rinse, leave to drain and chop up finely. Melt 20 g/ ¾ oz (1½ tablespoons) butter or margarine in a pan, add 200 g/7 oz rice, the garlic, ginger and chilli and fry. Pour in 400 ml/14 fl oz (1¾ cups) unsweetened coconut milk. Now add 1 piece of star anise, 1 stick cinnamon, ½ teaspoon each curry powder and cumin and a little salt. Bring to the boil, cover and cook the rice over low heat for about 15–20 minutes, stirring occasionally. If you wish, adjust the seasoning by adding a little salt and spices and herbs. Heat 1 tablespoon olive oil in a pan, add 50 g/ 2 oz cashew nuts and brown lightly. Sprinkle with ½ teaspoon curry powder and nutmeg. Pour the cashew nuts over the rice before serving.

Recipe variation 5: To make **rice pudding**, bring to the boil 1 litre/ 1¾ pints (4¼ cups) milk with 1 pinch salt, 20 g/¾ oz (2 table-spoons) sugar, 1 packet vanilla sugar and 2–3 pieces of the zest of an untreated, unwaxed lemon. Add 175 g/6 oz pudding rice, stir well, bring to the boil, put the lid on slightly askew so the steam can escape and cook over low heat for about 35 minutes, stirring occasionally. Serve as a dessert or as a sweet main meal with browned butter and cinnamon sugar or stewed fruit.

Lasagne
POPULAR (ABOUT 6 SERVINGS)

Preparation time:
about 45 minutes
Baking time: about 35 minutes

For the Bolognese sauce:
2 onions
1 cloves garlic
2 tablespoons olive oil
300 g/10 oz minced
(ground) pork
2 cans (400 g/14 oz each)
chopped tomatoes
125 ml/4 fl oz (½ cup)
vegetable stock
1 tablespoon tomato purée
1 bay leaf
½ tablespoon chopped basil
salt
Tabasco sauce

For the béchamel sauce:
30 g/1 oz (2 tablespoons)
butter or margarine
25 g/1 oz (4 tablespoons) plain
(all purpose) flour
300 ml/10 fl oz (1¼ cups) milk
200 ml/7 fl oz (⅞ cup)
vegetable stock
200 g/7 oz grated cheese
salt, pepper, nutmeg

12 sheets lasagne
(just under 250 g/9 oz)

Also:
some fat

Per serving:
P: 27 g, F: 31 g, C: 38 g,
kJ: 2293, kcal: 548, CU: 3.0

1 To make Bolognese sauce, peel and chop the onions and the clove of garlic. Heat the oil in a pan. Add the minced (ground) pork and fry (sauté), stirring all the time. Crush any lumps with a fork. Add the chopped onions and garlic and continue frying.

2 Now add the tinned chopped tomatoes together with the juice, the vegetable stock, tomato purée, bay leaf and basil to the minced pork and cook gently for about 5 minutes. Season with salt and Tabasco sauce. Preheat the oven:
Top and bottom heat:
about 200 °C/400 °F (Gas mark 6)
Fan oven:
about 180 °C/350 °F (Gas mark 4)

3 To make the béchamel sauce, melt the butter or margarine in a pan. Stir in the flour and continue stirring until the mixture has turned pale yellow. Then add the milk and vegetable stock and stir briskly with a whisk, making sure there are no lumps. Bring the sauce to the boil. Stir one-third of the cheese into the sauce and season generously with salt, pepper and nutmeg.

4 Remove the bay leaf from the sauce. Take a rectangular gratin dish, about 20 x 30 cm/8 x 12 in with a capacity of about 2.5 litres/ 4¼ pints (11 cups). Spread a layer of Bolognese sauce on the bottom

(photograph 1). Cover with a layer of lasagne sheets, then another layer of Bolognese sauce and sprinkle 3 tablespoons béchamel sauce on top (photograph 2). Continue alternating lasagne sheets, Bolognese sauce and béchamel sauce until you have four layers of lasagne, ending with a layer of béchamel on top (photograph 3).

5 Sprinkle the rest of the cheese on top and put the lasagne on the middle shelf of the preheated oven and bake for about 35 minutes.

6 Then take the lasagne out of the oven, leave to cool a little and serve.

Recipe variation: To make a spinach lasagne, heat 2 tablespoons olive oil in a pan. Peel and chop 1 clove garlic and 2 onions, add to the oil and fry. Now add 450 g/1 lb defrosted frozen spinach and continue frying for a further 4 minutes. Season with salt and pepper. Make a béchamel sauce with 60 g/2¼ oz (4½ tablespoons) butter, 50 g/2 oz (½ cup) plain (all purpose) flour, 600 ml/21 oz (2½ cups) milk, 200 ml/7 fl oz (⅞ cup) vegetable stock and the various condiments as described in the recipe. Arrange the lasagne in the gratin dish and sprinkle with 500 g/18 oz of mozzarella, torn into shreds. Bake for abour 35 minutes at the oven temperature indicated in the recipe.

Vegetable gratin
VEGETARIAN

Preparation time:
about 45 minutes
Baking time: about 45 minutes

1 kg/2¼ lb floury potatoes
salt
250 g/9 oz leeks
250 g/9 oz aubergines
(eggplant)
250 g/9 oz courgettes
(zucchini)
125 ml/4 fl oz (½ cup) hot milk
150 g/5 oz whipping cream
ground nutmeg
30 g/1 oz (2 tablespoons)
butter or margarine
freshly ground pepper
2 tablespoons chopped
flat-leaved parsley
150 g/5 oz grated medium
Gouda or Emmental cheese
about 3 tablespoons
sunflower seeds

Also:
some fat

Per serving:
P: 20 g, F: 38 g, C: 37 g,
kJ: 2449, kcal: 585, CU: 3.0

1 Peel the potatoes, rinse and leave to drain. Then cut into pieces and put in a pan. Sprinkle 1 teaspoon salt over the potatoes. Add enough water to cover the potatoes and bring to the boil. Cover and cook for 20–25 minutes.

2 Meanwhile prepare the leeks, cut in half lengthways, wash them thoroughly, leave to drain and cut into strips. Wash the aubergines (eggplants) and courgettes (zucchini), wipe them dry and cut the ends off. Cut both aubergine and courgettes into slices.
Preheat the oven:
Top and bottom heat:
about 200 °C/400 °F (Gas mark 6)
Fan oven:
about 180 °C/350 °F (Gas mark 4)

3 Drain the potatoes, dry them by tossing over the heat, then push them immediately through a potato press or mash with a potato masher. Stir the milk and cream into the mashed potatoes. Season with salt and nutmeg.

4 Melt the butter or margarine in a pan. Add the prepared vegetables and fry (sauté) for 1–2 minutes while stirring. Season with salt and pepper. Take a rectangular gratin dish, about 20 x 30 cm/8 x 12 in with a capacity of about 2.5 litres/4¼ pints (11 cups). Grease it well, transfer the vegetables to it and sprinkle with parsley. Sprinkle half the cheese on the vegetables

(photograph 1). Now spread the mashed potatoes on top (photos 2 and 3). Finally sprinkle the rest of the cheese and sunflower seeds on top.

5 Put the vegetable gratin on the middle shelf in the preheated oven and bake for about 45 minutes.

6 Take the gratin out of the oven, allow to cool a little and serve.

Recipe variation 1: To make a vegetable gratin with carrots and Comté cheese, use carrots instead of aubergines. Prepare the carrots, peel, rinse, leave to drain and cut into slices. Put the carrots in the melted butter or margarine, cover and braise over low heat for about 2 minutes; only then add the other vegetables. Prepare the vegetables as described in the recipe and put in the gratin dish. Replace the Gouda or Emmental cheese with Comté.

Recipe variation 2: To make a vegetable gratin with fish fillets, leave out the aubergines. Rinse 4 fish fillets (about 120 g/4 oz each) under running cold water, pat dry and season with salt and pepper. Arrange the fish fillets next to each other in the greased gratin dish and sprinkle 1 tablespoon chopped dill on top. Add the fried vegetables and the rest of the ingredients on top as described in step 4 of the recipe and bake as indicated there.

Scrambled eggs

QUICK (3 SERVINGS)

Preparation time:
about 10 minutes
Cooking time: about 5 minutes

6 eggs (medium)
6 tablespoons milk or
whipping cream
salt
freshly ground pepper
ground nutmeg
40 g/1½ oz (3 tablespoons)
butter or margarine
2 tablespoons chopped chives

Per serving:
P: 15 g, F: 27 g, C: 2 g,
kJ: 1301, kcal: 311, CU: 0.0

1 Beat together the eggs with the milk or cream and season with salt, pepper and nutmeg (photograph 1). Melt the butter or margarine in a pan (diameter 26–28 cm/10–11 in). Add the egg mixture to the pan and allow to set over low heat.

2 As soon as the egg mixture begins to set, loosen it from the bottom of the pan with a wooden spatula (photograph 2), constantly pushing the scrambled eggs away from the edges of the pan towards the middle until the entire mixture has set and no liquid remains (cooking time: about 5 minutes). Scrambled eggs should be fluffy and still moist inside. Sprinkle with chives before serving.

TIP ›› For scrambled eggs as a main dish, this quantity makes three servings: serve with fried potatoes (p. 168) and mixed salad. For a snack, the same quantity will make 4–6 servings, served with wholemeal bread. Instead of milk or cream you can use sparkling mineral water which will make the scrambled eggs particularly fluffy.

Recipe variation 1: For **garlic scrambled eggs**, peel 6 cloves of garlic, cut into thin slices and fry (sauté) in the butter or margarine. Whisk together the eggs with the milk or cream, season with salt, pepper and nutmeg. Add to the pan with the garlic and cook the scrambled eggs as described in the recipe.

Recipe variation 2: For **scrambled eggs with prawns**, defrost 200 g/ 7 oz frozen cocktail prawns, following the instructions on the packet, and pat dry. Whisk together the eggs with the milk or cream and season with salt, pepper and a little Worcestershire sauce. Melt the butter or margarine in the pan and add the eggs. As soon as the eggs begin to set, add the prawns. Continue cooking the scrambled eggs as described in the recipe.

Recipe variation 3: For **Mexican-style scrambled eggs**, peel and chop 2 cloves of garlic and 1 small onion. Wash 2 tomatoes, leave to drain, make a cross-shaped cut in the non-stalk end, plunge briefly in boiling water, then in cold water. Peel the tomatoes, cut in half, remove the seeds and cut out the stalks. Chop up the tomatoes. Cut in half 1 red pepper and 1 chilli, cut out the stalks, remove the seeds and the white membranes. Wash both, leave to drain and chop up. Fry the chopped garlic and onion in the butter and margarine. Add the chopped chilli and pepper and fry over low heat for about 5 minutes. Beat the eggs with 3 tablespoons milk or cream and season with salt and pepper. Add the chopped tomatoes. Add the egg mixture to the pan and continue cooking as described in the recipe. Sprinkle with 2 tablespoons chopped flat-leaved parsley before serving.

Fried eggs

EASY (4 EGGS)

Preparation time:
about 5 minutes
Frying time: about 5 minutes

**20 g/¾ oz (1½ tablespoons)
clarified butter or margarine
4 eggs (medium)
salt**

Per egg:
P: 7 g, F: 11 g, C: 0 g,
kJ: 540, kcal: 129, CU: 0.0

1 Melt the clarified butter or margarine in a 28-cm/11-in frying pan (skillet). Carefully break the eggs and slide them into the pan (photograph 1).

2 Sprinkle a little salt on the egg whites and fry (sauté) the eggs for about 5 minutes over medium heat until the egg white has set. Remove the fried eggs from the pan and serve immediately.

TIP » As a main meal, allow 2 eggs per person and serve, for instance, with vegetable salad or fried potatoes (p. 168), pickled gherkins or leaf spinach (p. 130).

Recipe variation 1: To make **fried eggs and bacon**, fry 4 slices of bacon in the butter or margarine, break the eggs, add them to the pan, season with pepper and fry as described in the recipe. Sprinkle chopped chives on the fried eggs before serving.

Recipe variation 2: To make a **farmer's sandwich** (photograph 2), prepare about 100 g/3½ oz vegetables (for instance carrots, radishes) and salad (for instance iceberg or rocket lettuce), chopped up small. Fry (sauté) 8 slices of bacon in a pan without fat until crisp, then remove from the pan. Fry the eggs

as described in the recipe, then turn them over and fry for about another 2 minutes. Cut 4 hamburger buns in half and spread 50 g/ 2 oz (4 tablespoons) butter on all the rolls. Arrange the prepared vegetables and lettuce, the eggs and the bacon on the bottom halves of the buns, sprinkle with freshly ground pepper and cover with the top halves.

TIP » As eggs get older the air chamber at the flat end of the egg becomes enlarged because some of the moisture evaporates during storage. In addition, the egg white becomes thinner as time goes by. Moreover these ageing processes are speeded up by higher storage temperatures and a reduction in air moisture. For these reasons it is recommended that eggs should always be stored in a refrigerator.

Freshness test: How to test the freshness of an egg broken on a plate:
» The egg white of a fresh egg encloses the egg yolk which is spherical.
» The egg white of a 7-day old egg begins to be runny and it is no longer firm.
» The egg white of a 3-week old egg is watery and the egg yolk is flat.

Poached eggs

SOPHISTICATED (8 EGGS)

Preparation time:
about 10 minutes
Standing time: 3–4 minutes

1 litre/1¾ pints (4½ cups)
water
3 tablespoons vinegar,
e.g. white wine vinegar
8 eggs (medium)
1 tablespoon chopped herbs,
e.g. chives, parsley or chervil
(optional)

Per egg:
P: 7 g, F: 6 g, C: 1 g,
kJ: 355, kcal: 85, CU: 0.0

1 Bring water and vinegar to the boil in a pan. Break the eggs one by one into a ladle and let them slide slowly into the simmering (but not briskly boiling) water (photograph 1). Using 2 tablespoons, push the egg whites towards the egg yolks (photograph 2). Cook the eggs over low heat without a lid for 3–4 minutes (only cook a maximum of 4 eggs at a time).

2 Take the poached eggs out of the water with a skimming ladle, plunge them briefly in cold water, leave to drain and trim the edges to make them smooth (photograph 3). Arrange the eggs on plates and garnish with chopped herbs if you wish.

TIP » You can add poached eggs to soups and serve them with fried potatoes (p. 168). Use only the freshest eggs possible; the fresher the egg, the better the egg white will set round the egg yolk.

Recipe variation 1: Serve poached eggs with a mixed salad (photograph 1). To make the mixed salad, remove the outer wilted leaves of ½ head each of Lollo Rosso and Oak Leaf lettuces or other crinkle-leaved lettuce. Wash the lettuces, pat dry or spin dry and tear into bite-size pieces. Wash 250 g/9 oz cocktail tomatoes, pat dry and cut into quarters. Wash 250 g/9 oz cucumbers, cut off the ends and slice. Prepare 200 g/7 oz baby carrots, peel, wash, leave to drain and cut into thin slices or grate. Peel and chop 1 onion. Mix together all the ingredients you have prepared for the salad. Stir together 2–3 tablespoons sherry vinegar and season with salt, pepper and 1 teaspoon liquid honey. Whisk in 5 tablespoons olive oil. Pour the dressing over the salad ingredients, mix well and arrange on 4 plates. Serve with 2 poached eggs on ciabatta bread. Garnish the eggs and salad with sprigs of dill.

Recipe variation 2: To make poached egg on toast, toast 4 slices of sandwich bread. Spread each piece of toast – while still hot – with ½ teaspoon pesto and garnish with 2 slices of tomatoes. Poach the eggs as described in the recipe (but do not dip in cold water) and place immediately on the slices of tomatoes. Sprinkle a little grated Parmesan and pepper on top and serve immediately.

Boiled eggs

EASY (4 EGGS)

Preparation time:
about 10 minutes

4 fresh eggs (medium)

Per egg:
P: 7 g, F: 6 g, C: 0 g,
kJ: 355, kcal: 85, CU: 0.0

1 Prick the rounded end with a needle or egg-pricker (photograph 1) to ensure that they do not crack. Bring water to the boil in a pan.

2 Place the eggs on a spoon or skimming ladle and gently slide them into the boiling water (photograph 2); the eggs must be completely covered by the water. Bring to the boil again, start timing and continue boiling the eggs without a lid over low heat. Medium eggs will take about 5 minutes to be soft-boiled, about 8 minutes to be semi-hard-boiled (hard-cooked) eggs and 10 minutes for hard-boiled eggs.

Large eggs will require about 1 minute longer in each case.

3 Remove the boiled eggs from the water with a spoon or skimming ladle and put briefly under running cold water to stop the eggs from cooking further. It will also make the shell easier to peel.

TIP » If you are using eggs directly from the refrigerator, increase the cooking time by about 1 minute. Very cold eggs should pre-warmed in lukewarm water to prevent the shells from cracking.

Eggs stuffed with anchovies

INEXPENSIVE (8 SERVINGS, TOP LEFT IN PHOTOGRAPH)

Preparation time:
about 25 minutes

**4 hard-boiled (hard-cooked)
medium eggs
1 slightly heaped tablespoon
mayonnaise
1 slightly heaped teaspoon
mustard
salt
freshly ground pepper
1 pinch sugar
a few lettuce leaves
8 salted anchovy fillets
about 3 gherkins (from a jar)
a few cherry tomatoes
roughly chopped dill**

1 Shell the hard-boiled (hard-cooked) eggs, cut in half lengthways, remove the egg yolk and rub through a fine sieve. Mix the egg yolk with mayonnaise and mustard to make a smooth mixture. Season with salt, pepper and sugar, put in an icing-bag with a large star-shaped nozzle and pipe the mixture into the scooped-out egg whites.

2 Wash the lettuce leaves and pat dry or spin dry. Pat the anchovies dry. Leave the gherkins to drain and cut into strips. Wash the cocktail tomatoes, pat dry and cut into slices. Arrange the egg halves on the lettuce leaves and garnish with the anchovy fillets, strips of

gherkins and sliced tomatoes. Decorate with a few sprigs of dill.

TIP » Serve these stuffed eggs as part of salad platters at a buffet meal or as a starter with toast or baguette. Roll the egg halves in chopped chives, sesame seeds or chopped peanuts.

Recipe variation 1: To make **eggs stuffed with herb-flavoured quark low-fat curd cheese** (at the bottom in the photograph), stir 1 tablespoon of each creme fraîche, herbs and herb-flavoured quark into the egg yolk, rub through a sieve, then season with salt and sugar. Stuff the egg halves with the mixture and garnish with thin strips of red, yellow and green peppers.

Recipe variation 2: To make **eggs with Parmesan filling,** stir 1 tablespoon creme fraîche, 1 table-spoon finely grated Parmesan and a few chopped pink peppercorns into the egg yolk you have rubbed through a sieve. Season with salt and pepper and pipe into the egg

halves. Garnish with 1 tablespoon roasted pine nuts and 1 tablespoon of rocket, cut into strips.

Recipe variation 3: To make **eggs stuffed with tomato-flavoured quark** (top right in the photograph), stir 2 tablespoons quark, 1–2 teaspoons tomato purée and 1 teaspoon drained, finely chopped capers into the egg yolk you have

just rubbed through a sieve. Season with salt, pepper and sugar. Pipe the mixture into the egg halves. Garnish with 50 g/2 oz ham, cut into thin strips, and capers.

Per egg:
P: 5 g, F: 6 g, C: 1 g,
kJ: 328, kcal: 78, CU: 0.0

Pancakes

FOR CHILDREN (ABOUT 7 PANCAKES)

Preparation time:
about 40 minutes,
excluding rising time

250 g/9 oz (2½ cups) plain (all
purpose) flour
4 eggs (medium)
1 tablespoon sugar
1 pinch salt
375 ml/13 fl oz (1⅝ cups) milk
125 ml/4 fl oz (½ cup)
sparkling mineral water
about 80 g/3 oz (6 tablespoons)
clarified butter or
8 tablespoons cooking oil,
e.g. sunflower oil

Per piece:
P: 9 g, F: 17 g, C: 30 g,
kJ: 1309, kcal: 313, CU: 2.5

1 Put the flour in a mixing bowl and make a well in the middle. Whisk together the eggs, sugar, salt, milk and mineral water. Pour a small amount of this mixture in the well (photograph 1). Starting from the middle, mix the flour and egg-mixture together. Add the rest of the egg mixture little by little, making sure there are no lumps. Leave the batter to rest for 20–30 minutes.

2 Heat a little clarified butter or oil in a 24-cm/9½-in non-stick frying pan (skillet) and pour a small amount of batter into the pan, rotating it so that the bottom is evenly covered with a thin layer of batter (photograph 2). As soon as the edges begin to turn golden yellow, carefully turn over the pancake using a wooden spatula or slide onto a plate and return to the pan, having turned it over (photograph 3). Cook the second side until it too is golden yellow. Before turning over the pancakes, add a little more butter or oil to the pan.

3 Cook the rest of the batter in the same way, stirring the batter each time before spooning it into the pan.

TIP ›› Serve the pancakes with stewed fruit, cinnamon sugar, maple syrup or fresh fruit.

EXTRA TIPS ›› The pancakes will be even more delicious if you separate the eggs and at first only add the egg yolk to the batter. Just before cooking the pancakes, beat the egg whites stiff and fold into the batter.
›› Keep the finished pancakes warm in the preheated oven: top and bottom heat about 80 °C/180 °F, fan oven: 60° C/140 °F.
›› Before piling the pancakes on top of each other, sprinkle each one with a little sugar. This will prevent them from sticking together. Pancakes are also suitable for freezing.

Recipe variation 1: To make apple pancakes, make the batter as described in the recipe. Now peel 1 kg/ 2¼ lb tart apples (for instance, Boskoop apples), cut into quarters, core and cut into thin slices lengthways. Divide into 7 servings. Add a little of the butter or oil in the pan, add 1 servings of sliced apples and fry (sauté) for 2–3 minutes. Pour a thin layer of batter over the apples and cook over medium heat until the batter sets, occasionally loosening the pancake from the bottom, and continue cooking as described in the recipe. Cook the rest of the apples and batter in the same way. Sprinkle the pancakes with cinnamon sugar.

Recipe variation 2: To make crêpes, melt 20 g/¾ oz (1½ tablespoons) clarified butter or margarine in a pan and leave to cool a little. Mix together 100 g/3½ oz (1 generous cup) plain (all purpose) flour with 1 tablespoon sugar and 1 pinch of salt in a mixing bowl. Add 2 eggs (medium), 250 ml/8 fl oz (1 cup) milk and clarified butter or margarine and mix well. Leave the batter to rest for 20–30 minutes. Brush a small frying pan (diameter 16–18 cm/6–7 in) with a little fat and make the crêpes as described in the recipe. Keep the finished crêpes in a warm place. To make the filling, drain a small can of apricot halves (drained weight 240 g/8½ oz) in a sieve. Make a custard with a small packet of custard powder (vanilla pudding mix) and only 300 ml/10 fl oz (1¼ cups) milk, following the instructions on the packet, but without any sugar. Stir 200 g/7 oz cream cheese into the custard. Cut the apricot halves into small pieces and heat in a pan with 100 g/3½ oz apricot jam (jelly) and 1 tablespoon lemon juice. Fill the crêpes with the custard and apricot mixture and, if you wish, garnish with lemon balm leaves before serving.

Kaiserschmarren
(sweet pancake pieces with raisins)
QUICK (2 SERVINGS)

Preparation time:
about 30 minutes

4 eggs (medium)
100 g/3½ oz (1 cup) plain (all
purpose) flour
1 pinch salt
1 packet vanilla sugar
200 g/7 oz (⅞ cup) whipping
cream or 200 ml/7 fl oz
(⅞ cup) milk
50 g/2 oz (⅓ cup) raisins
about 50 g/2 oz
(4 tablespoons) clarified
butter or 4 tablespoons
cooking oil, e.g. sunflower oil
icing (confectioner's) sugar

Per seerving:
P: 22 g, F: 52 g, C: 70 g,
kJ: 3574, kcal: 854, CU: 6.0

1 Separate the eggs. Beat the egg whites until they form stiff peaks. Put the egg yolks, flour, salt, vanilla sugar, cream or milk in a mixing bowl. Mix the ingredients with a hand-mixer with the whisk attachment until you obtain a smooth batter. Fold in the stiffly beaten egg whites and raisins (photograph 1).

2 Heat a little clarified butter or oil in a 28-cm/11-in frying pan (skillet). Add half the batter and cook over medium heat until the underside has turned a pale yellow. Now cut through the still rather "liquid" top of the pancake to make 4 servings, using 2 spatulas, turn them over (photograph 2) and cook until golden yellow, adding a little more fat if necessary.

3 Then tear the servings of pancakes into small pieces, using 2 spatulas (photograph 3), put on a plate and keep in a warm place. Cook the rest of the batter in the same way. Sprinkle with icing (confectioner's) sugar before serving.

TIPS » These raisin pancakes will serve 2 as a sweet main meal or 4 as a dessert. Serve with plum or apricot compote.
» You can learn how to separate eggs in the recipe for semolina pudding (p. 214).

EXTRA TIP » When beating the egg whites, the bowl and whisk must be absolutely fat-free and the egg white must not contain any trace of egg yolk. Egg whites should only be beaten just before they are used.

Variation: Soak the raisins in 1–2 tablespoons warmed brown rum for 30 minutes before using them. Then add the raisins with the rum to the batter as described in the recipe.

Recipe variation 1: To make Kaiserschmarren with nougat, replace the raisins with 100 g/ 3½ oz chopped nougat and stir into the batter together with 50 g/2 oz almonds. Continue preparing the pancakes as described in the recipe.

Recipe variation 2: To make Kaiserschmarren with apples and morello cherries, only use 150 g/ 5 oz cream or 150 ml/5 fl oz (⅝ cup) milk and replace the raisins with 1 grated apple and 75 g/3 oz dried morello cherries: fold these into the batter. Continue making the pancakes as described in the recipe.

1

2

3

Omelette stuffed with mushrooms

INEXPENSIVE (2 SERVINGS)

Preparation time:
about 60 minutes

For the filling:
400 g/14 oz mushrooms
1 onion
50 g/2 oz streaky bacon
20 g/¾ oz (1½ tablespoons)
clarified butter or
2 tablespoons cooking oil,
e.g. sunflower oil
salt
freshly ground pepper
50 g/2 oz (4 tablespoons)
whipping cream
2 tablespoons chopped parsley

For the omeletts:
6 eggs (medium)
1 pinch salt
1 pinch sweet paprika
30 g/1 oz (2 tablespoons)
clarified butter or
3 tablespoons cooking oil,
e.g. sunflower oil

Per serving:
P: 34 g, F: 59 g, C: 4 g,
kJ: 2822, kcal: 674, CU: 0.0

1 To make the filling, prepare the mushrooms, rub clean with a kitchen paper towel and slice. Peel the onion. Chop up the onion and bacon.

2 Heat the clarified butter or oil in a pan. Add the diced bacon and cook briefly to sweat out the fat. Now add the chopped onion, sliced mushrooms and fry (sauté). Season with salt and pepper and continue frying over medium heat for about 8 minutes, stirring occasionally.

3 Stir in the cream, season again with salt and pepper, stir in the parsley and put aside. keeping it warm.

4 Beat the eggs for the omelette and season with salt and paprika (photograph 1).

5 Melt half the clarified butter or heat half the oil in a non-stick frying pan (skillet) with a diameter of 22–24 cm/8½–9½ in. Add half the egg mixture, cover and cook over low heat for 4–5 minutes (photograph 2). The underneath must be golden brown (photograph 3).

6 Slide the omelette onto a pre-warmed plate, put half the mushroom filling on it and fold the omelette over. Keep in a warm place. Prepare the second omelette in the same way.

TIPS)) Serve the omelettes as a main dish with a mixed leaf salad or lamb's lettuce. An omelette should only be made just before it will be eaten.
)) If you would like the omelette to be lighter and fluffier, beat the egg whites stiff and then fold into the yolk mixture.

Recipe variation: Instead of the mushroom filling you can make an omelette with mozzarella and tomatoes. To do this, drain 125 g/4½ oz mozzarella cheese and cut into thin slices. Wash 2 tomatoes, wipe dry and cut out the stalks. Cut the tomatoes into slices. Put half the cheese and half the sliced tomatoes on one half of the omelette. Sprinkle with salt and pepper and fold the omelette over. If desired, garnish the omelette with a few basil leaves.

French toast

INEXPENSIVE (6 PIECES)

Preparation time:
about 40 minutes

300 ml/10 fl oz (1¼ cups) milk
2 eggs (medium)
50 g/2 oz (¼ cup) sugar
6 slices about 1.5 cm/
½ in thick white loaf bread
(2–5 days old)
50 g/2 oz (4 tablespoons)
clarified butter or
5 tablespoons cooking oil,
e.g. sunflower oil

Per piece:
P: 6 g, F: 11 g, C: 25 g,
kJ: 953, kcal: 228, CU: 2.0

1 Mix together the eggs, milk and sugar. Put the slices of white bread in a bowl and pour the egg-milk mixture on top. Leave to soak, turning the slices of bread over very carefully once or twice while they are soaking, until all the milk has been absorbed (but be careful that the bread is not too wet).

2 Melt the clarified butter or heat the oil in non-stick pan. Add the slices of bread, a few at a time, and fry (sauté) on both sides for about 8 minutes over medium heat until they are brown and crisp. French toast must be served hot.

TIP » French toast can be served as a pudding or as a sweet main meal with, for instance, stewed plums (p. 210), stewed apples (p. 210), icing (confectioner's) sugar or vanilla sauce.

Recipe variation 1: To make almond-flavoured French toast, stir together 3 tablespoons almond liqueur with milk and eggs. Instead of white sandwich bread, use 12 small baguette slices. After soaking in the egg-milk mixture, coat them with 75 g/3 oz peeled, ground almonds and continue cooking as described in the recipe.

Recipe variation 2: To make savoury French toast, instead of adding sugar to the milk and eggs, stir in 1 level teaspoon salt, a little pepper and grated nutmeg. Coat the slices of baguette in 100 g/ 3½ oz (1 cup) ground sunflower seeds or in about 75 g/3 oz (¾ cup) finely ground almonds and cook as described in the recipe. After turning the slices, you can also garnish them with 1 slice of salami, 1 slice of tomato and 1 slice of cheese. Sprinkle with dry oregano, cover and continue cooking until the cheese has melted. If you wish, serve with a lettuce or vegetable salad.

TIP » Savoury French toast (recipe variation 2) is also delicious served with soup or ratatouille. If you like a touch of garlic, peel 1–2 cloves of garlic, push through a garlic press, add to the milk and leave to stand for about 20 minutes. Pour the milk through a sieve and sir into the eggs and condiments. Soak the bread in it and cook as described in the recipe.

Vegetable sticks with dips
FOR GUESTS

Preparation time:
about 40 minutes

800 g/1¾ lb vegetables,
e.g. celery, carrots,
cucumber, peppers, kohlrabi

For the soft goat's cheese dip:
100 g/3½ oz soft goat's cheese
1 carton (125 g/4½ oz) crème
fraîche with herbs
1 chilli pepper
some Tabasco sauce
salt, pepper

For the garlic dip:
2 cloves garlic
1 tablespoon capers
2 tablespoons chopped parsley
2 tablespoons chopped chives
100 g/3½ oz cream cheese
75g/3 oz yoghurt (3.5 % fat)
salt, pepper

For the honey and mustard dip:
1 carton (150 g/5 oz)
crème fraîche
1 tablespoon medium strong
mustard
1 tablespoon runny honey
turmeric
salt, pepper

Per serving
(vegetables and dips):
P: 9 g, F: 33 g, C: 15 g,
kJ: 1630, kcal: 393, CU: 1.0

1 Prepare the vegetables, wash them and leave to drain. Cut into sticks and put into glasses.

2 To make a piquant soft goat's cheese dip, stir together the soft goat's cheese and crème fraîche. Cut the chilli in half, then remove the stalk, the seeds and the white membranes. Wash the chilli, leave to drain and cut into small pieces, then stir into the cheese-crème fraîche mixture. Season the dip with Tabasco sauce, salt and pepper.

3 To make the garlic dip, peel the cloves of garlic, then push them through a garlic press. Drain the capers and finely chop. Mix together the fromage frais and yoghurt and stir in the capers and garlic as well as the chopped parsley and chives. Season with salt and pepper.

4 For the honey and mustard dip, stir mustard and honey into crème fraîche and season with turmeric, salt and pepper

5 Serve the vegetable sticks with the dips.

Filled baguette rolls

EASY (4 PIECES, PHOTOGRAPH)

Preparation time:
about 15 minutes

2 tomatoes
150 g/5 oz cucumbers
100 g/3½ oz cooked ham
200 g/7 oz Camembert
a few lettuce leaves
a few herb leaves,
e.g. basil, parsley
4 baguette rolls
(about 80 g/3 oz each)
40 g/1½ oz (3 tablespoons)
butter

Per piece:
P: 23 g, F: 22 g, C: 42 g,
kJ: 1928, kcal: 461, CU: 3.5

1 Wash the tomatoes, wipe dry and cut out the stalks. Wash the cucumbers, wipe dry and cut off the ends. Cut both the tomatoes and cucumbers into slices. Cut the ham into strips and the Camembert into slices. Rinse the lettuce leaves and herbs and pat dry.

2 Cut the rolls in half horizontally and spread with butter. Garnish each of the bottom halves of the rolls in succession with lettuce leaves, sliced tomatoes, sliced cucumbers, slices of camembert, strips of ham and herbs. Put the top halves back on.

TIP » If you like you can sprinkle salt and pepper on the sliced cucumbers and tomatoes.

Recipe variation: To make filled pitta bread, coarsely grate 150 g/5 oz prepared carrots. Prepare 70 g/3 oz iceberg lettuce, wash, pat dry and cut into thin strips. Cut 100 g/3½ oz sliced smoked cured pork into strips. Stir together 1–2 teaspoons balsamic vinegar with salt and pepper and 2 tablespoons oil. Add 1 tablespoon chopped chives and the ingredients you have just prepared. Warm 1 round pitta bread and cut into quarters, then cut each horizontally but not completely through. Open them up and fill with the salad.

Tomatoes with mozzarella

CLASSIC

Preparation time:
about 15 minutes

7 tomatoes
250 g/9 oz mozzarella

For the sauce:
basil leaves
about 2 tablespoons balsamic
vinegar
salt, pepper, sugar
4 tablespoons olive oil

Per serving:
P: 13 g, F: 23 g, C: 4 g,
kJ: 1151, kcal: 275, CU: 0.0

1 Wash the tomatoes, wipe dry and cut out the stalks. Cut into slices. Leave the mozzarella to drain, then cut it too into slices. Arrange the sliced tomatoes and sliced mozzarella alternately on a serving dish.

2 Rinse and pat dry the basil leaves. To make the dressing, stir together the vinegar, salt, pepper and sugar. Stir in the oil. Pour the dressing over the ingredients you have just prepared and garnish with the basil.

TIP » Serve with ciabatta.

Recipe variation: To make tomatoes and courgettes (zucchini) with mozzarella, wash 200 g/7 oz courgettes (zucchini), wipe dry and cut off the ends. Cut into slices. Heat 2 tablespoons olive oil, add the sliced courgettes and fry (sauté) briefly. Sprinkle with salt and leave to cool. Arrange the sliced courgettes with the sliced tomatoes and mozzarella.

Desserts

Whether served as a pudding or as a main meal, sweets and desserts are always almost irresistible.

Creamy desserts
Creamy desserts can made over hot steam or in a hot bain-marie.

Preparation over hot steam
This method combines the effect of heating and whisking the egg yolk with the sugar until the mixture becomes creamy and airy. It is essential that the bowl containing the creamy mixture should fit perfectly into the pan containing the hot water or that the bowl is larger than the pan. If the bowl is too small, there is a risk that some water might get into the creamy mixture and spoil it.
Use a stainless steel bowl for the creamy mixture because this material is a better conductor of heat than china or glass. Then prepare the creamy dessert as described in the recipe.

Preparation in a bain-marie
To make creamy desserts in a bain-marie, grease the moulds or ramekins generously and sprinkle with a little sugar, if you like.
Then pour the creamy mixture you have prepared into the moulds or ramekins. Put the them in a pan or a roasting tin in the oven. Then very carefully pour boiling water into the pan or roasting tin until it reaches halfway up the ramekins. Now continue cooking as described in the recipe.

Fruit jellies
These can be red, green or yellow, depending on your choice and the fruit used. To make fruit jelly, berries or chopped up fruit are brought to the boil with fruit juice and thickened with cornflour (cornstarch).
Another alternative is to bring only the juice to the boil, then to thicken it and only then add the fruit to the thickened juice. In this way the aroma and intense colour of the fruit will be preserved.
If using frozen fruit, make sure that the juice is very thick and then stir the frozen fruit into the boiling hot juice (but do not bring to the boil again).

Ice cream and sorbets
The basic ingredients of ice cream are sugar, eggs, milk or cream and flavouring ingredients such as vanilla, chocolate, lemon or strawberries. The ingredients are first whisked together over a hot bain-marie and then frozen to set. It is important to stick to the amounts specified in the recipe. This is because ice cream may become granular if too little sugar is used and it will not set if too much sugar is added.
Sorbets are made from fruit purée and sugar syrup, sometimes with the addition of stiffly beaten egg whites; they are then frozen. If you want your sorbet to be creamy it is important to stir it several times during the freezing process (photograph 1).

An ice cream machine can be used to make both ice cream and sorbets (follow the manufacturer's instructions).

Fruit salads

Fruit salads will have more flavour and aroma if they are prepared with fresh, ripe fruit in its season. It will be sweeter and therefore will not need any more sugar. First put a little freshly squeezed grapefruit or orange juice into the bowl, then stir in the fruit you have previously prepared. Instead of the citrus juice you can use fruit which themselves contain juice such as grapes, melons or strawberries. The acid substances in the juice will ensure that more vulnerable fruit such as bananas and apples retain their colour and not turn brown. As well as being a feast for the palate, fruit salads are also a feast for the eyes because they combine fruits with different consistencies, textures and colours, for instance juicy peaches, crisp apples, soft, creamy bananas and acid kiwis.

Blancmange (vanilla pudding)

To make blancmange you need 500 ml/17 fl oz (2¼ cups) milk, 50 g/2 oz (¼ cup) sugar, 40 g/1½ oz (5 tablespoons) cornflour (cornstarch) and, if desired, flavouring agents such as lemon rind or vanilla essence. Start by bringing 375 ml/13 fl oz (1⅝ cups) milk to the boil and add the flavouring ingredients. Now stir the cornflour (cornstarch) and sugar into the rest of the milk, then stir this mixture into the boiling milk. Bring back to the boil, then leave to cool. It is much quicker to use ready-to-use custard (vanilla

pudding) powder. Whether you have made "real" blancmange or used ready-mix powder, you can always give it a more sophisticated touch by adding chocolate sprinkle, fruit or beaten egg whites.

In addition: Blancmange need not only be eaten cold, it is also delicious warm!

All about gelatine

Gelatine is easy to use and being a perfect gelling and setting agent, it plays an essential part in the preparation of custards, fruit jellies and sweets. Gelatine is transparent and has a neutral taste and smell.
» Red and white gelatine is available in shops either in powdered form or as gelatine leaves.
» 1 packet powdered gelatine (9 g/⅓ oz) is sufficient to set 500 ml/17 fl oz (2¼ cups) liquid and corresponds to 6 gelatine leaves (10 g/⅓ oz).
» Leaf or powdered gelatine can be interchanged according to your preference.
» Leaf gelatine needs to be soaked in sufficient cold water for about 5 minutes. Then squeeze the gelatine lightly, transfer to a small pan and dissolve over low heat while stirring (do not allow it to boil and follow the instructions on the packet).
» When using powdered gelatine, put it in a small pan, add 6 tablespoons cold water and stir over low heat until dissolved. Leave the gelatine to swell for about

5 minutes in the pan, then stir over low heat until dissolved (do not allow it to boil).
» Depending on the recipe, it is also possible to dissolve the soaked leaf gelatine or swollen gelatine powder in hot liquid such as fruit juice (photograph 2).

» To set whipped cream: whip the cream until almost stiff and fold in the sugar. Now stir in the dissolved, cooled but still lukewarm gelatine and whip the cream completely stiff. Continue as described in the recipe.
» Fresh pineapple, kiwis, papayas and figs influence the gelling properties of the gelatine because of the enzymes they contain. It is therefore recommended that these fruits should be blanched in hot water before combining them with the gelatine. Another possibility is to use tinned fruit.

Tip: Desserts containing gelatine must stored in the refrigerator in order to set properly.

Stewed apples

CLASSIC (AT THE FRONT OF THE PHOTOGRAPH)

Preparation time:
about 15 minutes
Cooking time: about 15 minutes

750 g/1½ lb sharp apples,
e.g. Boskop or Elstar
5 tablespoons water
about 50 g/2 oz (¼ cup) sugar

Per serving:
P: 0 g, F: 1 g, C: 30 g,
kJ: 537, kcal: 129, CU: 2.5

1 Peel the apples, cut into quarters, core and cut into small pieces. Bring the water and apple pieces to the boil, cover and cook over low heat for about 15 minutes.

2 Purée the cooked apples and add sugar to taste.

TIPS » Stewed apples can be served as a pudding in their own right or as an accompaniment to potato fritters (p. 164).
» Cook 1 cinnamon stick with the apples.

» You can also cook the apples without peeling them. In this case, wash the apples, remove the stalk and the remains of the flower at the other end. Cut the apples into pieces and cook as described in the recipe. Push the cooked apples through a sieve.

Recipe variation: To make apple compote, another form of stewed apples, coarsely chop the peeled and cored apples. Cook with water for about 10 minutes as described in the recipe, add sugar to taste but do not purée.

Pear compote

EASY (AT THE BACK OF THE PHOTOGRAPH)

Preparation time:
about 10 minutes,
excluding cooling time
Cooking time: about 10 minutes

500 g/18 oz pears
250 ml/8 fl oz (1 cup) water
50 g/2 oz (¼ cup) sugar

1 packet vanilla sugar
1 stick cinnamon
3 cloves
1–2 tablespoons lemon juice
a little sugar (optional)

Per serving:
P: 0 g, F: 0 g, C: 26 g,
kJ: 451, kcal: 107, CU: 2.0

1 Peel the pears, cut in half, core and cut into quarters. Bring the water to the boil in a pan together with the sugar, vanilla sugar, cinnamon and cloves.

2 Add the cut-up pears, bring to the boil again, cover and simmer over low heat for about 10 minutes. Stir in the lemon juice and leave to cool.

3 Add sugar to taste and remove the cloves and cinnamon stick.

TIP » You can replace half the water with 125 ml/4 fl oz (½ cup) white wine.

Recipe variation: To make a plum compote (in the middle in the photograph), wash 500 g/18 oz plums, leave to drain and wipe dry with a cloth, if necessary. Remove the stalks, cut in half and take out the stone. Bring 125 ml/4 fl oz (½ cup) water or red wine with 50 g/2 oz (¼ cup) sugar to the boil in a pan. Add the halved plums, 1 cinnamon stick and 3 cloves, bring to the boil again, cover and simmer over low heat for about 8 minutes. Remove the cinnamon stick and cloves. Leave to cool a little and add sugar to taste.

Red fruit jelly

CLASSIC (ABOUT 6 SERVINGS)

Preparation time:
about 20 minutes,
excluding cooling time

**250 g/9 oz each blackberries,
red currants, raspberries,
strawberries (all fruits well
prepared)
35 g/1¼ oz cornflour
(cornstarch)
100 g/3½ oz (½ cup) sugar
500 ml/17 fl oz (2¼ cups) fruit
juice, e.g. morello cherry or
red currant juice**

Per serving:
P: 3 g, F: 1 g, C: 39 g,
kJ: 808, kcal: 193, CU: 3.5

1 Sort out the blackberries if necessary, removing any damaged ones, rinse gently and leave to drain thoroughly. Wash the red currants, leave to drain thoroughly and strip the currants off the stalks. Sort out the raspberries but do not wash. Wash the strawberries, leave to drain, remove the stalks and, depending on the size of the fruit, cut in half or into quarters.

2 Mix the sugar and cornflour (cornstarch) together, then add 4 tablespoons of the juice and stir to obtain a homogenous paste (photograph 1). Bring the rest of the juice to the boil in a pan. Stir the cornflour mixture into the boiling juice (photograph 2) and bring to the boil again, then remove the pan from the heat. Add the fruit.

3 Put the red fruit jelly in a glass bowl or in individual glass serving dishes and put in the refrigerator.

TIP ›› Serve red fruit jelly as a pudding with vanilla custard or cream. As a sweet main meal, accompanied by milk, it will serve 4. To make vanilla custard, cut 1 vanilla pod open lengthways with the back of a knife and scrape out the pulp. Mix together 25 g/1 oz (3 tablespoons) cornflour and 50 g/2 oz (¼ cup) sugar. Take 3 tablespoons from the 500 ml/ 17 fl oz (2¼ cups) milk and stir into the cornflour-sugar mixture. Add the vanilla pulp to the rest of the milk and bring to the boil in a pan. Remove the pan from the heat and stir in the cornflour mixture with a whisk. Bring briefly to the boil again. Serve the sauce hot or leave to cool, stirring occasionally.

Recipe variation: To make green fruit jelly, wash 500 g/18 oz gooseberries, then leave to drain thoroughly. Top and tail the gooseberries. Peel 250 g/9 oz kiwis, first cut in half, then into smaller pieces. Wash 250 g/9 oz white seedless grapes, leave to drain, pull off the stalks and, if necessary, cut the larger grapes into half. Mix together 20 g/¾ oz cornflour (cornstarch) with 150 g/5 oz (⅔ cup) sugar. Take 4 tablespoons from 375 ml/13 fl oz (1⅝ cups) white grape juice and stir into the cornflour-sugar mixture. Bring the rest of the juice to the boil, stir in the cornflour-sugar mixture and bring to the boil again. Stir in the gooseberries and grapes and bring briefly to the boil again. Remove the pan from the heat and stir in the kiwis. Transfer to a glass bowl and put in the refrigerator.

Semolina pudding

FOR CHILDREN

Preparation time:
about 20 minutes,
excluding cooling time

½ **vanilla pod**
500 ml/17 fl oz (2¼ cups) **milk**
75 g/3 oz (⅓ cup) **sugar**
**grated zest of ½ organic
lemon (untreated, unwaxed)**
50 g/2 oz (⅓ cup) **semolina
(farina)**
1 **egg (medium)**

Per serving:
P: 7 g, F: 5 g, C: 33 g,
kJ: 922, kcal: 221, CU: 2.5

1 Cut the vanilla pod open lengthways, using the back of a knife, and
scrape out the pulp. Bring the milk
to the boil together with the sugar,
grated lemon zest, vanilla pod and
pulp in a pan, previously rinsed in
cold water. Sprinkle the semolina
(farina) into the milk while stirring,
bring to the boil again and simmer
for about 1 minute while stirring.

2 Remove the pan from the heat and
take out the vanilla pod. Separate
the eggs and stir the egg yolk briskly
into the semolina mixture. Beat the
egg white stiff and fold into the hot
semolina.

3 Pour the semolina pudding into a
mould, bowl or individual dishes,
all previously rinsed in cold water.
Leave to cool and then put in the refrigerator for about 3 hours.

4 Before serving, carefully loosen the
semolina from the edge with a
knife, then turn over onto a plate.

Advice: **only use very fresh eggs
which are not over 5 days old –
check the date when they were laid!**
Keep the semolina pudding in the
refrigerator and consume within
24 hours.

TIPS » Serve semolina pudding
with fresh fruit and whipped
cream, plum compote (p. 210)
or apricot halves.

» Because the semolina mixture
sometimes bubbles and splashes, it
is a good idea to use a spoon or
whisk with a long handle when
stirring.

EXTRA TIP » **Separating eggs.**
Break the egg on a hard edge, break
the shell open and tip the egg yolk
from one half-shell to the other
above a bowl to collect the egg
white as it slides out. You may find
it easier to use an egg separator. In
this case, simply crack the egg into
the egg separator; the white will run
away while the egg yolk remains in
the trough.

Recipe variation 1: To make
polenta pudding, bring the milk,
sugar, lemon zest, vanilla pod and
pulp to the boil together with 20 g/
¾ oz (1½ tablespoons) butter.
Instead of semolina, use 50 g/2 oz
(⅓ cup) polenta and cook the
pudding as described in the recipe.

Recipe variation 2: To make
**semolina-quark cream cheese
pudding**, after folding in the stiffly
beaten egg white, stir 125 g/4½ oz
quark (20 % fat) into the lukewarm
pudding (add more sugar if you
like).

Recipe variation 3: To make
semolina pudding with cinnamon,
replace the vanilla pod with a
cinnamon stick.

Vanilla dessert with zabaglione

WITH ALCOHOL (4-6 SERVINGS)

Preparation time:
about 30 minutes,
excluding cooling time

For the vanilla dessert:
3 sheets clear gelatine
250 ml/8 fl oz (1 cup) milk
100 g/3½ oz (½ cup) sugar
1 packet vanilla sugar
250 g/9 oz chilled whipping
cream

For the zabaglione:
250 ml/8 fl oz (1 cup) dry
white wine
2 egg yolk (medium)
40 g/1½ oz (3 tablespoons)
sugar
1 tablespoon lemon juice
1 teaspoon cornflour
(cornstarch)

Per serving:
P: 5 g, F: 20 g, C: 34 g,
kJ: 1572, kcal: 376, CU: 3.0

1 To make the vanilla dessert, soak the gelatine in cold water, following the instructions on the packet. Bring the milk, sugar and vanilla sugar to the boil in a pan, rinsed in cold water, then remove from the heat and transfer to a mixing bowl. Squeeze the gelatine lightly and dissolve in the hot milk while stirring. Allow the milk-gelatine mixture to cool a little, then put in the refrigerator, stirring occasionally with a whisk.

2 Whip the cream until stiff and as soon as the gelatine-milk mixture begins to set fold the whipped cream into it. Transfer the pudding immediately into a bowl or individual serving dishes and put in the refrigerator.

3 To make the zabaglione, pour the white wine into a stainless steel bowl, stir in the egg yolk, sugar, lemon juice and cornflour (cornstarch), place in a hot bain-marie and beat with a whisk until the mixture becomes creamy (about 5 minutes). The zabaglione is ready when the mixture has doubled in volume and thickened.

4 Place the bowl in cold water to cool the sauce, stirring occasionally with a whisk. Keep the vanilla dessert and zabaglione refrigerated until serving.

Advice: **only use very fresh eggs which not over 5 days old – check the date when the eggs were laid!** The finished dishes should always be kept in the refrigerator and consumed within 24 hours.

TIP » Put the zabaglione on the vanilla dessert just before serving.

EXTRA TIP » Rinse the pan in cold water before bringing the milk to the boil. The cold water prevents the milk from burning on the bottom of the pan.

Recipe variation 1: To make **alcohol-free zabaglione**, replace the white wine with 125 ml/4 fl oz (½ cup) apple juice and 2 tablespoons lemon juice.

Recipe variation 2: To make **Italian zabaglione**, whisk together 3 egg yolks (medium), 60 g/2 oz (½ cup) sugar and 125 ml/4 fl oz (½ cup) Marsala as described in the recipe.

Recipe variation 3: To make **chocolate-flavoured zabaglione**, use 3 egg yolks from medium eggs, 40 g/1½ oz (scant ¼ cup) sugar and stir in 50 g/2 oz finely chopped plain chocolate.

Recipe variation 4: To make **cinnamon and rum zabaglione**, stir 2 tablespoons rum and a pinch of ground cinnamon into the zabaglione mixture.

Upside-down Bavarian pudding

CLASSIC (4–5 SERVINGS, AT BOTTOM OF PHOTOGRAPH)

Preparation time: about 40 minutes, excluding cooling time

1 vanilla pod
250 ml/8 fl oz (1 cup) milk
6 sheets clear gelatine
3 egg yolks (medium)
75 g/3 oz (⅓ cup) sugar
250 g/9 oz chilled whipping cream

Per serving:
P: 7 g, F: 23 g, C: 21 g,
kJ: 1374, kcal: 329, CU: 1.5

1 Cut the vanilla pod open length-ways with a knife and scrape the vanilla pulp out with the back of a knife (photograph 1). Bring the milk and vanilla pulp to the boil in a pan. Soak the gelatine in cold water, following the instructions on the packet.

2 Stir the egg yolk and sugar together in a stainless steel bowl, using a whisk. Add the hot milk, stirring all the time. Heat all the ingredients in a hot bain-marie over medium heat, whisking the mixture all the time until the mixture begins to thicken and turns white (photograph 2). Neither the water nor mixture must be allowed to come to the boil or the mixture will curdle. Remove the pan from the heat.

3 Squeeze the gelatine. Add it to the still hot mixture (photograph 3) and dissolve it, stirring all the time. Pour the mixture through a fine sieve and leave to cool, stirring continuously.

4 Whip the cream until stiff. As soon as the mixture begins to set, fold in the whipped cream. Transfer the mixture into 4–5 individual moulds or cups, each with a capacity of 150–200 ml/5–7 fl oz (⅝–⅞ cup), rinsed out in cold water. Put in the refrigerator for about 3 hours to set.

5 Before serving, loosen the edges away from the moulds with a sharp knife. Plunge the moulds briefly in hot water and turn out the puddings onto dessert plates.

TIP ›› Serve Bavarian pudding with whipped cream and fruit, puréed fruit or chocolate sauce.

Recipe variation 1: To make Bavarian cappuccino pudding, dissolve 5 teaspoons instant espresso coffee powder together with the gelatine in the egg yolk and milk mixture, then prepare as described in the recipe. Pour the mixture into cappuccino cups and put them in the refrigerator. Before serving, whip 125 g/4½ oz (½ cup) whipping cream and put a dollop on top of each Bavarian cappuccino pudding, then sprinkle with cocoa powder.

Recipe variation 2: To make Bavarian orange pudding , stir 3 tablespoons orange liqueur into the egg yolk and milk mixture, then prepare as described in the recipe. Put the mixture in individual glass bowls or glasses and decorate with orange segments and refrigerate.

Recipe variation 3: To make Bavarian chocolate pudding (at the top in the photograph), chop up 150 g/5 oz plain chocolate, add to the egg yolk and milk mixture and stir until melted. Then dissolve the gelatine (use only 4 leaves since otherwise the mixture would become set too much) and prepare as described in the recipe. This will make 6 servings of 150 ml/5 fl oz (⅝ cup) each.

Lemon pudding

FRUITY (AT THE FRONT IN THE PHOTOGRAPH)

Preparation time:
about 30 minutes,
excluding cooling time

4 sheets clear gelatine
150 ml/5 fl oz (⅝ cup) lemon
juice (from about 3 lemons)
125 g/4½ oz (⅝ cup) sugar
150 g/5 oz yoghurt (3.5 % fat)
300 g/10 oz chilled whipping
cream

Per serving:
P: 4 g, F: 24 g, C: 35 g,
kJ: 1662, kcal: 398, CU: 3.0

1 Soak the gelatine in cold water, following the instructions on the packet. Heat the lemon juice in a small pan (but do not let it boil!).

2 Squeeze the gelatine thoroughly and dissolve in the hot lemon juice, stirring all the time, then stir in the sugar. Leave the gelatine mixture to cool a little, then stir in the yoghurt. Cover the mixture with clingfilm (plastic wrap) and put in the refrigerator until it begins to set, stirring occasionally.

3 As soon as the mixture begins to set, whip the cream stiff and fold into the mixture. Transfer the pudding into a glass bowl or individual glass serving dishes and put in the refrigerator for at least 3 hours.

TIP » Garnish the lemon pudding with whipped cream or lemon, lime or orange segments before serving.

Recipe variation 1: Serve the lemon pudding with **chocolate sauce**. For the chocolate sauce, coarsely chop 100 g/3½ oz plain (unsweetened) chocolate and melt in 3 tablespoons water in a stainless steel bowl placed in a hot bain-marie over low heat, stirring all the time. Serve immediately.

Recipe variation 2: You can also replace the lemon juice with orange, lime or grapefruit juice. When making **orange or lime pudding** (in the middle and at the back of the photograph) use only 100 g/3½ oz (½ cup) sugar.

Recipe variation 3: To make **apricot pudding**, put 1 small can of apricot halves (drained weight 250 g/9 oz) in a sieve, leave to drain and reserve the juice. Cut 2 apricot halves into segments and chop the rest into chunks. Soak 3 leaves clear gelatine in cold water, following the instructions on the packet. Mix together 250 g/9 oz quark low-fat curd cheese, 150 g/5 oz vanilla-flavoured yoghurt, 4 tablespoons of the apricot juice you have reserved, 50 g/2 oz (¼ cup) sugar and 1 packet vanilla sugar. Dissolve the soaked gelatine in a small pan, following the instructions on the packet, stirring all the time. Now stir about 4 tablespoons of the quark-yogurt mixture into the dissolved gelatine, then stir this mixture into the rest of the quark-yoghurt mixture. Whip 200 g/7 oz (⅞ cup) refrigerated whipping cream until stiff and fold into the mixture together with the chopped apricots. Now transfer the pudding into a glass bowl or into individual glass serving dishes, cover with clingfilm (plastic wrap) and keep refrigerated for at least 3 hours. Garnish the pudding with the apricot segments just before serving.

Fruit salad

Preparation time:
about 30 minutes

1 each apple, small mango,
nectarine, peach, orange, kiwi
fruit, banana
100 g/3½ oz strawberries
3 tablespoons lemon juice
1 tablespoon sugar or honey
(optional)

Per serving:
P: 2 g, F: 3 g, C: 20 g,
kJ: 525, kcal: 126, CU: 1.5

1 Peel the apples, cut into quarters and core. Cut the mango flesh away from the stone and peel the fruit. Wash the nectarine and peach, wipe dry, cut into half and remove the stone. Cut the prepared fruit into pieces. Peel the orange in such a way that the white pith is removed at the same time (photograph 1), then cut out the segments with a sharp knife so as to remove the membranes (photograph 2).

2 Peel the kiwi and banana, then cut both into slices. Wash the strawberries, leave to drain, cut out the stalk and cut into pieces.

3 Pour the lemon juice on top and stir in sugar or honey if liked. Put the fruit salad in a bowl and serve immediately. Otherwise cover with clingfilm (plastic wrap) and keep in the refrigerator.

TIP ›› Garnish the fruit salad with mint leaves before serving.

EXTRA TIP ›› You can vary the fruit salad endlessly, according to the season and your taste. You will need about 1 kg/2¼ lb fruit in all.

Quark dessert with fruit

Preparation time:
about 20 minutes,
excluding cooling time

1 can peach halves
(drained weight 450 g/16 oz)
grated zest of ½ organic lime or
lemon (untreated, unwaxed)
2 tablespoons lime or
lemon juice
250 g/9 oz each low-fat quark
and regular quark (20 % fat)
150 g/5 oz yoghurt (3.5 % fat)
3–4 tablespoons sugar

Per serving:
P: 18 g, F: 4 g, C: 41 g,
kJ: 1226, kcal: 292, CU: 3.5

1 Put the peach halves in a sieve, leave to drain, then cut into small pieces and sprinkle with the zest and juice of a lime or lemon.

2 Stir together both kinds of quark, yoghurt and sugar, using a whisk. Put half the quark mixture in a glass bowl. Spread the peach mixture on top, then cover with the rest of the quark mixture. Cover the bowl and refrigerate the quark dessert for at least 30 minutes.

TIP ›› Decorate the quark pudding with lemon balm leaves before serving. It also makes an excellent party pudding.

Recipe variation: To make chocolate quark with bananas, break 100 g/3½ oz of plain chocolate into pieces, put in a stainless steel bowl in a hot bain-marie over low heat and stir into dissolved. Stir together 500 g/18 oz low-fat quark with 4–6 tablespoons milk or whipping cream until smooth and homogenous. Stir in the chocolate together with 1 packet of vanilla sugar. Sweeten with ½ tablespoon sugar. Peel 4 small bananas, place 1 banana on each plate and spoon the chocolate quark over the bananas and next to them.

Baked apples

WITH ALCOHOL (8 SERVINGS)

Preparation time:
about 20 minutes,
excluding soaking time
Cooking time: about 40 minutes

1 tablespoon raisins
about 100 ml/3½ fl oz (½ cup)
rum
8 apples, e.g. Holsteiner Cox
or Boskop
20 g/¾ oz (1½ tablespoons)
soft butter
20 g/¾ oz (1½ tablespoons)
sugar
1 packet vanilla sugar
2 tablespoons finely ground
almonds
2 tablespoons slivered
almonds

Per serving:
P: 2 g, F: 7 g, C: 23 g,
kJ: 814, kcal: 194, CU: 2.0

1 Soak the raisins overnight in 2 tablespoons of the rum.

2 Preheat the oven:
Top and bottom heat:
about 200 °C/400 °F (Gas mark 6)
Fan oven:
about 180 °C/350 °F (Gas mark 4)

3 Remove the stalks of the apples, wash and wipe dry. Core the apple with an apple-corer from the non-stalk end but do not push completely through (photograph 1). Place the apples in a well-greased baking tin.

4 Stir together the butter, sugar, vanilla sugar, almonds and soaked raisins. Using a teaspoon, stuff the apples with this mixture (photograph 2). Arrange the slivered almonds on top and press lightly. Pour the rest of the rum on the apples in the baking tin (photograph 3).

5 Put the baking tin on a shelf in the bottom third of the preheated oven and bake for about 40 minutes.

6 Remove the apples when they are done and serve hot.

TIPS » Serve the baked apples sprinkled with icing (confectioner's) sugar, vanilla custard or semi-whipped cream.
» Baked apples can be served as a pudding or at tea-time.

Recipe variation: To make **baked apples without alcohol**, soak the raisins in 2 tablespoons orange or apple juice, leave to drain and use as described in the recipe. Instead of rum, pour orange or apple juice over the apples in the baking tin.

Buying and storing food

Most food tastes best when it is fresh. Nevertheless, storing a small amount of food can be very useful. If you store food correctly, you will reduce the time you spend shopping and the food will retain its goodness. Always check the sell-by-date and refrigerate perishable food as soon as possible.

Storing food correctly in the refrigerator

» The temperature in a refrigerator should range between +2 °C and +8 °C/35 °F and 46 °F.
» Fruit and vegetables will keep fresh longer when stored in the special vegetable and fruit compartments.
» Store mushrooms in a paper bag, this will keep them fresh longer.
» Always cover food to prevent it drying out and to stop smells being transferred.
» Transfer any food or condensed milk left in a can into different containers to prevent them acquiring a "tinny" taste.
» Allow cooked food to cool before putting it in the refrigerator.

Freezing correctly

» Frozen food can be stored for a long time.
» Make sure that the food to be frozen is frozen as quickly as possible (to a temperature of at least -18 °C/0.4 °F). This will prevent the formation of ice crystals within the food. The appearance and taste of frozen food can also be affected during the defrosting process.

Defrosting correctly

» Frozen food which is being defrosted should not be in contact with the defrosting liquid. When defrosting food, place the item in a sieve.
» Only season the food after it has completely defrosted – salt and sugar draw the juices out of the food and condiments lose some of their taste.
» Food should be defrosted slowly in the refrigerator.
» Process defrosted food within the following 24 hours.
» Never refreeze defrosted food, because bacteria may develop and multiply on the surface during the defrosting process which would not be killed if deep-frozen again. These organisms continue to develop after the defrosting process and they could be dangerous to your health.
» Raw defrosted food which has been cooked after defrosting can be frozen again in the same way as cooked dishes, having been allowed to cool first.
» Do not defrost frozen vegetables before preparing and cooking them.
» Small servings of fish and meat can be processed when they are still slightly frozen.
» Food that is still slightly frozen may easily be cut into very small pieces.
» Before putting food in the micro-wave to defrost, leave it standing at room temperature for a few minutes.

Avoiding danger

Treating and dealing with food correctly will protect your health. This is why it is important to pay particular attention to the storage of certain foods:
» Meat and fish should always stored in the refrigerator at a temperature below +7 °C/45 °F because they perish very easily.
» Food which in certain circum-stances could carry salmonella bacteria, such as eggs and poultry, should always be stored and prepared away from other foods.
» When defrosting poultry and meat, make sure that the defrosting liquid does not come into contact with any other food which might become contaminated by it. Poultry and meat should always be processed and prepared on washable work surface.
» Poultry and minced (ground) meat should always be cooked through properly. If possible minced meat should always be prepared on the day it has been processed.
» For dishes prepared with raw eggs, such as mayonnaise, only use eggs which are not over 5 days old – check the date the eggs were laid. Once prepared, keep the food in the refrigerator and consume within 24 hours.
» Wash your hands with soap and warm water before preparing food and also as often as possible during the preparation.

Cooking herbs and spices

Cooking herbs and spices always enhance the taste of any dish and add a variety to your menu. Herbs can be used on their own or in combination with other herbs. Some herbs will also enable you to use less salt. They will definitely add a sophisticated touch to your dishes.

Buying herbs
Traditional herbs such as parsley, chives, chervil, dill, basil, rosemary and thyme are usually sold in pots and also in bunches in the supermarket or at farmers' markets. Make sure the herbs have firm stems and that the leaves are neither too pale not too thick and leathery.

Storing herbs correctly
» Fresh herbs from the garden or a window-box can be harvested whenever you need them.
» Bunches of herbs will remain fresh for 1–2 days if you cut off the ends of the stems and place the herbs in fresh water or in a sealed freezer bag filled with air which is then stored in the refrigerator.
» If you are planning to dry the herbs, it is important to harvest them before they flower. After harvesting, tie them together in a bunch and hang to dry in a well-ventilated, dark place at a temperature of 21–32 °C/ 69–90 °F. Then you can transfer the dried herbs into tightly closed jars and store them in a dark, dry place where they will keep for 1 year.
» It is also very useful to freeze the herbs in servings. To do this, prepare the herbs, chop them up, place in small freezer bags and freeze.
» Another method is to preserve them in oil and vinegar. During this process, the oil and vinegar absorb the flavour of the herbs. These herb-flavoured oils and vinegar are much used in preparations of dressings for salads, as well as for roasts and grilled (broiled) dishes.

Processing the herbs properly
» Rinse the herbs in a bunch under running cold water (photograph 1), then pat dry or shake until completely dry.
» To remove the leaves of small-leaved herbs such as rosemary, oregano and thyme, grip the herbs at the top of the stems and strip the leaves from top to bottom against the direction of the growth (photograph 2).
» Chop the herbs with a sharp knife just before serving. This will ensure that they preserve their full flavour.

Spices
Spices are aromatic or pungent seasonings which exist in an incredible range of flavours. They are mostly of vegetable origin with essential oils which not only enhance the flavour of food – they also make them more digestible. Spices will emphasise and bring out the flavour of your dishes.

Tips
» If possible, always buy unground spices. Only grind them just before you will be using them – in a mortar, pepper mill or with a nutmeg grater.
» Buy ground spices only in small quantities and store them in closed containers in a place where they are protected from the light and from other smells.
» Watch out for steam and water vapours! Do not hold ground spices (for instance in a shaker) directly above food while it is cooking. The steam and water vapours will make the spices clump together and ruin them. Instead place the condiment in a tablespoon or the palm of your hand and sprinkle over the food. In this way it will easier to add the correct amount.
» Never add spices to hot fat or they will burn and become bitter.

Cooking methods and types of cookers

Food can be prepared and cooked in a very wide variety of ways. Which method you choose will depend on the recipe, your cooking experience and, last but not least, how you like your food cooked. A low-fat cooking method which will preserve the nutritional properties of the food, such as steaming or braising, is always the best. As a rule of thumb: the ideal cooking time is as long as is necessary and as short as possible. Ready-to-eat dishes should only be heated briefly.

» **Frying (sautéing):** This is cooking in a little fat – cooking oil, clarified butter, butter or margarine – over a high heat in a frying pan (skillet) or saucepan without a lid. When food is fried, no liquid such as stock, wine or water is added.

» **Roasting in the oven:** Here the food is cooked by browning in an open container with or without the addition of fat. This method is particularly suited to large pieces of meat such as joints or poultry.

» **Steaming:** This is the slow cooking of food in a sieve above steam (about 100 °C/212 °F) in a covered container or saucepan. It is an ideal cooking method because the nutrients contained in the food are preserved. Herbs and spices are added directly to the water, where the steam absorbs their flavours and aromas. Steaming in a steamer is particularly easy (but as always if it

is important to follow the manufacturer's instructions).

» **Braising:** With this method the food is cooked more or less in its own juices with a little fat and liquid in a covered container. The temperature is less than 100 °C/212 °F.

» **Simmering:** The food is cooked very gently at relatively low temperatures ranging between 80 and 90 °C/180 and 200 °F in simmering liquid. Important: the liquid must not bubble briskly; it should only move very gently.

» **Grilling (broiling):** Here the food is cooked and browned with a little or no fat through radiation or contact heat at a high temperature (in the oven, over charcoal or on an electric grill. Grilled food should only be seasoned with salt after grilling because the salt tends to draw out the meat juices which would make the meat bland and tough. When grilling over charcoal it is recommended to use a disposable aluminium foil grill pan.

» **Cooking in foil:** This is a particularly healthy cooking method whereby the food is cooked in its own juices wrapped in heat-resistant foil in the oven heated to 200 °C/400 °F (Gas mark 6). Do not wrap the foil too tightly round the food because there must be sufficient space round the food for the steam to develop. Make sure the foil is sealed tightly so that no liquid

can escape. Then place the packet on the oven shelf, in a dish if you like. The time needed for cooking in foil is about one-third longer than traditional cooking. Foil bags are available which are heat-resistant to about 230 °C/450 °F. Chose a large enough bag or tube and close it tightly because the bag will become inflated. When cooking in foil bags, make sure you follow the manufacturer's instructions.

» **Boiling:** Cooking in a large amount of boiling liquid at a temperature of 100 °C/212 °F.

» **Sautéing:** With this technique, food is cooked in a little fat in a frying pan (skillet) without a lid. The food is briskly fried in hot fat for a short time. The heat is lowered when the food has turned brown.

» **Deep-frying:** Food such as chips, croquettes, doughnuts, fish and meat in breadcrumbs are deep-fried in very hot fat until brown and crispy. After cooking, allow to drain on a kitchen paper towel to reduce the amount of fat. Be careful: the fat should not be "as hot as possible"! Temperatures over 175° C/350 °F will contribute to the development of carcinogenic substances.

» **Stewing:** This method combines sautéing and boiling. The food is first browned briskly on all sides over high heat. This has the effect of contributing to the development of tasty aromatic substances. Then stock, wine, gravy or water is added and the food is cooked slowly with the lid on.

» **Bain-marie:** The slow warming of food in a saucepan or stainless steel bowl, placed in a pan filled with hot (not boiling) water is ideal for the preparation of dishes which could curdle or stick to the bottom such as Hollandaise sauce or Bavarian cream.

» **Poaching:** This is the slow cooking or simmering of food in stock or other liquid such as water. It can be used for eggs, fish, vegetables and dumplings.

The electric cooker

Electric cookers are available either with 4 individual cooking plates or with the cooking plates covered by a ceramic hob, which provides a smooth, easy-to-clean surface. The heat settings are controlled by knobs and numbered, but there is no standardisation of the numbering system.

As the name suggests, fast-heating plates heat up more quickly and are therefore particularly suited to boiling, sautéing and stir-frying.

The induction cooker

Also powered by electricity, induction cookers use alternating electro-magnetic fields to generate heat directly in the cooking pots placed upon it. The heat is pro-

duced immediately so such cookers are very quick and efficient. Meanwhile the glass ceramic hob itself remains cold. It is important to realise that induction cookers will only work with iron or steel pots (not aluminium, copper or glass) and it is best to use cooking pots specially designed to be used on them.

The gas cooker

The burners on a gas cooker are usually ignited automatically by an electric spark when the gas is turned on. Heat is delivered immediately to the cooking pot and it can controlled instantly and directly. For this reason many cooks prefer gas cookers.

Oven

Ovens are available with various heating functions and many models offer the possibility of selecting different kinds of heating:

» Top and bottom heat: The heating elements at the top and bottom of the oven generate heat which produces air currents and radiation round the food. To achieve the best heat transmission only one shelf can be used. The level of the shelf depends on the recipe and the manufacturer's instructions. Regardless of the cooking time, the oven should always be preheated as indicated in the recipe.

» Fan: A fan built into the back of the oven circulates hot air throughout the entire oven. This type of heating makes it possible to cook food on several shelves at the same time.

» Grilling (broiling): in large and small grill (broiler), it is possible to adjust the surface area that is heated to the amount of food to be cooked. Flat items are cooked by radiant heat and become crisp on the surface.

Microwave

In microwave ovens the water molecules in the food are caused to oscillate which results in the production of heat. This makes it possible to defrost, reheat or cook food in a very short time. But only non-metallic containers suitable for use in microwave ovens can be used. It is important to follow the manufacturer's instructions.

Technical cooking terms

Ball shapes, making (photograph 1)
Ball-shaped servings are taken from dough or other mass with a couple of moistened spoons and shaped with them before the next stage of the recipe.

Binding, thickening
The addition of a thickening agent, for instance, flour, cornflour (cornstarch) or gravy thickener, to liquids, thus giving them a creamy consistency.

Blanching
Food is first immersed briefly in boiling water, then quickly plunged into ice-cold water. This process loosens the skin (e.g. of tomatoes) and enhances the colour of green vegetables.

Breadcrumbs, covered with
Food, first seasoned with spices or herbs, is coated in flour, beaten egg and breadcrumbs before being fried (sautéed) or deep-fried. This gives the food a tasty crusty outer coating while keeping the meat moist and tender.

Caramelising
Food such as carrots or potatoes are covered in liquid sugar (caramel). The sugar hardens quickly, thus creating a sweet-tasting coating and beautiful glossy shine.

Carving (photographs 3 and 4)
The cutting of cooked food into slices or pieces for serving.

Cold water, rinsing in
The purpose of doing this is to stop the cooking process immediately and to cool food quickly.

De-boning (photograph 2)
The removal of the bones from game, venison, meat or poultry.

Deep-frying
The process of cooking meat, fish, fruit and vegetables (often wrapped in batter) by being submerging in hot oil or fat.

Deglazing
This term describes the process where liquid is added to remove the cooking residues from the base of a pan and stirred to make the basis for a gravy or sauce.

Degreasing
Removal of the fat that has risen to the surface of a stock, stew or sauce with a spoon or kitchen paper towel.

Drying
Drying removes the remaining liquid from food which has been cooked in water, such as potatoes or rice. To do this the pan may be tossed over the heat until all the water has evaporated. Alternatively, putting a tea-towel over the top of a saucepan under the lid will absorb moisture as it is given off as steam.

Filetting
The careful removal of the skin and bones from meat or fish, which may then be cut into pieces. Filetting also describes the freeing of the flesh of citrus fruit from the membrane enveloping each segment.

Flambéing
A small amount of heated alcohol is poured over food and then set alight.

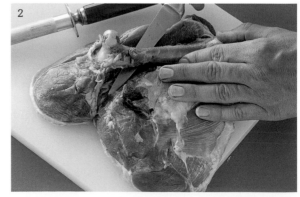

Flour, coating with
Food with a moist surface, such as liver or veal escalopes, is first wiped dry with a kitchen paper towel before being coated in flour and then fried.

Folding-in
The process of gently stirring and distributing beaten egg whites or whipped cream into a mixture. The word describes the action; it is important not to stir too briskly.

Marinating
Meat and fish is left in a marinade for a period of time; as well as tenderising, the process adds flavour. Unlike pickling, the marinade can be used as the basis for the sauce later. Meat is sometimes left in an oil-based marinade before being grilled (broiled).

Maturing (hanging)
The process of storing meat, venison or game in a cool place for a time before it is processed further. This make the meats more tender

and more digestible, as well as enhancing the flavour.

Peeling
The removal of the skin of fruit or vegetables such as potatoes, cucumbers, bananas and onions.

Poaching
The slow cooking of food by gently simmering it in liquid, for instance eggs in water with vinegar.

Reducing
Stock, soup and sauces are cooked in a large container without a lid so that the liquid evaporates; thus they become concentrated and thick. The process gives stocks, soups and sauces a more intense aroma.

Rendering
The process of frying fatty meat cut into small cubes (such as bacon), so that the fat is melted and extracted.

Setting
This describes the solidifying of an egg mixture in a bain-marie (such as crème caramel), in the oven (as in

a quiche), or in a pan (for instance, scrambled eggs).

Sieving
Soft raw or cooked food is rubbed through a sieve to reduce the solids to a pulp.

Skimming
The process of using a skimming ladle to remove the foam which forms on broth, stock or fruit after the initial boiling.

Thickening
Stirring an egg yolk, cream or butter into a liquid which is off the boil

Trussing
Fixing prepared food in its desired shape before cooking, using skewers, clips or needle and thread. It is used on poultry and rolled joints of meat.

Whipping, beating
The process of working air into the food with a whisk – for instance, whipped cream and beaten egg white.

3

4

CONTENTS

CONTENTS

CONTENTS

CONTENTS

ALPHABETICAL INDEX

If you have any questions, suggestions or comments, please contact the Consumer Service of the Dr. Oetker Test Kitchen
Telephone: + 49 8 00 71 72 73 74 Mon–Fri 8 am–6 pm, Sat 9 am–3 pm
or the staff of Dr. Oetker Verlag
Telephone +49 521 520651 Mon–Fri, available hours: 9 am–3 pm.
Or you can write to us: Dr. Oetker Verlag KG, Am Bach 11, 33602 Bielefeld (Germany), or visit us on the Internet at: www.oetker-verlag.de oder www.oetker.de.

Environmental notice

This book and its cover were printed on chlorine-free bleached paper. The shrinkwrapping to protect it from getting dirty is made from environmentally-friendly recyclable polyethylene plastic.

Copyright

© 2010 by Dr. Oetker Verlag KG, Bielefeld

Editorial

Carola Reich
no:vum, Susanne Noll, Leinfelden-Echterdingen

Editorial Consultancy

Dr. Judith Borgwart, Frankfurt

Cover photograph Photographs in the book

Thomas Diercks (Fotostudio Diercks), Hamburg
Kai Boxhammer (Fotostudio Diercks), Hamburg
Mariusz Mocak (Fotostudio Diercks), Hamburg
Christiane Pries, Borgholzhausen (pp. 44, 112, 113)

Food styling

Rocco Dressel, Hamburg
Maik Schacht, Hamburg

Recipe development and advice

Dr. Oetker Versuchsküche, Bielefeld

Translation

Rosetta Translations SARL, France

Nutrition calculations

Nutri Service, Hennef

Graphic concept and design Cover design

BCW Gesellschaft für Kommunikation mbH, Hamburg
kontur:design, Bielefeld

Reproduction Typesetting Printing and binding

Repro Ludwig, Zell am See, Österreich
JUNFERMANN Druck & Service, Paderborn
Firmengruppe APPL, aprinta druck, Wemding

With thanks for their generous assistamce

Masterfoods GmbH, Verden

ISBN: 978–3–7670–0933–2

Conversions and abbreviations

CONVERSIONS

For each recipe, measurements are given in metric and Imperial quantities, with American equivalents where appropriate. Conversions given are inevitably approximate; 1 oz is equivalent to 28.34981 g, so exact conversion would involve unwieldy measurements such as 1¹⁄₁₆ oz. Therefore 25 g has normally been rounded up to 1 oz and 30 g has been rounded down to 1 oz.

The tables on these pages show the conversions normally used in the recipes. It is important to use all metric or all Imperial measurements in a recipe, not a mixture of the two. Please note that the metric measurements are more precise than the Imperial ones.

WEIGHT

Metric	Imperial	Metric	Imperial
10 g	⅓ oz	375 g	13 oz
15 g	½ oz	400 g	14 oz
20 g	¾ oz	450 g	16 oz
25 g	1 oz	500 g	18 oz
30 g	1 oz	600 g	1¼ lb
40 g	1½ oz	700 g	1½ lb
50 g	2 oz	750 g	1½ lb
60 g	2 oz	800 g	1¾ lb
70 g	3 oz	900 g	2 lb
75 g	3 oz	1 kg	2¼ lb
100 g	3½ oz	1.1 kg	2½ lb
125 g	4½ oz	1.2 kg	2½ lb
150 g	5 oz	1.3 kg	2¾ lb
175 g	6 oz	1.4 kg	3 lb
200 g	7 oz	1.5 kg	3⅜ lb
225 g	8 oz	2 kg	4½ lb
250 g	9 oz	2.5 kg	5½ lb
275 g	9½ oz	3 kg	6½ lb
300 g	10 oz	4 kg	9 lb
325 g	11 oz	5 kg	11 lb
350 g	12 oz	6 kg	13 lb

OVEN TEMPERATURES

Celsius	Fahrenheit	Gas mark
140 °C	275 °F	1
150 °C	300 °F	2
160 °C	325 °F	3
180 °C	350 °F	4
190 °C	375 °F	5
200 °C	400 °F	6
220 °C	425 °F	7
230 °C	450 °F	8
240 °C	475 °F	9

LENGTH

Metric	Imperial	Metric	Imperial
3 mm	⅛ in	11 cm	4½ in
5 mm	³⁄₁₆ in	12 cm	5 in
1 cm	⅜ in	20 cm	8 in
2 cm	¾ in	22 cm	8½ in
2.5 cm	1 in	25 cm	10 in
3 cm	1¼ in	26 cm	10½ in
4 cm	1½ in	28 cm	11 in
5 cm	2 in	30 cm	12 in
10 cm	4 in	40 cm	16 in